The
BEST of
Reader's
Digest

Reader's
Digest
New York / Montreal

A READER'S DIGEST BOOK

Copyright © 2022 Trusted Media Brands, Inc.
44 South Broadway
White Plains, NY 10601

The credits that appear on pages 279–280 are hereby made part of this copyright page.

ISBN 978-1-62145-840-1 (retail hardcover)
ISBN 978-1-62145-838-8 (dated hardcover)
ISBN 978-1-62145-839-5 (undated hardcover)
ISBN 978-1-62145-841-8 (e-pub)

Component numbers 116600107H (dated); 116600109H (undated)

We are committed to both the quality of our products and the service we provide to our customers. We value your comments, so please feel free to contact us at TMBBookTeam@TrustedMediaBrands.com.

For more Reader's Digest products and information, visit our website:
www.rd.com (in the United States)
www.readersdigest.ca (in Canada)

Printed in the United States

10 9 8 7 6 5 4 3 2 1

Text, photography and illustrations for *The Best of Reader's Digest* are based on articles previously published in *Reader's Digest* magazine (rd.com).

CONTENTS

INTRODUCTION

Before there was a magazine, there were stacks of three-by-five-inch slips of paper onto which *Reader's Digest* founder DeWitt Wallace would jot notes and quotes from everything he read. After he returned from serving in World War I, Wallace decided to share his condensed versions of articles. He and his wife, Lila Acheson Wallace, worked together on the first issue of *Reader's Digest*, published in February 1922. It contained 33 articles, all condensed from other publications, and sold for $3 a year through direct mail subscriptions.

Since then, *Reader's Digest* has grown through the decades, showcasing original stories from then-emerging writers, such as James Michener and Mary Roach; influencing public health campaigns including those against tobacco and drunk driving; and curating the best

Four million reprints of this story—which described in graphic detail the preventable carnage of a car wreck—were handed out with license plates at motor vehicle departments around the country.

articles from other magazines around the country and the world. The first foreign edition of the magazine was launched in 1938; it is now available in more than 43 countries and 19 languages, and continues to bring readers stories that inform, inspire and entertain.

But its influence reaches beyond the magazine. *Reader's Digest* was instrumental in supporting the research that went into two enormously influential and successful books: Cornelius Ryan's *The Longest Day*, a journalistic account of D-Day, published in 1959, and Alex Haley's *Roots*, a novel about a young slave and his descendents, published in 1976. Since 1950, *Reader's Digest* has also been publishing condensed versions of popular books. And nonprofit organizations founded by the Wallaces support literacy and art.

As we set out to put together a collection to celebrate and honor 100 years of publishing history, we strove to include stories that our readers have enjoyed most over the years: stories that make us laugh until we cry; stories that show ordinary people in extraordinary circumstances; stories that move and inspire us and remind us that we have more in common with each other than not.

In this popular health series, which ran from 1967 to 1990, readers heard detailed accounts from 36 body parts of Joe and his female counterpart, Jane.

Along with these curated stories, *Reader's Digest* has nurtured several beloved columns, including Laughter, the Best Medicine, Quotable Quotes and Your True Stories, and this material has been incorporated here as well. Since publishing its first two-color illustration in 1939, the magazine has also featured many artists and photographers. In this volume you'll find selections from C.F.

Payne, who drew an exclusive series of illustrations for *Reader's Digest*'s back covers; Glenn Glasser, who documented some of the unique Faces of America; and many others.

We know you'll be moved by the story of the prospector who earns a trapped wolf's trust in order to save her pups from starvation and release her from a hunter's snare; you might laugh unexpectedly at a comedy writer's last moments with her dying father when, true to form, he makes sure to remind her and her siblings of joy, even in his passing; and your heart will race when a high school principal puts his life on the line to stop a school shooter from inflicting more harm. In addition to these stories, we've also included award-winning photographs that will take your breath away, make you think and feel, and expose you to a world beyond your own.

Originally reprinted from Guideposts in 1983, this timeless story about an acquaintance who knows just how to help someone in mourning was reprinted again in 2017 and went viral on rd.com.

We hope that as you read through this collection, you'll feel a sense of connection in being part of the *Reader's Digest* legacy. After all, it is the readers who have inspired us for over 100 years to find the best stories, jokes, cartoons and images. Enjoy this volume that highlights the best of the best, as we look forward to bringing you powerful, thought-provoking and entertaining stories for another 100 years.

—The Editors of *Reader's Digest*

When Does Education Stop?

by James A. Michener

It doesn't. A noted author offers convincing evidence that to learn is to live.

The war had passed us by on Guadalcanal in 1945, and we could see certain victory ahead. Relieved of pressure, our top officers in the South Pacific Force could have been excused if they loafed, but the ones I knew well in those days used their free time to educate themselves in new fields. One carrier admiral studied everything he could get on tank warfare. The head of our outfit, Vice Admiral William Lowndes Calhoun, spent six hours a day learning French.

I asked him about it. "Admiral, what's this big deal with French?"

"How do I know where I'll be sent when the war's over?" he replied.

A few nights later I happened to participate in an officers study group. As we were breaking up, the leader asked me, "By the way, Michener, what are you studying?" The question stunned me, for I had been studying exactly nothing.

As I walked back to my quarters, the challenge implicit in his probably idle question touched in me a profound response, and that very night I started work on something that I had been toying with for months. In a lantern-lit, mosquito-filled tin shack, I began writing *Tales of the South Pacific*.

I know now that the good work of the world is accomplished principally by people who dedicate themselves unstintingly to the big, distant goal. Weeks, months, years pass, but the good workman knows that he is gambling on an ultimate achievement which cannot be measured in time spent. Responsible men and women leap to the challenge of jobs that require enormous dedication and years to fulfill, and are happiest when they are so involved. This means that men and women who hope to make a real contribution to American life must reeducate themselves periodically or they are doomed to mediocrity.

In the United States the average man (let's leave out doctors and highly specialized scientists) can expect to work in three radically different fields before he retires. The lawyer is dragged into a business reorganization and winds up a college president. The engineer uses his slide rule for a while, then finds himself a sales expert and ends up in labor relations. The schoolteacher becomes a principal, and later on heads the town's automobile agency. I have been the typical American in that I have had widely scattered jobs: teacher, businessman, soldier, traveler, writer. No college education could give me specific preparation for any of these jobs, but mine did inspire me with the urge to reeducate myself constantly.

By fantastic luck, I got to Swarthmore College, outside Philadelphia, just as it was launching an experiment. At the end of my sophomore year, the faculty assembled a group of us and said, "Life does not consist of taking courses in small segments. A productive life consists of finding huge tasks and mastering them with whatever tools of intelligence and energy we have. We are going to turn you loose on some huge tasks. Let's see what you can do with them."

Accordingly, we were excused from all class attendance and were told, "Pick out three fields that interest you." I chose logic, English history and the novel.

The faculty said, "Go to the library and learn what you can about your fields. At the end of two years, we'll bring in some experts from Harvard and Yale whom you've never seen, and they will determine whether you have educated yourself."

What followed was an experience in intellectual grandeur. The Swarthmore professors, realizing that when I was tested they would be tested too, helped me to gain as thorough an education as a young man could absorb. When the two years ended, the visiting experts arrived, and for a week they queried, probed and heckled. At the end, one of the examiners said to me simply, "You have the beginnings of a real education."

He was right: It was only the beginnings. Nothing I studied in college has been of direct use to me in my various occupations. If my education had ended the week I stood before those examiners, I would have proved a useless citizen. But what I did learn was how to learn, how to organize, and how to educate and reeducate myself.

From my own experience and observation, I realize today that it is not so much the education that counts: It's the self-reeducation—the discipline that keeps a man driving toward hard and distant goals, the human values he believes in.

Specialization is not enough; what the world needs for the big jobs—historically, culturally, morally—are well-rounded human beings.

I remember a day in 1942 when the U.S. Navy was hungry for talent. Four of us were shivering in our shorts in a small room. A grim-faced selection committee asked the first would-be officer, "What can you do?" and the man replied, "I'm a buyer for Macy's, and I've trained myself to judge very quickly between markets and prices and trends." The board replied, "Can't you do anything practical?" And they shunted him off to one side.

When the board asked the next man, a lawyer, if he could do anything practical, he had to confess, "I can weigh evidence and organize information." He was rejected.

I was third and when I answered, "I know language and a good deal of history," the board groaned and I went shivering away.

Then the fourth man said boldly, "I'm a college-trained engineer, and I can overhaul diesel engines." The committee practically embraced him, and made him an officer on the spot.

But this is not the end of the story. When the war was over, the Macy's buyer was assistant to the secretary of the Navy, in charge of many complex responsibilities requiring instant good judgment. He had given himself courses in naval management and government procedures and had become a top expert. The lawyer wound up as assistant to Admiral Halsey, and in a crucial battle deduced logically from intelligence reports just where the Japanese fleet had to be. He came out covered with medals.

I got the job of naval secretary to several congressional committees who were determining the future of America in the South Pacific.

What was the engineer doing at the end of the war? He was still overhauling diesel engines.

Condensed from an address delivered at Macalester College. Originally published in the December 1962 issue of *Reader's Digest* magazine.

James A. Michener won the Pulitzer Prize for Fiction in 1948 for Tales of the South Pacific *and went on to write more than 40 books before his death in 1997.*

A MOTHER'S LOVE

I was rushed to the emergency room with complications from my high-risk pregnancy. After weeks of mandated bed rest in the hospital, I found myself suffering from an unfamiliar sadness. One day, my nurse brought a surprise to my room— a newborn named James.

James's mom (who also experienced a high-risk pregnancy) sent her precious, healthy son for me to hold…along with an encouraging message: "This is the reason you are here in the hospital." Three decades later, my heart is still full of gratitude for Baby James and his mom. And, I am thankful for my own healthy son, Hunter.

—Lisa Steven, *The Woodlands, Texas*

IN-FLIGHT PLAYDATE

On a recent flight, I sat next to a mom with a baby on her lap and a slightly older son. She was having trouble holding on to the baby while helping her son and herself, so I offered to hold the baby. Baby and I hit it off right away—so much so that when Mom reached to take her back, Baby started screaming! So Mom left her with me. For two hours, we played tickle and moved the tray table up and down. After we landed, I handed the baby back. Mom smiled and said, "Thank you!"

—Raymond Drago, *Glen Mills, Pennsylvania*

The Undelivered Letter

by Fulton Oursler

Once upon a time, a man's soul
rose from the dead.

Some years ago there lived in an English city a man whom I shall call Fred Armstrong. He worked in the local post office, where he was called the dead-letter man because he handled missives whose addresses were faulty or hard to read. He lived in an old house with his little wife, an even smaller daughter and a tiny son. After supper he liked to light his pipe and tell his children of his latest exploits in delivering lost letters. He considered himself quite a detective. There was no cloud on his modest horizon.

No cloud until one sunny morning when his little boy suddenly fell ill. Within 48 hours the child was dead.

In his sorrow, Fred Armstrong's soul seemed to die. The mother and their little daughter, Marian, struggled to control their grief, determined to make the best of it. Not so the father. His life was now a dead letter with no direction. In the morning Fred Armstrong rose from his bed and went to work like a sleepwalker; he never spoke unless spoken to, ate his lunch alone, sat like a statue at the supper table and went to bed early.

Yet his wife knew that he lay most of the night with eyes open, staring at the ceiling. As the months passed his apathy seemed to deepen.

His wife told him that such despair was unfair to their lost son and unfair to the living. But nothing she said seemed to reach him.

It was coming close upon Christmas. One bleak afternoon Fred Armstrong sat on his high stool and shoved a new pile of letters under the swinging electric lamp. On top of the stack was an envelope that was clearly undeliverable. In crude block letters were penciled the words "Santa Claus, North Pole." Armstrong started to throw it away when some impulse made him pause. He opened the letter and read:

> Dear Santa Claus:
>
> We are very sad at our house this year, and I don't want you to bring me anything. My little brother went to Heaven last spring. All I want you to do when you come to our house is to take Brother's toys to him. I'll leave them in the corner by the kitchen stove; his hobby-horse and train and everything. I know he'll be lost up in Heaven without them, most of all his horse; he always liked riding it so much, so you must take them to him, please. You needn't mind leaving me anything, but if you could give Daddy something that would make him like he used to be, make him smoke his pipe again and tell me stories, I do wish you would. I heard him say to Mummie once that only Eternity could cure him. Could you bring him some of that, and I will be your good little girl.
>
> Marian

That night, through the lighted streets, Fred Armstrong walked home at a faster gait. In the winter darkness he stood in the dooryard garden and struck a match. Then as he opened the kitchen door he blew a great puff from his pipe, and the smoke settled like a nimbus around the heads of his startled wife and daughter. And he was smiling at them just as he used to do.

Originally published in the December 1950 issue of *Reader's Digest* magazine.

Our America

Earth Day
—C. F. PAYNE
APRIL 2004

Humor Hall of Fame

My friend's daughter Chelsea found a baby tooth that her kitten had lost. She and her sister decided to put one over on the tooth fairy. They placed the tooth under Chelsea's pillow. It worked. But the tooth fairy left a can of sardines.

—SANDRA E. MARTIN

My father's secretary was visibly distraught one morning when she arrived at the office and explained that her children's parrot had escaped from his cage and flown out an open window. Of all the dangers the tame bird would face outdoors alone, she seemed most concerned about what would happen if the bird started talking.

Confused, my father asked what the parrot could say.

"Well," she explained, "he mostly says 'Here, kitty, kitty.'"

—TERRY WALKER

"He's a high-tech watchdog."

Code of the Navajos

by Bruce Watson, from *Smithsonian*

It was a secret weapon that helped win the war in the Pacific.

Like all members of his generation, Keith Little remembers exactly where he was when he heard the news of Pearl Harbor. A Navajo, he was attending boarding school in Ganado, Arizona, on the reservation. "Me and a bunch of guys were out hunting rabbits with a .22," he recalls. "Somebody went to the dorm, came back and said, 'Pearl Harbor was bombed.' One of the boys asked, 'Where's Pearl Harbor?'"

"In Hawaii."

"Who did it?"

"Japan."

"Why'd they do it?"

"They hate Americans. They want to kill all Americans."

"Us too?"

"Yeah, us too."

Then and there, the boys made a promise to one another. They'd go after the Japanese instead of the rabbits.

The next morning, the superintendent of the reservation looked out

The Navajo language formed the basis of an unbreakable secret code.

his office window and saw a crowd of ponytailed young men carrying hunting rifles, ready to fight.

Philip Johnston, the son of missionaries, also grew up on the reservation and was fluent in Navajo. When the war broke out, Johnston got an extraordinary idea. Early in 1942, he visited the Marine Corps' Camp Elliott, north of San Diego, and proposed to use the Navajo language as an up-to-date code, guaranteed unbreakable.

The Marines were skeptical. At the time, military codes were encrypted by high-tech black boxes that used rotors and ratchets to shroud messages in a thick alphabet soup. Still, Johnston returned with a few Navajo friends. For 15 minutes, while the iron jaws of Marine brass went slack, messages metamorphosed from English to Navajo and back.

In the spring of 1942, as the Japanese sent American prisoners on the Bataan Death March, Marine recruiters came to the Navajo Nation in the high-desert country of Arizona and New Mexico. There, among the sagebrush and sandstone, they began looking for a few good men fluent in Navajo and English.

Fewer than 80 years had passed since the Navajos had fought *against* the U.S. military. Kit Carson's scorched-earth campaign had broken their resistance in 1864. Why would men volunteer to fight for a nation that had humbled their ancestors and wouldn't even let them vote?

Soldiers enlist for reasons of jobs, adventure, family tradition—and patriotism. Says Albert Smith, a Navajo who fought in World War II, "This conflict involved Mother Earth being dominated by foreign countries. It was our responsibility to defend her."

Few Navajos—who call themselves *Dineh* (the People)—had ever been off the reservation. For the most part, they had met "Anglos" only on trading posts. Yet they proved to be model Marines. Accustomed to walking miles each day in the high desert, they marched on with full packs after others buckled. When training was finished, the first group of Navajos became the 382nd Platoon, USMC, and was ordered to make a code.

On the reservation the language was primarily oral, and the Code Talkers were told to keep it that way. There would be no code books, no cryptic algorithms. Navajo itself was puzzling enough. Germans deciphering English codes could tap common linguistic roots. Japanese eavesdropping on GIs were often graduates of American universities. But Navajo was known to few outsiders. It is a tonal language. Its vowels rise and fall, changing meaning with pitch. A single Navajo verb, containing its own subjects, objects and adverbs, can translate into an entire English sentence.

To devise the code, the Navajos turned to nature. They named planes after birds: *gini*—chicken hawk (dive bomber); *ne-as-jah*—owl (observation plane); *tas-chizzie*—swallow (torpedo plane). They named ships after fish: *lo-tso*—whale (battleship); *ca-lo*—shark (destroyer); *besh-lo*—iron fish (submarine).

To spell out proper names, the Code Talkers made a Navajo bestiary, turning the Marines' *Able Baker Charlie* into *Wol-la-chee Shush Moasi* ...*Ant Bear Cat*. They also played word games. "District" became the Navajo words for "deer ice strict," and "belong" became "long bee."

The finished code was a hodgepodge of everyday Navajo and some 400 newly devised code words. One Code Talker told how, as a test, Navy intelligence officers spent three weeks trying, and failing, to decipher a single message. New Navajo recruits untrained in the code could not break it. Yet it seemed too simple to be trusted. Codes normally took hours to translate. These Indians were encoding and decoding sensitive military information almost instantly. How could that be?

"In Navajo, everything—songs, prayers—is in memory," said William McCabe, one of the code's designers. "That's the way we was raised up. So we didn't have no trouble."

Two Code Talkers stayed behind to teach the next group; the rest were shipped to Guadalcanal. There, Code Talkers met skepticism in the flesh. One colonel agreed to use the Navajos only if they won a man-versus-machine test against a cylindrical gizmo that disguised words and broadcast in coded clicks. The Code Talkers won handily.

Back on the reservation, Navajo instructors led by Sergeant Johnston kept searching for the best and brightest volunteers. Of the 3,600 Navajos who served in World War II, only 420 became Code Talkers. In boot camp, Keith Little was just another Indian, and few cared from which tribe. Then a drill instructor took him aside and asked, "By any chance, are you a Navajo?" He was sent to Code Talkers' school.

Eventually, Marine commanders came to see the code as indispensable for the rapid transmission of classified dispatches. Lent to the Navy, the Code Talkers kept the Japanese from learning of impending air attacks. On Saipan, an advancing U.S. battalion was shelled from behind by friendly fire. Desperate messages demanded, "Hold your fire," but the Japanese had imitated Marine broadcasts all day. Mortar crews weren't sure what to believe. The shelling continued. Finally headquarters asked, "Do you have a Navajo?" A Code Talker sent the same message to his buddy, and the shelling stopped.

Code Talkers were sometimes given bodyguards to protect them from

Marines who couldn't tell a Navajo from a Japanese. On Saipan, Navajo Samuel Holiday joined his buddies bathing in a shell hole filled with rainwater. He made the mistake of being the last man out. A military policeman saw the short, black-haired man wearing his birthday suit instead of a private's stripe. "I turned around, and he held a bayonet right between my eyes," Holiday recalled. His captain had to identify him for the MP.

During the first two days on Iwo Jima, six networks of Code Talkers transmitted more than 800 messages without error. On the morning of February 23, 1945, the Stars and Stripes were hoisted on a mountaintop. The word went out in code, ending with: "*Na-as-tso-si Than-zie Dibeh Shi-da Dah-nes-tsa Tkin Shush Wol-la-chee Moasi Lin A-chi.*" Cryptographers translated the Navajo words for "*Mouse Turkey Sheep Uncle Ram Ice Bear Ant Cat Horse Intestines,*" then told their fellow Marines in English: The American flag flew over Mount Suribachi. Signal officer Major Howard Conner recalled, "Were it not for the Navajos, the Marines would never have taken Iwo Jima."

When the war ended, the Navajos headed home to their reservation. Some returned to school; others worked where they could find jobs. Many had nightmares. When George Kirk began dreaming of enemy soldiers leaping into his foxhole, his wife sent him to a medicine man. "The Enemy Way," a ceremonial slaying of the "enemy presence," cured him. Samuel Smith told his medicine man the story. The healer said, "Don't tell it no more to nobody. That way you won't be bothered in the future."

The code itself remained top secret. Asked about the war, Code Talkers simply said, "I was a radioman." Finally, in 1968, the code was declassified, and the secret was out. In 1992, Keith Little was invited to the Pentagon, where he translated a prayer for peace phoned in by a Code Talker in Arizona. Then Little and other Navajo vets helped dedicate a permanent exhibit on the Code Talkers.

When the country needed them, the *Dineh*, often known for their silence, had spoken volumes.

Originally published in the December 1993 issue of *Reader's Digest* magazine.

Astonishing America

When winter winds pour in, the Great Lakes are easily mistaken for oceans. Living near Lake Erie, photographer Dave Sandford has been making a visual study of the liquid peaks that result when gale-force gusts sculpt surface water into towering waves up to 25 feet high. Because Erie is the shallowest of the Great Lakes, it is also the most temperamental; of the 8,000 shipwrecks estimated to speckle the lakes, a fourth are thought to lie below Erie.

Photograph by Dave Sandford

INTERCONTINENTAL COINCIDENCE

I recently took my son to his very first piano lesson with a lady named Carol. I thought it was funny because my first piano teacher was also named Carol, but that was decades ago in West Germany. (My dad was in the Air Force and we were stationed there.) When we met Carol, I thought she looked familiar. She stood shocked for a moment, then gave me a huge hug and said she remembered me. From West Germany to Georgia—32 years later—our paths crossed again. It sure is a small world!

—Paul Wiles, *Evans, Georgia*

VACATION CONNECTION

My wife and I were on vacation in Yellowstone. During a cruise around Elk Island, one of the boat's workers asked everyone where they were from. The couple directly behind us said that they were from New Jersey. I'm originally from there, so I turned around and recognized my best friend from high school. I joined the service soon after graduating 40 years ago, and we had lost touch—but we've stayed in touch ever since we reconnected.

—David Moeller, *Millville, Delaware*

The Husband Who Vanished

by Joseph P. Blank

*For 15 years, Anne McDonnell lived
in limbo, not knowing whether her Jim was
dead or alive. Then one afternoon
the doorbell rang.*

T he McDonnells lived in a small brick house in Larchmont, a sub-
urb of New York City. Jim was foreman of mail carriers at the post
office where he had worked for 25 years. A gentle, soft-spoken man, he
had a wave-of-the-hand acquaintance with hundreds of people in town.
Married in 1960, he and Anne were childless.

During February and March 1971, when he was 50, Jim McDonnell
suffered a curious series of accidents. None was critical in itself, but the
combination appeared to trigger a strange result.

Carrying out the garbage one evening, he slipped on ice-coated steps,
bruised his back and struck his head. A few days later, driving to work,
he had a fit of sneezing, lost control of the car, hit a telephone pole and
banged his forehead against the windshield. The following day, a dizzy
spell at work sent him tumbling down a flight of steps, and again he
banged his head.

Ten days later he again lost control of his car and hit a pole. Found unconscious, he was hospitalized for three days with a cerebral concussion.

On March 29, 1971, Jim borrowed a friend's station wagon and drove to Kennedy Airport to pick up Anne's brother and family. Then he took them to Anne's sister's house. When he returned the borrowed car at 10 p.m., he was unaware that the leather folder containing his identification had slipped out of his pocket onto the floor of the station wagon. Jim declined the offer of a ride home: "I have a terrible headache and the walk will help clear my head." Ordinarily the walk would have taken about 15 minutes.

Anne had faith that Jim would return. She kept his clothes in the closet. His razor and shaving cream remained in the bathroom cabinet.

At 11:15 p.m. Anne called the owner of the station wagon; he had no idea why Jim had not yet reached home. It was unlike Jim not to telephone if he was delayed. At 2 a.m., Anne called the police and reported her husband missing.

After 24 hours, the police sent out an all-points bulletin and wrote letters to Jim's friends and relatives. They followed through on every anonymous tip and checked unidentified bodies in New York morgues.

Detective George Mulcahy was assigned to head the investigation. He knew Jim was a man of probity and openness—the two attended the same church—and Mulcahy was sure the disappearance had nothing to do with wrongdoing by Jim McDonnell. Investigation confirmed that McDonnell's personal and professional records were impeccable, and turned up no tendencies toward self-destruction nor any evidence that he had been a victim of an accident or attack.

For Mulcahy, the only explanation was amnesia.

The phenomenon of amnesia is clouded in mystery. Why it occurs in some patients and not in others is open to medical speculation. What is known is that loss of memory can be caused by stroke, Alzheimer's disease, alcoholism, severe psychological trauma—or by blows to the head. Any individual whose brain has suffered such injuries can simply wander aimlessly away from the place where he lives, with all knowledge of his past blacked out.

"For weeks," Anne's sister recalls, "Anne walked the house wringing her hands and praying. She agreed that Jim could be a victim of amnesia—and she worried about his health. Anne was sustained by her deep trust in God. She felt that one day he would provide an answer."

Anne remained alone in the house, waiting. At night, watching television, she would stare at the overstuffed hassock where Jim had dozed off evenings. She often dreamed he had come home, only to wake up and find he wasn't there.

Soon after Jim's disappearance, Anne realized she had to earn a living. She took babysitting jobs, was a supermarket checker and worked in a hospital cafeteria. In 1977 she took a job as a nursing attendant.

Anne fell into the habit of working at the hospital on holidays because it was easier if she kept busy. *I've got to go on, live as best I can,* she told herself. She had faith that Jim would return. She kept his clothes in the closet covered to protect them from dust. His razor and can of shaving cream remained in the bathroom cabinet.

*   *   *

During his walk home, Jim had indeed blacked out, losing all ability to remember who he was and where he lived. What happened then is unclear. He may have taken the train to Grand Central Terminal, then another train or a bus south. The next thing he knew, he was in downtown Philadelphia, a city he had never visited before.

Seeing signs advertising the services of a James Peters, a real estate broker, Jim adopted James Peters as his own name. It never occurred to him to seek assistance at a police station or hospital. He had no past; his only reality was the present.

James Peters got a Social Security card, which could be obtained at that time without showing a birth certificate, and took a job in the luncheonette of a health club. He next worked at a cancer-research institute, cleaning out animal cages. He also got a night-shift job at the P&P luncheonette, where he became well-known for his omelets as well as for his courtesy and good humor. After a year he felt he was established at P&P and quit his job at the cancer institute.

Jim made new friends, joined an American Legion post and the Knights of Columbus, and became an active member of the St. Hugh Roman Catholic Church.

He never talked about his past, and his friends didn't pry. One once said to him, "From your accent, you must be from New York."

Jim replied, "I guess so."

To Cheryle Sloan, a waitress at P&P, Jim was special: "He loved kids. At Christmastime, he played Santa Claus at orphanages. He grew a big white beard to make his appearance more authentic. Of course we wondered about his past. My mother decided that he had to be an ex-priest or an ex-criminal." Bernadine Golashovsky recalls: "Soon after Jim started at P&P, I took a job there as a waitress. My father had died and Jim apparently had no family, so we adopted each other. He became my father figure, and we—my husband, Pete, our four children, and I—were his family. The children loved him."

About a month before Christmas 1985, Bernadine noticed that Jim had grown unusually quiet and subdued. Something seemed to be turning in his mind.

On Thanksgiving Day, Jim visited the family and sat watching television with Pete. A scene appeared in which a mail carrier was making deliveries on a miserably rainy day. Pete said, "Boy, that's one job I wouldn't want."

Jim frowned and said, "I think I used to be a postman."

"Really? Where?"

"I don't know," Jim answered.

"New York?"

"I'm not sure. But I think I remember my parents. A little."

Jim spent every major holiday with Bernadine and Pete. On Christmas Eve he always arrived late because the Golashovskys were his last stop on his rounds of wishing friends a happy holiday. On this Christmas Eve he never arrived. Bernadine and Pete stayed up all night waiting for him.

On December 22, Jim had fallen and banged his head. The next day at work he seemed distracted, and late that afternoon he had fallen again, striking his head. On December 24, he awoke feeling confused, yet elated. After almost 15 years, he knew who he was! He was James A. McDonnell Jr. of Larchmont, New York. His wife's name was Anne. Then, suddenly, he was scared: *Is Anne alive? Has she remarried? If not, how will she greet me?*

* * *

Anne had just returned home from Christmas Mass, where she'd lit candles and prayed for Jim. A light snow was falling, and she was in a hurry to leave for Christmas dinner at her sister's before the roads grew slick.

Then the doorbell rang. *Oh, my*, she thought, *this is not a good time for a visitor.*

Jim frowned and said, "I think I used to be a postman."

Anne opened the door—and peered at a man with a full white beard. Immediately she recognized Jim. She couldn't speak.

To Jim, Anne looked a little older, but prettier too. His heart overflowed. "Hello, Anne," he said.

"Jim," she gasped. "Is it true?" Her breathing came in bursts, as if she had been running. "Oh, I'm glad you're home. Come in; come in." They barely touched hands. They were too stunned to fall into each other's arms. The embraces and the tears would come later.

Anne led Jim to his favorite seat, the overstuffed hassock. They began to talk, trying to fill in the gaps in time. Finally, Jim's eyes grew heavy. Exhausted and happy, he dozed off.

After 15 years, Jim McDonnell was home at last.

* * *

On the day after Christmas, Jim reported his return to the police. That evening the Golashovskys received a phone call from a *New York Daily News* reporter who told them Jim was fine. Bernadine phoned Jim's friends with the good news.

A week after his return, Jim had a complete physical, including a CAT scan of his brain. The conclusion: He was in normal health.

Jim and Anne have had no problems resuming their lives as a married couple. "Each day we are together," Jim says, "makes the time we were apart seem shorter."

Originally published in the January 1987 issue of *Reader's Digest* magazine.

Jim and Anne remained together until Anne's death in 1999 at the age of 75. Jim died in 2007 at age 85. They are buried next to each other.

Sit, Stay, Whoa!

by P. J. O'Rourke, from *Garden & Gun*

Faced with conflicting and useless parenting advice, P. J. O'Rourke consulted his gun-dog training manual.

I have three badly behaved children and a damn good bird dog. My Brittany spaniel, Millie (age seven), is far more obedient than my daughters, Muffin (eleven) and Poppet (nine), and has a better nose than my son, Buster (five). Buster does smell, but in his case it's an intransitive verb.

Millie hunts close, quarters well, points beautifully, is staunch to wing and shot, and retrieves with verve. My children...are doing OK in school, I guess. They look very sweet—when they're asleep.

As my family was growing, I got a lot of excellent advice about discipline, responsibility, respect, affection and cultivation of the work ethic. Unfortunately, this advice was from dog trainers and was directed to my dog. In the matter of child rearing, there was also plenty of advice, all of it contradictory—from family and family-in-law, wife, wife's girlfriends, pediatricians, nursery school teachers, babysitters, neighbors and random old ladies on the street, plus Dr. Spock, Dr. Phil and, for all I know, Dr Pepper: Spank them/Don't spank them. Make them clean their plate/Keep them from overeating. Potty train them at one/Send them to Potty Training Camp at 14. Hover over their every activity/Get out of their faces. And none of this advice works when you're trying to get the kids to quit playing video games and go to bed.

It took me years to realize that I should stop asking myself what I'm doing wrong as a parent and start asking myself what I'm doing right as a dog handler.

The first right thing I did was read and reread *Gun Dog*. "Start 'em young" is the message from its author, the late Richard A. Wolters. That's why, if we have another child, he's going to learn to walk pushing on the handle of a lawn mower instead of teetering around the sofa.

Although Wolters was sure that waiting until the traditional one-year mark before teaching a puppy to hunt was like carrying your kid in a Snugli until he was seven, he wasn't sure why. Then he came across the work of John Paul Scott, a founder of the Animal Behavior Society. Scott was involved in a project to help Guide Dogs for the Blind, Inc. Seeing Eye dog training was considered almost too difficult to be worthwhile. When litters were used from even the best bloodlines, the success rate was only 20 percent. Scott discovered that if training began at five weeks instead of a year and continued uninterrupted, the success rate rose to 90 percent.

It goes without saying that the idea of Seeing Eye kids is wrong—probably against child labor laws and an awful thing to do to blind people. But I take Scott's point. So did Richard Wolters, who devised a regimen that had dogs field-ready as early as six months. That's three and a half in kid years. My kids weren't doing anything at three and a half, other than at night in their Pull-Ups.

Commands should be short, brisk single words. In the case of my kids, that will be "getajob" or at least "marrymoney."

The Start-'Em-Young program turns out to be a surprise blessing for dads. Wolters writes in *Gun Dog* of a puppy's first 28 days (equal to about six months for a kid), "Removal from Mother at this time is drastic." That's just what I told my wife about the care and feeding of our infants—drastic is the word for "leaving it to Dad." According to Wolters, I'm really not supposed to get involved until the kid is about one (equivalent to a 56-day-old pup).

Then I can commence the nurturing (Happy Meals) and the "establishing rapport" (sitting together on the couch watching football).

Next the training proper begins. "Repetition, more repetition and still more repetition," enjoins Wolters. I've reached the age where I'm repeating myself all the time, so this is easy. "Commands should be short, brisk single words: 'sit,' 'fetch,' 'whoa,' 'come,' 'no,' etc." In the case of my kids, the *etc.* will be "getajob" or at least "marrymoney."

"Don't clutter up his brain with useless nonsense," warns Wolters, who is opposed to tricks such as "roll over" or "play Dick Cheney's lawyer" for dogs that have a serious purpose in life. Therefore, no, Muffin, Poppet and Buster, I am not paying your college tuition so you can take a course called "Post-Marxist Structuralism in Fantasy/Sci-Fi Film." And meanwhile, no, you can't have a Wii either.

Wolters favors corporal punishment for deliberate disobedience. "Failure to discipline is crueler," he claims. I do not recall my own dad's failure to discipline as being crueler than his pants-seat handiwork, but that may be my failing memory. In any case, a whack on the hindquarters is a last resort. Wolters prefers to use psychology: "You can hurt a dog just as much by ignoring him. For example, if you're trying to teach him 'sit' and 'stay,' but he gets up and comes to you, ignore him." When I was a kid, we called this "Dad working late every day of the week and playing golf all Sunday."

The basic commands for a gun dog are "sit," "stay," "come" and "whoa." Those are exactly the four things my boy Buster will have to learn if he wants a happy marriage. My girls, Muffin and Poppet, on the other hand, seem to have arrived from the womb with a full understanding of these actions—and how to order everyone to do them.

Wolters begins with "sit" and "stay." Kids today are given frequent encouragement to "Stand up for this and that." But "Sit tight 'til it blows over" is wiser counsel. Wolters employs a leash to pull the head up as he pushes the rump down. I've found that the collar of a T-shirt works just as well. Wolters uses praise in the place of dog biscuits. He writes, "I do

not believe in paying off a dog by shoving food into his mouth." I, on the other hand, try to make sure the kids eat their green, leafy vegetables once I've got them seated.

Wolters teaches "stay" by slowly moving away from the dog while repeating the command and making a hand signal with an upright palm. But I've found that if your kids get Nickelodeon on the TV, you don't have to say or do anything. They'll stay right there for hours.

Once "sit" and "stay" have been mastered, you can go on to "come." Wolters lowers his palm as a signal, but a cell phone call will also work if your kids are properly trained. Mine aren't. Getting a kid to come when he's called is a lot harder than getting a dog to, probably because the dog is almost certain that you don't have green, leafy vegetables in the pocket of your shooting jacket. Wolters suggests that if you're having trouble teaching "come," you should run away, thereby enticing the dog to run after you. This has been tried with kids in divorce after divorce all across America, with mixed results.

The command that's the most fun to teach using Wolters's method is "whoa":

"The dog," writes Wolters, "is ready to learn 'whoa' as soon as he will 'stay' on hand signal alone and 'come' on command. When he has this down pat, my system is—scare the hell out of the dog. Put the pup in the 'sit stay' position. Walk a good distance away from him. Command 'come.' Run like hell away from him. Make him get up steam. Then reverse your field. Turn, run at the dog. Shout 'whoa.' Thrust the hand up in the 'stay' hand signal like a traffic cop. Jump in the air at him. Do it with gusto. You'll look so foolish doing it that he'll stop."

Personally, I don't have to go to this much trouble. Just my morning appearance—hungover, unshaven, wearing my ratty bathrobe and slippers Millie chewed—is enough to stop my children cold. I reserve the antics that Wolters describes for commands to this idiot computer I'm writing on. *Gun Dog* was authored in the days of the simple, reliable Royal Portable. Thus Wolters has nothing to say about computers. Besides, dogs don't use computers. (Although, on my Visa bills, I've noticed some charges to rottenmeat.com.)

Children don't need computer training either. Muffin, Poppet and Buster—who can't even read—have "good computing instincts." When the Internet says "come," they come. I'm the one who should be taught some basic commands to make this darned PC...

"What's the matter, Daddy?" Muffin asks. With one deft flick of the mouse, she persuades the balky printer to disgorge all that I have composed. Reading it, she frowns. "Daddy, Millie chews everybody's shoes. She bit the teenager who mows the lawn. She killed Mom's chickens. And..."

And here is where my Richard A. Wolters theory of parenting goes to pieces. There is one crucial difference between children and dogs. You can teach a dog to lie. Down.

Originally published in the March 2011 issue of *Reader's Digest* magazine.

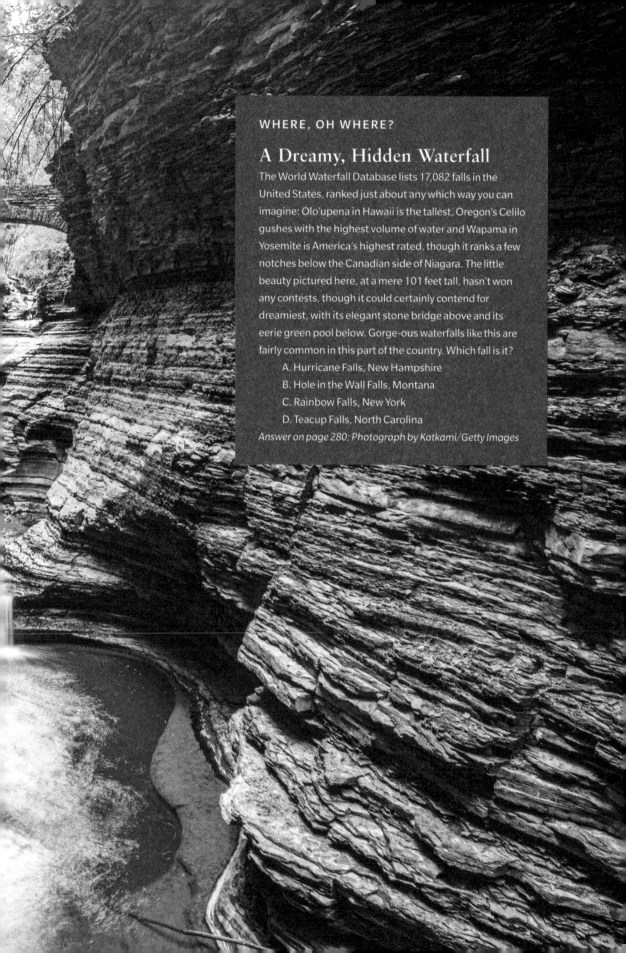

A Dreamy, Hidden Waterfall

The World Waterfall Database lists 17,082 falls in the United States, ranked just about any which way you can imagine: Olo'upena in Hawaii is the tallest, Oregon's Celilo gushes with the highest volume of water and Wapama in Yosemite is America's highest rated, though it ranks a few notches below the Canadian side of Niagara. The little beauty pictured here, at a mere 101 feet tall, hasn't won any contests, though it could certainly contend for dreamiest, with its elegant stone bridge above and its eerie green pool below. Gorge-ous waterfalls like this are fairly common in this part of the country. Which fall is it?

    A. Hurricane Falls, New Hampshire

    B. Hole in the Wall Falls, Montana

    C. Rainbow Falls, New York

    D. Teacup Falls, North Carolina

Answer on page 280; Photograph by Katkami/Getty Images

A Soldier's Last Bedtime Story

by Kenneth Miller

With a handful of videos, Lieutenant Florence Choe helped shape her daughter's life—even after she lost her own.

W hen the package arrived in the mail, Commander Chong "Jay" Choe stared at it in shock. This was the fifth delivery since his wife had been shipped overseas. On previous occasions, he'd brought the padded envelopes to his three-year-old daughter, Kristin, as soon as he saw the return address. She would eagerly help him open the seals, and they'd watch the DVDs together right away. But this delivery was different. Florence must have sent the disc shortly before the gunman opened fire, he thought. He wondered what she'd chosen for the reading that would be her last gift to her daughter. He could feel the square plastic case inside the pouch. But he couldn't bring himself to pull it out, let alone watch it. So the package sat on his desk for weeks, unopened.

Jay and Florence had met at the National Naval Medical Center in Bethesda, Maryland, where he was doing his internship in general surgery. Shy and unassuming but fiercely disciplined, Jay hit the hospital gym nearly every day early in the morning before beginning his rounds.

Kristin (in pink) excitedly awaited each package from her mom, Lieutenant Florence Choe.

The only other person in the room at that hour was a small, beautiful woman who always wore headphones and seemed intent on avoiding eye contact. He ran into her again at a staff meeting and learned that she was a medical service corps officer named Florence Bacong. When he gathered his courage and asked her to dinner, she blurted "No!" and told him she had other plans. Sensing wariness, he tried another tack: "How about lunch this Sunday after church?" To his amazement, she agreed.

Over sandwiches, he learned that Florence was the daughter of a Navy cook; her parents were from the Philippines and she'd grown up in San Diego. She was the first in her family to earn a bachelor's degree, which she had topped off with a master's in public health. Two days after the 9/11 attacks, she'd followed her father into the service. Despite her manicured nails and well-coiffed hair, she shared Jay's taste for camping and hiking. Their romance bloomed on the trails of Virginia's Great Falls Park.

They were married in June 2004 and were deployed to Okinawa, Japan, soon afterward. At Camp Hansen, Jay was assigned to the Third Marine Logistics Group as a general medical officer, while Florence became officer in charge of the Headquarters and Service Battalion, overseeing nearly 100 sailors and Marines.

Kristin was born in November of the following year. The joys and stresses of parenthood—compounded by the demands of their jobs and the challenges of living abroad—tightened the couple's bond. Jay marveled at Florence's gung-ho performance as a mother and an officer, but it stung him when the strain of balancing both roles made her cry. In 2007, as their tour neared its end, he applied to do his residency at the Naval Medical Center in San Diego, where his in-laws could provide a support network. And then, in May 2008, Lieutenant Florence Choe was called for duty in Afghanistan.

Florence and Jay's immediate concern was how she could remain in her little girl's life from more than 7,500 miles away. Soon after landing at Bagram Airfield, she found the answer: United Through Reading (UTR).

Run by a San Diego–based nonprofit, the program enables military parents to be recorded on DVD reading storybooks to their faraway children. UTR was founded in 1989 by Betty J. Mohlenbrock, the wife of a naval flight surgeon who was deployed when their daughter

Florence organized the UTR library/video room at Camp Mike Spann, Afghanistan.

was a baby; after his return, the child didn't recognize him, and their relationship had to be painstakingly rebuilt. Mohlenbrock, an educator who'd seen children lagging at school because no one read to them at home, designed the program as a way to sustain family closeness while boosting literacy.

For her first DVD for Kristin, Florence selected *Cinderella*. When the package arrived in San Diego, it was as if the Fairy Godmother herself was inside. Jay popped the DVD into the player and settled on the floor with Kristin while her grandparents sat on the sofa, craning their heads toward the TV. When Florence appeared on the screen, Kristin yelled "Mommy!" and ran to kiss her face. Kristin sat rapt throughout the performance, then demanded a replay. Over the next few weeks, she begged to watch the video every evening—and sometimes several times a day. Florence and Kristin had, indeed, been united through reading.

From Bagram, Florence flew to Camp Mike Spann, a coalition outpost within an Afghan National Army base near the northern city of Mazar-e-Sharif. Her assignment was to help organize administrative logistics at a new medical station for troops and civilians. In her off-hours, she got to work establishing a local branch of UTR. She lobbied camp authorities to set aside a small room for a library, which she furnished with handmade shelves, donated recording equipment and books collected through an e-mail drive.

Florence's next DVD, a reading of *Good Night, Gorilla,* was an even bigger hit. Kristin watched it over and over; she made Jay or her grandparents read her the book at bedtime as well. Several weeks later came *The Cat in the Hat,* followed by *Llama Llama Red Pajama.* Between deliveries, Florence checked in via Skype whenever she could, but the connection was often wonky, and Kristin would drift away midconversation. The readings, however, held the toddler's attention with an almost hypnotic force. Like any young child, Jay thought, she thrived on repetition

> *Instead of waiting for a call, Kristin could summon Mommy's face and voice whenever she chose.*

and ritual; the comfort of these virtual visits with her mother was heightened by their utter predictability and the gentle rhythms of the stories. The element of control was another factor: Instead of waiting for a call, Kristin could summon Mommy's face and voice whenever she chose.

The DVDs were a balm to Jay as well. The tenderness of Florence's gaze and the avidity of Kristin's response provided a countercurrent to the worries that come with military life. It felt deeply soothing to tap into that circuit of love.

In January 2009, when Florence came home on leave, Kristin climbed into her lap as if she'd never been away. The family spent a week in Hawaii, reveling in the sun, the sea and one another before Florence boarded a plane back to the war zone.

* * *

Two months later, on March 27, Jay's department chair told him the admiral wanted to see him. Jay's first thought was that he had bungled some task and was due for a dressing-down. But when he saw the faces of the dozen people gathered in the wood-paneled office, he knew the news would be infinitely worse. "I'm so sorry," the admiral said.

It had happened when Florence and three friends were on their afternoon run. As they jogged along the base's perimeter fence, an Afghan soldier swung his AK-47 toward the group. The first bullet passed through Captain Kim Lebel's arm; the second struck Florence's thigh. Lieutenant Junior Grade Francis Toner, 26, charged the shooter, giving his life in an attempt to save the others. The assailant stood over Florence and finished her off before turning his weapon on himself. No one knew whether he was a Taliban infiltrator or had some other grievance.

A chaplain accompanied Jay to his in-laws' house. As Florence's parents wept, Jay carried Kristin down the street. "Can we visit Mommy in heaven?" she asked.

"No, sweetie," Jay told her. "She's an angel now, watching over us." Kristin hugged him tighter and buried her face in his shoulder.

Florence was only 35 when she was buried at Fort Rosecrans National Cemetery in San Diego, on a hillside with a view of the sea. The last DVD arrived a few weeks after she died. When Jay finally mustered the strength to watch it, he discovered that the disc had been damaged in transit. He stared through his tears at the blank blue screen—an emblem of all he and his family had lost.

For a long time, Jay and Kristin visited Florence's resting place frequently, bringing a blanket, snacks, and cards that Kristin had drawn herself. But inevitably, life began to pull them in new directions. They moved in with Jay's mother, who relocated from Maryland to lend a hand. The DVDs wound up stashed in a closet. Jay couldn't bear to watch them anymore, and Kristin eventually stopped asking to.

Today, Jay is married again, to a fellow surgeon. Kristin, now 11, has two younger sisters—a 23-month-old, Dana, and a newborn baby. Yet Florence remains a presence in the lives of the family members she left behind. Like her mother, Kristin is outwardly prim, with a tomboyish streak just below the surface; on fishing trips with her dad, she insists on being the one to gut the catch. She also inherited Florence's studiousness, her focus, and something of her toughness and adaptability. She recently won the local Rotary Club's "Character Counts" essay contest with an entry that described her time of bereavement. "Losing my mom made me feel different from the other kids," Jay remembers Kristin writing. "But it taught me perseverance."

As for the storytelling DVDs, Jay keeps them tucked away on a shelf in the closet. He plans to present them to Kristin as a keepsake someday. "The time will have to be right," he says, "for her, for me, for the family. I have no idea when that will be. But when she's older, I want her to have those treasures. None of us ever knew how significant they would be in our lives."

> *The legacy of those DVDs is right there in the family living room.*

Yet in a sense, the legacy of those DVDs—of the gift that a soldier-mother created for her daughter—is right there in the family living room. In the evenings, when the adults take out their medical journals and Kristin cracks a volume of *Harry Potter*, little sister Dana invariably climbs into her elder sibling's lap holding a picture book. "Kristin loves to read to her," Jay says. "When Dana is old enough for *Good Night, Gorilla*, we'll really have come full circle."

Originally published in the March 2017 issue of *Reader's Digest* magazine.

Philanthropy was a key part of DeWitt and Lila Wallace's legacy. Today, the Reader's Digest Foundation continues to support many of the causes they held dear, including literacy, through its donations to organizations such as United Through Reading.

"Don't Go Away! I'm Alive!"

by Joe Austell Small

When search planes failed to spot his crashed helicopter or signal fire time after time, the injured pilot lost all hope. Then he decided to make one last effort.

It sounded as if a baseball bat had hit the tail end of the helicopter. Immediately the aircraft shivered and started a slow spin. Having lost control of the tail rotor, Walter Yates knew he was going to crash.

A spruce forest blanketed the British Columbia marshland 700 feet below him. Almost automatically he put the helicopter into a dive to build up enough speed to resume a straight course. But he was running out of sky. Yates decided to go into a sweep of spindly spruce trees to break his fall. At the last moment he pulled the aircraft up sharply to stop its forward speed. He was now in the treetops, drilling a hole in the forest. Yates called out "God, help me!" and braced himself.

It was a nightmare of cracking, chopping, jolting, confusion. The rotor blades were slicing the trees into chunks. One section crashed through the bubble, hit Yates's side and glanced off his face.

Impact! The right door flew off, and fire instantly swept the shattered bubble. Releasing his safety belt, Yates dived through the angry flames. When he looked back, his Bell Ranger helicopter had become an inferno.

Fearing that the aircraft's fuel tanks might explode, he began crawling away through a muck of moss, water and mud. After 30 feet, he collapsed in a depression full of brackish water and watched as flames consumed his beautiful aircraft. Then he passed out.

When he came to, the fire had burned out, and it was raining steadily. Shivering from the cold, Yates started to get to his feet, then realized he could not stand. The pain in his back and chest was agonizing. He could feel his broken ribs rubbing together as he moved. Yates crawled closer to the remains of his helicopter to absorb the little heat that was still radiating from it. The classy machine that had carried him across the Alaskan and Canadian wilderness was nothing but a pile of molten, twisted metal, sizzling in a swamp.

Walter Yates, 55, had passed the summer prospecting for gold near Alaska's Kuskokwim River. That morning, September 2, 1979, he had left Fort Nelson on his four-day flight home to Cedar Park, Texas, where his wife and four children waited. There had been many adventures and close calls in Walter Yates's life—as a Marine in World War II and as a pilot in the North country for the past 12 years. But now death seemed closer than ever before.

That night Yates lay in cold water, half awake. In the morning he was weak from the loss of blood. He crawled to the wreckage. Just as he had thought, a component of the tail rotor had come off, causing the loss of control.

Sifting through the ashes, he found a charred box of prunes. They would sustain him for two days. The ashes also yielded his pocketknife, a camera lens, a hacksaw, some wire and a bucket he could catch rainwater in. Thrown from the wreck lay his heavy boots and jacket. In the jacket pocket were seven matches—a find that brightened his spirits.

Concerned that his broken ribs might puncture a lung, Yates carved some splints from spruce limbs and bound them together in a rough corset that he hoped would keep the ribs in place.

He had always taken great pride in his strength of will. That, plus his study of the art of survival, would now face the supreme test. But he knew that determination alone would not save him. He prayed then—for those who would be searching for him, for his family and friends, for strength.

How could anyone ever find him here? The chopper's blades had drilled straight down through thick growth 30 to 40 feet high. To see the wreckage, a pilot would have to fly directly over him in conditions of perfect visibility.

The rain did not let up, and those first three days and nights Yates drifted in and out of reality. By not allowing his thoughts to travel beyond one day, he was able to fight off despair. Even without the constant rain, it would have been impossible to keep dry. Anywhere he put his weight, the marshy ground sank several inches.

First he had to build a shelter—or die. On hands and knees, Yates pulled the chopper's right door on top of some three-foot-high tree stumps created by the rotor blades. Around this roof he placed parts of the wreckage, then banked it with spruce boughs.

He collected marsh grass and made a mattress, but when he lay down, the lower part of his body was still an inch deep in water. Wet boots and exposure were taking their toll. Now he was suffering from trench foot.

Foraging for food one day, Yates found some cranberry bushes. He had to dig underneath to find berries that wildlife had missed. The leaves and stems made a bitter "salad."

During his forays, Yates gathered dry wood for what he called his "mound of hope." When it stopped raining and the search planes came, this mound would be his signal fire.

On the fourth day Yates decided to try to move the tail section of the helicopter into an opening 20 feet away where it could be seen by search planes. He struggled with the tail for over an hour. It wouldn't budge. He gave up and crawled back to his shelter to await clear weather.

Just before dark on the fifth day, Yates heard something moving through the brush. It was a bear! The big bruin stopped 30 feet away, then stood up on its hind legs and sniffed the air. Yates took some aluminum fragments he had salvaged and banged them together. To his horror, this seemed not to disturb the bear at all. It dropped to all fours and came even closer; eight feet from him, it stood up again. Now it was baring its teeth and making low growls.

The animal was so close that all Yates could see was fur. He began praying. The bear made a circle around the shelter, then another, until it was out of sight. Yates wondered if the bear was merely waiting for darkness to attack. That night was the longest and most miserable one he had spent yet.

Day after day the rain continued. Yates would drag himself out of the shelter and crawl around in the wet bushes to pick berries and gather wood. It was a tedious routine, but it kept his mind occupied.

On the seventh day there was a strange quiet. Then Yates realized the rain had stopped! Lifting a radiant face toward the sky, he said aloud, "Lord, don't let it start again. Clear weather is my only hope."

The sun was shining late the next afternoon when Yates heard an aircraft. He shouted in elation and rushed to start a fire. The plane, belonging to a Canadian Armed Forces Search and Rescue Squadron, missed him by a quarter of a mile. In a few minutes it came back—and missed him again. It was one of the lowest feelings Yates had ever experienced.

When he had recovered from the disappointment, Yates figured the rescuers would probably try again the next morning. He would get his signal fire going early, and they would find him. He was certain. Feverishly he added wood to his mound of hope. He was really excited now; he didn't sleep all night.

At daybreak of the ninth day, Yates took off the corset he had made from limbs and used it for kindling. With only three matches left, he felt this would be his last signal fire. If they didn't find him today, it was all over. Later he heard an aircraft. He quickly piled moss and green limbs on the fire to produce smoke. But the wind played a cruel trick: As soon as the smoke reached treetop level, it rolled back into the forest.

The plane flew by twice. The rescuers hadn't seen anything! Yates couldn't believe it. They had passed by four times now. There wasn't one chance in a thousand they would come again.

As the drone of the engine grew dim, Yates slumped to the ground and wept. Then an odd peace came over him. He began crawling toward the tail section. *Why am I doing this? I failed before, and I'm weaker now.* But a powerful urge pulled him toward the wreckage. *If the rescuers do come back, they must have something to see on the ground.*

When he reached the tail section, Yates lay on his back, took hold of the 200-pound mass and began dragging it. Each exertion brought on blinding pain. His ribs had begun to mend, but now he could feel them breaking loose.

A mysterious new strength now enabled Yates to move the tail section. Then, just as his adrenaline began to flow, the metal snagged on a tree. In all, five trees, four to five inches in diameter, blocked his path. Yates retrieved the hacksaw and began cutting them. It took him two more days, but by the end of the 11th day, he had dragged the tail into the clearing.

When he awoke on the 13th day, Yates was horrified. Drizzle and fog had moved in, hiding the tail section he had worked so hard to move. *But the sun will come back out.*

That afternoon the clouds began to break, and for an hour the sun shone beautifully. Yates thought he heard an aircraft. Quickly he pulled some dry moss and twigs from his jacket. Only two matches were left. The first flared and went out. Only one match left—panic ate at his insides. He couldn't use it until he was sure.

Maybe the camera lens would work. He concentrated the sun through it onto the moss. Eventually a tiny curl of smoke arose. At last the blaze appeared, and Yates was able to keep it going for an hour. But no aircraft showed up.

Yates spent part of the 14th day of his ordeal writing notes to his family and changing his will. At ten o'clock he heard an engine. His heart pounding, Yates crawled outside, barely in time to see the aircraft pass directly over him.

As he reached the clearing, he heard the plane circling. *It's coming back!* Now he was shouting at the top of his lungs, "I'm saved! Thank you, God—I'm saved!"

Yates signaled with a piece of shiny metal as the plane swooped back over him. "I'm alive!" he shouted. "Don't go away!" The plane dipped its wings, a signal that the crew had seen him. It was too much. Tears of relief streamed down his face as he kept shouting, "I'm saved! I'm saved!" As the aircraft continued to circle, probably radioing for a helicopter, Yates lay back and rested.

Fifteen minutes later a giant yellow helicopter was hovering over him. Two rescue specialists came down on a cable, and one asked if he was Walter Yates. "Yes! Oh, my God, yes!" he answered, wanting to hug his rescuers.

Strapping Yates securely in a basket, the two members of the 442nd Search and Rescue Squad lifted him into the helicopter. "You're OK now," said one. Overwhelmed by gratitude, Yates pulled him close and whispered hoarsely, "You saved my life."

At the hospital in Fort Nelson, Yates was treated for a crushed vertebra, eight broken ribs and trench foot. While recovering, he learned that the rescuers would have missed him again—and perhaps for good—had they not seen the tail section he had dragged into the clearing—and had the weather in the area not, as a report stated, "mysteriously cleared." For Walter Yates, there is no mystery.

Originally published in the February 1982 issue of *Reader's Digest* magazine.

After surviving the 14-day ordeal, Yates returned to gold mining in the Yukon Territory and exploring deserted ghost towns in his helicopter. Yates was also a real-estate developer who built Breakaway Park in Cedar Park, Texas, a fly-in community where homes have spaces for private planes. Walter "Yukon" Yates died on March 2, 2015, at age 90.

Humor Hall of Fame

"Perhaps you've heard of me. I discovered a little thing called fire."

My dapper 51-year-old husband supervises scads of attractive younger women at his law firm. After friends divorced, I had to ask, "Honey, have you ever been tempted by the idea of a May-December romance?" "Not really," he replied. "I don't see myself dating older women."

—SUSAN FERGUSON

My friend Connie was very supportive of her husband's campaign to be elected vice president at his local union, but she missed seeing him off for work the day of the election.

Since she would be late arriving home, she left a special message for him on their home answering machine: "Good luck, honey, and don't worry. No matter how the election turns out, you'll always be vice president at our house."

—CHRISTY S. MARCHAND

GIVE AND TAKE

Since both my husband and I are right-handed, there were some basics we couldn't teach our left-handed daughter. She made up for this "loss" in reading skills. When she entered first grade, Ellen could read anything. I worried that her classmates might resent this skill—that it would cause her to have trouble making friends. Early in the school year, I asked her teacher if Ellen's reading ability affected her relationship with her peers. The teacher replied, "One of her friends summed it up best when she said, 'Ellen tells us the hard words and we tie her shoes.'"

—Wilmoth Foreman, *Columbia, Tennessee*

AGELESS SPUNK

Grandma was 96, and her mind was still sharp. One day she fell down and hurt her arm. We decided to take her to the local emergency room to have her checked out. We arrived and were shown into a room to await the doctor. He arrived shortly and started to examine Grandma's arm while asking her a few questions. "How old are you?" he asked. Grandma answered. "And what year were you born?" Grandma leaned forward and looked directly at the doctor. "Young man," she said, "the problem is in my arm, not my head."

—Barbara Phillips, *Eustis, Florida*

Surviving Whole Foods

by Kelly MacLean, from HuffingtonPost.com

A suburban woman braves a minefield of
mindfulness at the upscale market.

Whole Foods is like Vegas. You go there to feel good, but you leave broke, disoriented and with the newfound knowledge that you have a bacterial infection.

Unlike in Vegas, Whole Foods's clientele are all about mindfulness and compassion ... until they get to the parking lot. Then it's war. As I pull up this morning, I see a pregnant lady on the crosswalk holding a baby and groceries. A driver swerves around her and honks. As he speeds off, I catch his bumper sticker, which says NAMASTE. Poor lady didn't even hear him approaching, because he was driving a Prius. He crept up on her like a panther.

As the great sliding-glass doors part, I am immediately smacked in the face by a wall of cool, moist air that smells of strawberries and orchids. I leave behind the concrete jungle and enter a cornucopia of organic bliss, the land of hemp milk and honey. Think about heaven and then think about Whole Foods; they're basically the same.

The first thing I see is the gluten-free section, filled with crackers

and bread made from various wheat substitutes such as cardboard and sawdust. I skip this aisle because I'm not rich enough to have dietary restrictions. Ever notice that you don't meet poor people with special diet needs? A gluten-intolerant housecleaner? A cab driver with candida? Candida is what I call a rich-white-person problem. You know you've really made it in this world when you get candida. My personal theory is that candida is something you get from too much hot yoga. All I'm saying is, if I were a yeast, I would want to live in your yoga pants.

Next I approach the beauty aisle. There is a scary-looking machine there that you put your face inside of, and it tells you exactly how ugly you are. It calculates your wrinkles, your sunspots, the size of your pores, etc., and compares the results with those of other women your age. I think of myself as attractive, but as it turns out, I am 78 percent ugly, meaning less pretty than 78 percent of women in the world. On the popular "one to ten" hotness scale used by males the world over, that makes me a three (if you round up, which I hope you will). A glance at the extremely closeup picture it took of my face—in which I somehow have a glorious blond porn mustache—tells me that three is about right. Especially because the left side of my face is apparently 20 percent more aged than the right. After contemplating ending it all here and now, I decide instead to buy a bottle of delicious-smelling, silky-feeling cream that may raise me from a three to a four for only $108.

I grab a handful of peanut butter pretzels on my way out of this stupid aisle. I don't feel bad about pilfering these bites because of the umpteen times I've overpaid at the salad bar and been tricked into buying

$108 beauty creams. The pretzels are very fattening, but I'm already in the 70th percentile of ugly, so who cares?

Next I come to the vitamin aisle, which is a danger zone for any broke hypochondriac. Warning: Whole Foods keeps its best people in this section. The vitamin clerk talks me into buying estrogen for my mystery mustache along with women's acidophilus because apparently I do have candida after all.

I move on to the next aisle and ask a nearby clerk for help. He's wearing a visor inside, and it has one word on it in all caps. Yup: NAMASTE. I ask him where I can find whole wheat bread. He chuckles at me. "Oh, we keep the poison in aisle seven." Based solely on the attitudes of people sporting namaste paraphernalia today, I'd think it was Sanskrit for "go to hell."

I pass a table where a vendor invites me to join a group cleanse he's leading. For $179.99, I can not-eat not-alone ... not-gonna-happen. They're doing the cleanse where you consume nothing but lemon juice, cayenne pepper and fiber pills for ten days. What's that one called again? Oh, yeah ... anorexia. I went on a cleanse once; it was a mixed blessing. On the one hand, I detoxified, I purified, I lost weight. On the other hand, I fell asleep on the highway and fantasized about eating a pigeon. I think I'll stick with the whole eating thing.

You put your face inside the machine, and it tells you exactly how ugly you are.

I grab a couple of loaves of poison and head to the checkout. The fact that I'm at Whole Foods on a Sunday finally sinks in when I join the end of the line ... halfway down the dog-food aisle. I suddenly realize that I'm dying to get out of this store. Maybe it's the lonely feeling of being a carnivore in a sea of vegans or the revelation that some people's dogs eat better than I do, but mostly I think it's the fact that Yanni has been playing literally this entire time. Like sensory deprivation, listening to Yanni seems harmless at first, enjoyable even. But two hours in, you'll chew your own ear off to make it stop.

A thousand minutes later, I get to the cashier. She is 95 percent beautiful. "Have you brought your reusable bags?" @#$%! No, they are at home with their two dozen other once-used friends. She rings up my meat, alcohol, gluten and a wrapper from the chocolate bar I ate in line, with thinly veiled alarm. She scans my ladies acidophilus, gives me a pitying frown and whispers, "Ya know, if you wanna get rid of your candida, you should stop feeding it." She rings me up for $313. I resist the urge to unwrap and swallow whole another $6 truffle in protest. Instead, I reach for my wallet, flash her a quiet smile and say, "Namaste."

Originally published in the April 2014 issue of *Reader's Digest* magazine.

The Lady and the Gangsters

by Lester Velie

Min Matheson's war against the underworld was no ordinary labor dispute.

Perched on high heels, Min Lurye Matheson reaches only five feet three inches. Yet, where strong men feared to tread, Min waged a woman's war against the terror and force of the East's big underworld—and won.

Min Matheson is a regional manager of the International Ladies Garment Workers Union (ILGWU) at Wilkes-Barre, Pennsylvania. Trim at 47, she has the settled look of a housewife and mother. This is deceptive. Once torn by labor turmoil, Wilkes-Barre today is a model of union-management teamwork and, says the town's mayor, Luther Kniffen, "We owe it mostly to Min."

New York's garment center owes much to Min, too. For years gang-sters had kept the ILGWU out of "protected" shops in New York by cracking the skulls of union organizers. These protected employers paid substandard wages and threatened competing dress men with bankruptcy. Then, as the ILGWU gained strength, some nonunion employers "ran away" to Pennsylvania's distressed hard-coal country.

There, as late as 1946, they paid wives and daughters of idle miners as little as $16 weekly for sewing work.

Some of the invaded Pennsylvania towns became underworld cesspools where labor racketeers, fugitives from justice, and other flotsam and jetsam drained. Here, if uncurbed, the gangsters could not only destroy competing dress men in the industry's home base in New York, but their sweatshop wages could doom the depressed hard-coal country to permanent poverty.

To this new garment battlefield, in 1945, came Min Matheson. Her mission: to force union peace and union wages on the nonunion shops and underworld invaders. Her male predecessors had been able to unionize only five out of 100-odd shops. How could a woman do better? By being a woman, Min decided.

Min's daughters, ages five and four and dressed in starchy pinafores, came tripping down the street.

As an initial target Min picked a factory in Pittston, a hard-coal town near Wilkes-Barre—the stamping ground of underworld figure Russ Bufalino and a gang whose members had served time for crimes ranging from white slavery to passing counterfeit money. In Pittston, cronies of Bufalino's served on the school board, carried guns as constables, served as tax assessors. Many of the dress and other factories that line Pittston's streets are owned by Bufalino and his close friends.

First Min called on the sewing-machine operators at night. "I've got kids, too," she told them, "and I know you can't raise a family on $16 a week. Join the union and you'll have 400,000 friends helping you get better conditions."

"Easy said," the girls would reply, "but you don't live in Pittston. What do you know about bombed homes, wrecked cars, blood spilled?" Others simply said, "We're afraid."

"I don't think they'll hurt women," Min said. "Anyway, they can't kill all of us. Join me on the picket line and we'll find out together."

The women did join, and one summer day in 1946 Pittston was treated to something new: 30 female pickets laying siege to a Main Street dress factory—with the "union lady" parading at their head. A crowd soon gathered across the street, among them some of the town's most lurid characters.

This was war. If those "crazy skirts" won their union fight, they'd kill the "edge"—the competitive advantage enjoyed by nonunion, gangster-protected shops. Against male pickets the hoodlums knew their duty and would have done it by crippling a few. But "broads"? How do you fight them?

Maybe they could discredit the "union lady." They yelled obscenities at Min. "Slut!" they shouted. "You ain't fit to lead our girls."

Min rushed to the nearest phone and called a clerk at the union office in Wilkes-Barre. "Run to my home," she said. "Dress up the children like angels. Bring them here, quick." Soon, in tow of the clerk, Min's daughters, ages five and four and dressed in starchy pinafores, came tripping down the street.

"Clear the sidewalk," Min ordered her pickets, and seizing picket signs she handed them to her children. Together, mother and daughters took up the picketing, flouting the baffled hoodlums with motherhood and respectability.

The incident steeled the female pickets to hold fast in the war of nerves that followed. The hoodlums pushed the girls around, threatened their families and menaced Min herself with a shotgun. They ordered the owner of the strike-bound shop not to make peace and tided him over with money raised from other "protected" employers. For eight months Min's pickets stayed on the job, then withdrew when the place failed to open.

Neither side won. But Min showed the employers and their protectors that they were in for a costly war. Moreover, it was a war against a woman antagonist in which the thug's usual weapons—the knife and acid bottle—might not work. Doggedly Min tackled other employers, spending her nights preaching the union gospel and going on a picket line at dawn. Then tragedy struck, reminding Min that she was in no ordinary labor dispute. The underworld uses murder in the line of business.

The time was 1949. In New York the powerful ILGWU, goaded by honest dress men who were being ruined by protected sweatshops, launched a major drive against the underworld protectors. Unlike Min, the union wouldn't use female pickets, but brought in huskies from the Seafarers' Union instead. The hoodlums sent some of these to the hospital, then invaded union headquarters and beat top leaders senseless with chairs.

Into this turmoil plunged Min's younger brother, Will Lurye, a slight 135-pounder and the father of four children. Burning with union zeal, Will had given up his $150-a-week job as presser to join up as an $80-a-week union organizer. His first assignment: to captain a picket line blockading a shop protected by a partner of Albert Anastasia of Murder, Inc.

Min rushed to New York. "Get off that picket line," she pleaded. "Think of your wife and children." "Look who's talking!" said Will Lurye. So Min and Will took their argument to their 72-year-old father, Max, who was ill in a hospital. He had spent his life organizing unions and had survived a machine-gunning in Chicago.

"What do you think of your daughter telling me to quit, Pop?" joked Will Lurye.

The aged man raised himself on his elbow. "Never, never!" he said. Then he read them a lecture on "the need to organize"—a staple of Lurye household oratory that Min and Will knew from childhood up.

Next day, in the heart of the teeming garment center, Will Lurye was crowded into a telephone booth by two assassins and was so hacked with knives that he died soon after. And Pop Lurye, his heart breaking with remorse, died a few days later.

The Lurye slaying and the publicity that followed so spotlighted the gangsters' garment-center operations that many more fled to Pennsylvania. And the job of coping with the new invasion still rested with Min. Terror alone had not stopped her. Starting with a half dozen unionized shops and 700 members in 1945, she had signed contracts with 70 dress factories by 1953. Now, in a showdown struggle, Min's foes tried something new.

In the Pittston office of dress manufacturer Angelo Sciandra, crony of racket figure Bufalino, employers and their protectors laid plans to drive Min and her union out of northeastern Pennsylvania. The weapon: their own friendly union. Several years before, a Bufalino pal, known as both Nick Benfonte and Belfonte, had organized a union. This had been dissolved by court order because of the unsavory character of the leaders. Benfonte had gone into saloonkeeping instead. Now employer Sciandra, a swarthy husky of 30 with no criminal record but many underworld connections, joined up with Benfonte in pushing another "union," the Northeastern Pennsylvania Needle Workers' Association.

Sciandra and Benfonte made the rounds of the dress factories. "Sign up with our union," they said, "and we'll give you a good deal. You'll be sorry if you don't." Some dress men, already signed up with Min, showed them the door. But others signed up out of fear or greed.

Min counterattacked, and again her troops were girls. She picked Pittston's Main Street as the chief battleground, picketed one manufacturer who had embraced the racket union, and served notice on others that soon they would be blockaded too. Alarmed, Min's superiors sent orders from New York: "Don't tangle with them. We don't want another Lurye murder."

"The danger is exaggerated," Min assured them. But in Pittston the pressures were mounting.

"Tell your boss," female pickets were told, "to lay off our union. Or she'll get what her brother got."

Then came the cruelest pressure of all. As Min and her girls walked to the union hall one night, they heard a man's voice behind them. "Walk on. Don't recognize me," the man said, his voice choked with emotion. It was an employer who had signed with Min. "For God's sake, Min," he blurted, "they've ordered me to close my shop. They've threatened my family. If you don't think of yourself and your children, think of me and mine. Stop this. Get out of Pittston." The man broke into tears.

Min went on the radio. "To live by permission of goons is worse than death," she said, and wound up with: "Gentlemen, hoodlums, I don't scare easily."

Her foes responded by sending more thugs. When Min marched her six pickets to their stations one morning, some 100 toughs—new faces all—ringed the narrow strip of sidewalk on which her girls paced. In the face of catcalls and threats, the women held their ground. Meanwhile, threatened employers kept their shops going.

The hoodlums, baffled by the problem of battling with women, settled down to a cold war, alternating between terror and horseplay. Angelo Sciandra, the employers' leader, took to coming down to the picket line at 6 a.m. Climbing atop a car, he would sound a quavering taps on a trumpet as Min and her girls marched to their posts. "For your funeral," his pals would shout.

As Min pushed the racket union out of one shop after another, Sciandra took to sending her huge horseshoes of flowers, gangland-funeral size, ironically inscribed "Congratulations!"

With tension mounting as the weeks passed, friends in the Teamsters Union insisted on coming down from New York to protect the girls. One was beaten so severely he went to the hospital. Tasting blood, the hoodlums taunted the girls: "Go home and bring your husbands." Shouting loudest of all was "Murph" Loquasto, convicted robber and white-slaver. Min tidied her hair and adjusted her hat. "Don't move," she instructed her pickets, and with fists clenched—amid a sudden hush—Min marched across the 80 feet of no-man's-land to Bufalino.

She looked up at the scar-faced hoodlum. "I don't need my husband to protect me," she shouted so that both sides of the street could hear. "I'm twice the man you'll ever be, Russ Bufalino."

Bufalino fidgeted. His men snickered, then guffawed. Across the way the girls gulped, then cheered. That did it: The tension and fear were broken. Soon afterward the racket needle workers union withdrew from the dress shops.

Min had broken the back of the hoodlums' resistance. The risks she had run came into sharper focus when the racket union moved and a Durable Thread Co. took over its store headquarters. Arriving from New York as partner—and using local hoodlums as aides—came Vincent Macri, a bodyguard for Anastasia of Murder, Inc. Min, it turned out, had been fighting local allies of the big New Jersey–New York mob!

Min did a job on the gangsters and their friends that other union leaders—merely males—have not been able to do to this day. Driven from the dress factories, Benfonte and his needle workers "union" invaded cigar, woodworking, electrical and trailer plants. Even such mighty unions as the United Steel Workers and the International Brotherhood of Electrical Workers have not been able to drive them out.

Meanwhile, Min—freed from the hoodlum menace—has signed up all but a handful of the 150 garment factories in her area, including all of the once "protected" shops.

"I don't need my husband to protect me," she shouted. *"I'm twice the man you'll ever be."*

At Wilkes-Barre I called on the town's leading banker, Frank Anderson. With him was the head of the Chamber of Commerce, Bill Sword. They vied to tell me what the lady labor leader had done for their town. Min, the gangbuster, it turned out, had also won herself a place as Min, leading citizen. "She has woven her union into the very fabric of this community," said Anderson. "Little goes on here without Min taking a hand."

One of Min's hands is deep in the affairs of the Chamber of Commerce—unusual, since unions and chambers of commerce usually regard one another as "natural enemies." But in Wilkes-Barre, unions and businessmen had a common problem—new jobs for displaced hard-coal miners. So Min and other labor leaders joined the chamber's Committee of 100 to bring in industry. It was she who went to Washington to speak for Wilkes-Barre before a Senate committee probing distressed areas.

Min's 9,000 members and their families, 17,000 strong, provide a vanguard for launching civic projects. When the town's club ladies sought support for a symphony orchestra, for instance, the president of the local Wilkes College suggested they call Min. When the ladies got over the novelty of sharing their project with a labor leader, Min helped their orchestra by getting her girls to sign up for family subscriptions.

Once the $16-a-week victims of sweatshops, Min's members today average $65 for a 35-hour week in an industry that has become so stabilized it is the economic backbone of many Pennsylvania communities. Employers pay 5 to 8 percent of their payroll into a union welfare fund that provides a 28-doctor medical center for union members where employers, too, can get checkups. Members get hospital care, an average of two weeks' paid vacations, and life insurance.

More, Min's union gives its girls a way of life—dancing classes, swimming lessons and weekend "happiness clinics" where the girls can learn the latest hairdo or diet. Once a year Min's members put on a musical play with an assist from the school system's musical director—and the whole town turns out. At a time when other union people have been clouding the name of labor, Min against great odds has built a model local labor union.

Whenever Mayor Luther Kniffen gets up to make a speech, he always begins: "Honored guests, ladies and gentlemen—and Min Matheson..." For, as the mayor explains, "In Wilkes-Barre, Min is an institution."

Originally published in the January 1957 issue of Reader's Digest magazine.

Northeast Pennsylvania had grown rapidly in the 18th and 19th centuries as people flocked there to work in the booming coal industry. By the 1940s, however, the coal mines had begun to close, leaving families desperate for employment. Garment contractors in nearby New York, often controlled by the mob, seized the opportunity to take advantage of these impoverished workers, thus setting the stage for the vicious labor dispute described here.

Our America

Wireless Connection
—**C.F. PAYNE**
FEBRUARY 2007

Humor Hall of Fame

While my husband was stationed overseas, our four-year-old daughter decided that she needed a baby brother. "Good idea," I told her. "But don't you think we should wait till your father is home?" Lori had a better idea. "Why don't we just surprise him?"

—KAY SCHMIDT

One of my roommates during Air Force flight training was a tall, rangy lieutenant from Louisiana. After his first solo flight, he raced back to the barracks to call his folks. His grandmother answered the phone. "Do you know what I did today, Granny?" he said. "I took an airplane out all by myself and flew it around and landed it."

There was a pause on the other end. Then she said, "Don't you evah do that again, y'hear?"

—WILFRED K. WATANABE

"An impressive résumé, General, but remember—
department store security is different from national security."

Our division had to repaint our Humvees to a sand color for Desert Storm. The result was a pinkish hue, and the jokes began. One wag renamed us the Pink Panzer Division. But the best was the Humvee bumper sticker "Ask me about Mary Kay."

—DAVID K. DRURY

Our Marine Corps son, who was assigned to the Defense Language Institute in Monterey, California, was disappointed that his repeated requests for transfer to the Gulf were denied. We telephoned his apartment when the war started, and his answering machine message said it all: "I can't come to the telephone right now. I'm busy conjugating verbs for democracy."

—E.T. DURAND

Back to the Wild

by Matthew Shaer, from *Smithsonian*

*An experimental program in
eastern Russia raises hope that
one of the most endangered animals
on earth may once again thrive.*

On a frigid afternoon in February 2012, a pair of hunters stalking deer in Russia's remote Primorsky Province were halted by an unusual sight: a four-month-old Amur tiger cub lying listlessly on her side in the snow. The cat clearly had not eaten in days, and the tip of her tail was black with frostbite. The hunters carted her to the home of Andrey Oryol, a local wildlife inspector. Oryol made an enclosure for the tiger, who was eventually given the name Zolushka, and fed her meat, eggs and warm milk. After a few days, the tiger cub's vitals had stabilized; after two weeks, she was pacing restlessly. Heartened, Oryol reached out to Dale Miquelle, the director of the Russia Program of the Wildlife Conservation Society (WCS), an American nonprofit.

Miquelle arrived at Oryol's house with Sasha Rybin, a WCS colleague. Immediately, Zolushka began to snarl. Adolescent tigers, despite their relatively small stature, are dangerous animals, with sharp claws and teeth. Miquelle used a stick to distract her while Rybin jabbed her with a tranquilizer dart. Once she had collapsed, a pair of local veterinarians amputated the necrotic tip of her tail, and Zolushka was moved

*A male Amur tiger rescued
from poachers recovers at
Utyos Wildlife Rehabilitation
Center in Kutuzovka, Russia.*

63

to the Center for the Rehabilitation and Reintroduction of Tigers and Other Rare Animals, some 40 miles to the south in Alekseevka.

Opened months earlier by a coalition that included the Russian Geographical Society and the government-funded group Inspection Tiger, the Alekseevka Center spilled over eight acres thick with brush and vegetation. "There were two main goals," Miquelle recalled. "Don't let the animal get acclimated to humans. And teach her to hunt."

If orphaned cubs could be rehabilitated to the point of mating with wild tigers, they would not only provide a boost in the local population but, in the aggregate, perhaps reclaim regions that hadn't seen healthy tiger communities in decades.

Zolushka was the first tiger to arrive at Alekseevka. In the early months, she was fed primarily meat. In the summer of 2012, Zolushka was presented with rabbits—fast, but ultimately defenseless. The next step was wild boar. It seemed at first to confuse her. "It was like a kid trying to figure out a puzzle," says Miquelle.

Three boars in, and Zolushka was driving the animals to the ground with grace and skill. She did the same with much larger sika deer.

In May 2013, a little more than a year after she arrived at the Alekseevka Center, the decision was made to set Zolushka free.

*   *   *

The Amur tiger—also known as the Siberian—is, along with the Bengal, the biggest in the tiger family. An adult male can measure as long as 11 feet and weigh 450 pounds; the average female is closer to 260.

Tigers once roamed the shorelines of Bali, the jungles of Indonesia and the lowlands of China. But deforestation, poaching and the widening footprint of man have all taken their toll, and today there are few wild tigers in China and none in Bali. At the turn of the 20th century, it was estimated that 100,000 tigers were roaming the wild. Now, per the World Wildlife Fund, the number is probably much closer to 3,890.

The area comprising Primorsky and neighboring Khabarovsk Province is, in a way, the tiger's last fully wild range. Just two million people live in Primorsky Province, on a landmass of nearly 64,000 square miles.

Zolushka after her tail surgery in 2012.

In the fall of 2014, I flew to Vladivostok to meet with Dale Miquelle and tour his ward, which extends from the southern lip of Primorsky to the easternmost reaches of Siberia. At 7 on a dark morning in late October, a green pickup truck pulled up to my hotel, and the broad-shouldered, unruly-haired Miquelle—more bear than tiger—piled out.

Miquelle oversees what is generally agreed to be the longest-running field research project on the Amur in history. Using GPS collars and other tracking techniques, he has established an unrivaled library of data, from the size of the male Amur's territory to its preferred prey. That information has allowed him to advise the government on what areas need more protection and to help establish new reserves in Russia and China.

He had an itinerary ready for me: We'd make a daylong journey, by car and by ferry, to Udege Legend National Park. There, we would set up camera traps. The combined infrared and photographic lenses, activated by motion and heat, provide data that might otherwise take months of backbreaking work to obtain. A few cats had been seen in Udege Legend, Miquelle told me, and he wanted to get a grip on their numbers.

* * *

Beginning in late 2012, five new orphaned cubs were brought to the Alekseevka Center: three males and two females. In spring 2013, they were outfitted with GPS collars and reintroduced into the wild in two different areas. Two of the male cats ranged hundreds of miles across mountain ridges and soggy marshland. The third male and the females staked out an area and remained near it, making shorter trips to hunt.

Zolushka was released in Bastak Zapovednik, some 300 miles north of Alekseevka. "This was an area where there were once tigers, and now there weren't," Miquelle told me. "It was an opportunity to actually recolonize tiger habitat. That's totally unheard of."

From his home, Miquelle watched the GPS data for evidence of Zolushka's first kill in the wild. Five days after her release, her GPS signal went stationary—often an indication that a tiger has brought down prey and is feasting on the carcass. After Zolushka had moved on, rangers found the remains of a sizable badger at the site.

Then, in August, Zolushka's GPS collar malfunctioned. "I was really freaked out," Miquelle told me. "She'd survived the summer, but winter is critical. A cat has to be able to eat and stay warm." If it can't, it will often approach villages to search for easier pickings, like cattle or domestic dogs. Humans are put in danger, and the cat is often killed.

Dale Miquelle tracks tigers using radio collars and traditional bushcraft methods such as "pugmarks" in the snow (pictured) and scent-marking on trees.

In September, the monitoring team was able to use the radio signal from Zolushka's collar to roughly pin down her location near the Bastak River. That winter of 2013, Miquelle traveled to Bastak. He and a pair of Russian scientists found a set of recent tracks, which met at several points with boar prints. Curiously, there was a set of larger prints, too: another tiger. Camera trap images soon proved what Miquelle and others had previously dared only to hope: The second tiger was a healthy male.

*   *   *

In the morning it was still snowing. Three miles out on the ferry road, we saw cars in the undergrowth, stuck. The desolation was complete.

Battling poaching in the Far East has always been a tricky proposition: The sheer size of the area makes law enforcement difficult and, according to Miquelle, "Sometimes, poachers are poaching because they're starving, and they need food for their families." In the Far East, a dead tiger can go for thousands of dollars.

Yet there has been progress. In 2010, at an international tiger summit in St. Petersburg, 13 countries pledged to double the world's tiger population by 2022. And in 2013, Vladimir Putin spearheaded the enactment of a strict anti-poaching law that made possession of tiger parts a criminal offense punishable by a lengthy spell in prison. In addition, at the end of 2015, the Russian Federation created Bikin National Park, which will be the largest protected area for Amur tigers in the world.

At the Udege Legend ranger station, we were joined by a squad of inspectors and two WCS team members: David Cockerill, an American volunteer, and Kolya Rybin, Sasha's older brother. We piled into two trucks and made our way into the surrounding hills. The Udege Legend staff estimated that there were close to ten tigers in the area, so Miquelle had arranged to lend them 20 camera traps.

We drew to a halt in the shadow of a high ridge. Tigers often frequent the bottom of cliff faces, where there is shelter from the driving winds. It was a good place for a trap, Miquelle said.

Rybin strapped up two cameras about ten feet apart. To test the first

Zolushka was photographed by camera traps after she was returned to the wild.

lens, a ranger crouched down and passed in front of the camera. A red light blinked; motion had been detected. The rangers cheered.

*   *   *

One evening, Miquelle invited me to his home to look at pictures captured on camera traps in Bastak. Zolushka was strong, self-assured, completely at home in the wilderness. Finally, we came to the other tiger: a thickset male who had been given the name Zavetny.

Zavetny and Zolushka seemed to be sharing a range. Miquelle was hopeful that one day he would see a photo showing Zolushka, who was then of breeding age, with cubs. Two years after her release, he got his wish: The team received a photograph from a camera trap showing two cubs trailing behind Zolushka. "Zolushka has made history and made us all feel like godparents," Miquelle says with a smile.

Originally published in the 2017 *Reader's Digest* international editions.

I Can't Find My Apron Strings

by Louise Dickenson Rich, from *Woman's Day*

A protective mother recounts how she
learned what every parent comes to know.

There was a time when I would have said with all confidence that the life of my only son, Rufus, was an open book to me. I was acquainted with everyone with whom he was acquainted; I recognized his limitations and his abilities; at any hour I could tell approximately where he was and what he was doing; and I knew that were anything troubling him, I would sense it. At least, that was my smug assumption. Then one blizzardy Saturday afternoon he asked me as a favor to drive him around his paper route. I'd never had a paper route myself, but naturally I knew all there was to know about the business. You left the paper, collected the week's tariff, and that was that. If it had been any more complicated, my son couldn't have held the job for the past two years. He was, after all, only a child.

I not only agreed to furnish transportation, but, in my innocence, I even offered to help him in the delivery. "All right," he said, "you take the left-hand side of the street and I'll take the right. That's 14 *Enterprise*s for you, six *Globe*s and two *Record*s. The first three houses are all

*Enterprise*s. Stick the papers inside the storm doors, and the money will be on the porch rails. The fifth house you have to ring the bell or she'll holler. The seventh and ninth houses are *Globe*s, and the eighth you have to deliver at the back door. She owes for two weeks and make her give it to you. Seventy cents, and don't let her talk you out of it."

I was lost. "Wait. The first three houses the papers go in the storm doors. Then the next you ring the bell..."

"No-no," he said indulgently. "Wouldn't it be simpler if I did them all and you kept the route book?" Keeping the route book consisted of checking off payments. I guessed I could do that.

For about three streets everyone paid on schedule. At the end of the fourth street, pencil poised, I asked, "Check them all?"

"Yup, all except number 39. I collect there on Mondays instead of Saturdays." I asked why.

"Oh, he's always drunk on Saturdays. Half the time he doesn't understand what I want and the other half he tries to give me all his money." My face must have reflected my horror. "Don't start worrying about it," my sheltered little lamb begged me. "Him and me understand each other all right. Now," he changed the subject with finality, "want to count out 11 *Enterprise*s for me?"

It took me two streets to recover. Then I came to a name about ten weeks in arrears. When Rufus came plowing back through the drifting snow, I said, "How long are you supposed to let them go without paying? This one here..."

"Yeah, I know. We're supposed to drop them after a month, but the boss says to use our own judgment."

What judgment of deadbeats can you have at 12? I wondered. "This fellow's been having a hard time. He's been out of work for a long while, and now his wife's in the hospital. But he's just got a job, and he says he'll pay me when he gets caught up with himself."

"But what if he doesn't?"

"It comes out of my hide. But don't worry. He'll pay."

I kept my mouth shut, since this was my son's affair and he had to learn the ways of the world sometime, probably the hard way. For weeks

I studied his face every collection day, trying to read in it any signs of disillusionment. At last I couldn't stand it any longer, so I asked.

"Who?" Rufus looked blank. "Oh, him. Oh, sure, he paid me up a month ago and gave me an extra buck for carrying him so long."

I never did find out much about Rufus's job at the garage. In theory, he washed cars and pumped gas. However, I came out of the chain store one day to find my son in deep consultation with a well-dressed stranger. Rufus was shaking his head and looking judicious. "She shouldn't do that," he said. "Let me take a look." The man climbed into a brand-new Lincoln parked at the curb and released the hood, and Rufus plunged elbow-deep into the innards of the motor. I prevented myself with difficulty from screaming "Don't touch! Those things run into money!" I was in no financial position to replace Lincolns ruined by my son's feckless attention.

"Now try her," Rufus instructed with the confident aplomb of a high-priced specialist. The owner stepped on the starter, the motor purred into life and Rufus announced, "She's OK now."

When the stranger had driven away, I told him, "You mustn't fool around with other people's cars. Who was that, anyhow? What were you doing under his hood? You might have busted something, and..."

"Gee whiz, Ma," he expostulated, "you'd think I was born yesterday! There wasn't nothing much the matter with that Lincoln. You ought to have seen the job we had last week. Oh boy, timing off, feed line plugged, wiring shorted..."

Last winter Rufus told me that he was going to spend his Christmas vacation working at a turkey-processing plant two towns away where they killed turkeys and prepared them for market. He'd arranged for transportation: He'd meet Norm at Charlie's Diner at 6 in the morning. All I had to worry about was putting up a lunch and seeing that the alarm clock was set for 5:30. This seemed within my limited abilities, but one night I forgot to set the alarm. Rufus wasn't at Charlie's the next morning, Norm went off without him and it was up to me to see that he got to work, since I was the one who had failed with the alarm clock.

Shivering and hungry in the pitch-black of a winter predawn, I drove him by obscure back roads to a long tumbledown shed in a field. Dim lights burned within, illuminating vaguely some sinister figures bundled against the cold and wearing rubber aprons. An ugly black mongrel came tearing out, slavering and snarling savagely. *Good Lord*, I thought, *what a horrible setup! I can't leave my child here with this bunch of thugs. That dog is only waiting to rip his throat out. I'm going to take Rufus straight home.*

But before I could open my chattering teeth to say so, he'd jumped out of the car. "Hello, Bandit!" he greeted the dog affectionately, and the great beast swooned with silly joy. The men in the shed crowded to the door, laughing. "Sure as heck thought you weren't going to make it this morning, boy!" they shouted, and all the unshaven, villainous faces were transfigured with good humor and friendliness.

"OK, OK," said one who seemed to be in charge. "We haven't got all day. Shake the lead out of your pants, Rufus, and get an apron on. I want you to shackle today."

That's when I gave up. I didn't know what shackling was, and I didn't try to find out. Driving back home alone in the red sunrise, I faced the fact that my child had a life of his own that he was perfectly competent to handle. He'd been doing it for years, during which most of my fussing and worrying had been so much wasted energy. From now on, I resolved, I was going to bear in mind the truth that the young are much more resourceful, adaptable and capable than their poor mothers, who foster a delusion of indispensability, are willing to accept.

It'll be very good for both of us, if I can do it.

Originally published in the October 1957 issue of *Reader's Digest* magazine.

"They'll Never Find Us"

by Margot McWilliams

The three men were adrift—at the mercy of a fierce winter storm. Only a miracle could save them.

Rudy Musetti shivered as he re-entered the wheelhouse after a quick inspection of the *Harkness*, the 70-foot tugboat he captained. The vessel was chugging through one of the worst gales Musetti had seen in his 37 years on the treacherous North Atlantic. It was 5:30 p.m. on January 16, 1992, and as he settled in to steer he knew it would be a long night.

That morning the seas had been peaceful when the *Harkness* left Eliot, at the southern tip of Maine, for the 22-hour voyage up to its home berth in Northeast Harbor on Mount Desert Island. But the weather had suddenly changed. Now the thermometer registered four degrees Fahrenheit, the wind was blowing at 40 knots, seas were swelling from 10 to 15 feet, and every inch of the tug's exterior was covered with ice. A six-foot layer of sea smoke, an impenetrable vapor created by the difference between ocean and air temperatures, floated on the water's surface.

The *Harkness* was traveling 25 miles offshore to avoid the maze of islands closer in. There were no fishing boats this far out after dark,

Duane Cleaves, Rudy Musetti and Arthur Stevens.

especially in these conditions. Musetti's only contact with shore was via his VHF radio. Confident he could bring the *Harkness* to a safe mooring, the 57-year-old captain radioed ahead to Northeast Harbor just before 6 p.m.: "Our ETA is 5 a.m. tomorrow—as scheduled."

Ship's mate Arthur Stevens, 43, poured hot coffee for Musetti and passenger Duane Cleaves, 54, a friend who had come along for the ride. The sounds of amiable conversation competed with the raging winds outside. Cleaves and Stevens had full confidence in their captain.

As the chill began to leave Musetti's bones, he turned and cast a watchful eye back over the length of the tug—and couldn't believe what he saw. More than a foot of water was sloshing around the deck. *Where did that come from?* Musetti wondered. *Could the boat have split a hull seam?* He started the bilge pump and kept his eyes locked on the stern. The water was still rising. With a sinking heart, he soon knew that the pump had frozen.

At that moment the tug took a swell broadside, and the two 500-foot coils of tow rope stowed on the stern washed overboard. Musetti knew the *Harkness* would have to keep moving and stay straight or those hawsers would snarl the propellers and kill the engines.

"We've got a problem, boys," he said, and radioed the Coast Guard. "I've got a foot and a half of water on the stern, and it's coming on fast. I'm going to try for Frenchboro," he said, referring to a port 20 miles to the north.

"Forget Frenchboro," a voice came back. "You'll never make it. Try for Matinicus."

Matinicus? Musetti thought as he replaced the mike on its hook. *Is anyone on that Godforsaken rock in the winter?*

A little before 6 o'clock, Rick and Sue Kohls arrived for a lasagna dinner with their neighbors Vance and Sari Bunker. With virtually no ferry service to the mainland, the ten families that lived and lobster-fished year-round on Matinicus Island had to rely on one another. One of their unwritten laws was to help anyone in trouble, particularly anyone at sea.

That evening when the Kohlses and Bunkers settled down to eat, the ever-present VHF radio crackled in the background. Soon the four friends heard Rudy Musetti's exchange with the Coast Guard. They listened, disbelieving, as Musetti reported his location and the depth of water over his stern. Then they heard him being urged to try for Matinicus.

Vance Bunker rose and opened the porch door. The thermometer read six below, and the wind howled savagely. When he came back into the room, barely a word was spoken. As the men suited up in their foul-weather gear, they placed a call to island electrician Paul Murray to join them on the *Jan-Ellen*, the Bunkers' boat. *We don't have a chance of reaching them in time,* Vance thought. But he knew they had to try.

Musetti struggled with the idea of heading for Matinicus. Every instinct was telling him to stay on course and head for a place he knew. *If we change course,* he thought, *we're going to run afoul of those hawsers.*

The Coast Guard had radioed that a cutter was en route from Rockland. But Musetti was sure it couldn't reach them in time. *I have no choice,* he told himself as he turned the wheel toward Matinicus.

Sure enough, two-thirds of the way into the turn, the loose hawsers swept under the boat and like deadly snakes wrapped themselves around both propellers, killing the engines. The *Harkness* was adrift, dead in the water. All that could be heard now was the triumphant howl of the wind.

A few minutes later, at 6:40, Musetti picked up a voice on his radio. "This is the *Jan-Ellen* from Matinicus," Vance Bunker said. "We're on our way." *But can you get here in time?* Musetti thought grimly.

* * *

As the *Jan-Ellen* cleared the Matinicus breakwater, icing-up began. Bunker had never seen spray freeze as hard and as fast. When the boat left the harbor shortly before 7 p.m., Musetti had given his position over the radio and warned Bunker about the loose hawsers. If they got tangled in the *Jan-Ellen*'s propeller and the *Harkness* sank, Bunker's much smaller boat would be pulled down with it.

Along the coast of Maine, families were now glued to their VHF sets, listening to the drama unfolding on the seas. Soon they heard another frightening message. "It's up to our chests in the wheelhouse," Musetti reported. "We're going down." After that, there was silence.

Bunker knew now that the three of them were risking their lives for what were likely to be dead men. Survival time in these waters in January is usually measured in minutes. Still, he kept the *Jan-Ellen* moving ahead, as Kohls and Murray peered blindly into the sea smoke.

* * *

Inside the *Harkness*'s swamped wheelhouse, while Musetti talked to the Coast Guard on the radio, Duane Cleaves struggled to guide the captain's feet into one of the thinly insulated immersion suits that had been stowed on board. Musetti knew that the suits wouldn't keep them warm for long in icy waters. Yet this was all they had.

On the roof of the wheelhouse, Stevens was having trouble freeing an inflatable life raft from its protective canister. Cleaves pointed to the dinghy lashed to the bow and volunteered to climb over to it, but Musetti dismissed the idea, noting that their chances of survival would be greater if they stuck together. Cleaves grabbed a flashlight from the cabinet near the tug's wheel and went to the roof to help Stevens.

When the life raft wouldn't inflate, Cleaves yelled for the captain. By the time Musetti made it up to the roof, the tug's bow was pointing straight up at a 90-degree angle to the water. The men were now standing on the wheelhouse windshield, fighting for balance.

Suddenly, with a shuddering crash, the *Harkness*'s 500-pound anchor, which had been at rest on the point of the bow, thundered down toward the dinghy, narrowly missing Musetti and Cleaves as it crashed through the wheelhouse and into the sea below. The lifeboat was smashed.

"It's up to our chests," Musetti reported. "We're going down." After that, there was silence.

Musetti realized that if they were near the *Harkness* when it sank, suction would pull them right down with the tug. Before he could say a word, a wave washed over the boat and swept all three men into the water.

Musetti gasped as the paralyzing water sucked the air out of his lungs. While his ship slid silently into the water, he felt sick.

"Rudy, over here!" he heard through the deafening wind. Cleaves and Stevens were calling him. He found them holding on to an eight-foot wooden ladder that had somehow freed itself from the deck.

"Good. We're together," Musetti said. "If we drift apart, they'll never find us." *They'll never find us anyway*, he thought. But he had to keep up the two other men's courage.

*　*　*

Fifteen minutes later, the *Jan-Ellen* arrived at the last coordinates the *Harkness* had given. As expected, there was nothing there but the howling wind and the blackness. Suddenly a light pierced the sea smoke. "There she is, there she is!" Bunker yelled at Kohls and Murray.

Quickly he realized his mistake. The light was not from the *Harkness*, but from the Coast Guard cutter now arriving on the scene.

Bunker backed away and turned the *Jan-Ellen* in another direction, while the Coast Guard boat followed. Kohls and Murray kept looking.

*　*　*

In the water Musetti fell into a dreamlike state as his body began the slow shutdown of hypothermia. He thought about his children. He thought about Cleaves and Stevens and what this would mean to their families.

Suddenly a light appeared in the distance, and he jerked himself into wakefulness. But as quickly as it had appeared, the light was gone.

Moments later he saw a second light coming toward them—this time from the opposite direction. He had always heard that freezing to death was a peaceful way to go. *It's true*, he thought. *There really are angels!*

To his amazement, the angels began to shout at him. Suddenly there were boats around him and the others, and arms were reaching toward them. Slowly he understood. *We've been found!*

It took all the strength of the *Jan-Ellen*'s crew to haul the waterlogged bodies of Musetti and Cleaves into the boat while the Coast Guard retrieved Stevens. Kohls and Murray pulled their two passengers below, and they struggled to get the frozen clothes off the two violently shaking men while Bunker turned the boat homeward.

When the *Jan-Ellen* and the Coast Guard cutter pulled into Matinicus, cars and trucks were waiting with thermoses, blankets and extra clothing. The crew of the *Harkness* was immediately wrapped in the blankets and driven to the warmth of the Bunkers' house. Death from hypothermia could still occur. Sue Kohls and Sari Bunker did their best to make the three comfortable. They poured coffee, but the men's hands shook so violently that it spilled. When their shaking subsided, the men from the *Harkness* devoured reheated lasagna.

After they could talk, Musetti spoke up. "How did you find us?"

"The light," Kohls answered.

"What light?" Musetti asked.

"There was a flashlight frozen to Duane's glove," Kohls said. He retrieved it from the crew's wet belongings and banged it until it lit up.

Stevens's jaw dropped. "That's mine," he said. His 16-year-old daughter, Robyn, had given it to him for Christmas, and he'd assumed that it had gone down with the boat. Cleaves explained that he'd grabbed it when he left the wheelhouse.

There was stunned silence. "What are the chances," Musetti finally asked, "that a turned-on flashlight would freeze itself to the glove of a man whose hands were too cold to hold it?"

"Or that a ladder would free itself as we went down—and float right over to me?" asked Cleaves.

Arthur Stevens spoke last. "And why did Robyn choose a flashlight, of all things, as a Christmas present for me?"

Rudy Musetti shivered, but this time it wasn't from the cold. "Thank you, Captain," he said to Vance Bunker. *And thank you, too*, he mused in silent prayer, letting his thoughts lift upward.

Originally published in the October 1993 issue of *Reader's Digest* magazine.

Rudy Musetti became and remained friends with his rescuers until his death in 2003. Rick Kohls passed away in 2015, Arthur Stevens in 2018, and Duane Cleaves in 2019. Paul Murray still lives on Matinicus Island with his wife, Eva. Vance Bunker now lives on the mainland but is still lobstering at age 80.

Motorcycle Poet

"I kept getting a coffee cup [at Starbucks] that read 'A writer is someone who wrote today,'" says Phil Berg. "I must have gotten 30 or 40. One day, I just looked up in the sky and thought, *I get it—I'm going to write a book about all the funny things that happen when I ride my motorcycle.* People said, 'How are you going to write a book? You don't know how to write a book!' And I said, 'Get out of the way and watch!'"

Photograph by Glenn Glasser

Cowboy Doctor

"I grew up in Rockland, Maryland, and did my medical training in New York City. I was a city boy all the way through, so I'd never even seen a cow before," recalls Shahriar Anoushfar, MD. "One day, I was watching a Western and thought, *Looks beautiful—I'm gonna go out west and buy a ranch.* I bought one before I even moved!"
Photograph by Glenn Glasser

CHRISTMAS MAGIC

My daughter and only child, Talena, was killed by a drugged driver in 1994. It nearly destroyed me, but I kept going on somehow. I had a favorite picture from when she was about three: Christmas Day, me sitting on the floor and her sitting on my legs, opening a present, and we're looking at each other. The bond between us was so beautiful, and after she died, I lost that picture. On Christmas Day a few years later, I opened a book and found the picture inside! She sent me that picture as a Christmas present from heaven.

—Dayle Vickery, *Orange Park, Florida*

BLESSING FROM ABOVE

My stepfather, Marlin, bought a dancing Christmas tree in the mid-2000s as a gimmick decoration. Marlin passed away in 2014. My sister, Stacy, had taken possession of it along the way. Stacy got engaged to her longtime boyfriend on Thanksgiving night (Marlin had met him). The tree was unpacked but had no batteries. Later that evening, with all the ladies sitting around talking, the tree lit up and started to dance! The empty battery pack was in hand, and the only conclusion we could reach was that Marlin was sending his blessing and dancing a jig.

—Norman Powers, *Sheffield, Alabama*

Overtaken by Joy

by Ardis Whitman

*A writer celebrates the moments of awe
that lift us out of our day-to-day routine.*

It was a gray day in late June. My husband and I were driving to Nova Scotia for a much-needed vacation. We traveled glumly, hoping to reach rest and dinner before the rain came. Suddenly, on a lonely stretch of highway flanked by woods, the storm struck. The forest vanished in a great deluge. Cascades of water shut us in, making driving impossible. We pulled off onto the shoulder of the road and stopped.

Then, as though someone had turned off a celestial faucet, it ended. A thin radiance spread out from the clouds, catching the tops of the trees. The very road shone. And then a rainbow arched across the sky. But more than that: On our right was a pond, and in the pond was the end of the rainbow! It was as though this arch of living color had been built for us alone. We could hardly speak for awe and joy.

A friend of mine has described a similar experience. She had walked out on a lonely beach at twilight. It was a time of grief for her, and she wanted solitude. Offshore, across the darkening sea, was a single low island. Presently she was aware of a dim light moving on the island, and then came the splash of oars and the scrape of a boat leaving the shore. She made out the outlines of a fishing boat, and in it the figure of a man. He rowed a little way and anchored. My friend told me that, after a

83

while, she felt an intense sense of oneness with that silent figure. It was as though sea and sky and night and those two solitary human beings were united in a kind of profound identity. "I was overtaken by joy," she said.

Most of us have experienced such lighted moments, when we seem to understand ourselves and the world and, for a single instant, know the loveliness of all living things. But these moments vanish quickly, and we are almost embarrassed to admit that they have ever been, as though in doing so we betray a willingness to believe in what is not true.

However, psychologist Abraham Maslow of Brandeis University embarked some years ago on a study of average, healthy individuals and found that a great many report such experiences—"moments of great awe; moments of the most intense happiness or even rapture, ecstasy or bliss." He has concluded that these experiences are often the expression of buoyant health.

In his files is the story of a young mother. Getting breakfast for her family, she hurried about the kitchen pouring orange juice and coffee. The children were chattering; the sun streamed in on their faces; her husband was playing with the littlest one. All was as usual. But as she looked at them, she was suddenly so overcome by how much she loved them, by her feeling of good fortune, that she could scarcely speak for joy.

Here, too, is the story of a man who remembers a day when he went swimming alone and recalls "the childish joy with which he cavorted in the water like a fish." He was so overwhelmed by his great happiness at being "so perfectly physical" that he shouted again and again with joy.

Apparently almost anything may serve as the impetus of such joy. Joy may wait, too, just beyond danger when you have been brave enough to face a situation and live it out. It may come from such a simple thing as waking in the night on a train as it pulls into a station, hearing voices calling to one another out of the darkness, seeing a face smiling warmly in the light of the trainman's lantern. Whatever the source, such experiences provide the most memorable moments of human life.

Joy is much more than happiness. It is "exultation of spirit," says the dictionary, "gladness; delight; a state of felicity." Awe and a sense of mystery are part of it; so are the feelings of humility and gratitude.

Suddenly we are keenly aware of every living thing—every leaf, every flower, every cloud, the mayfly hovering over the pond, the crow cawing in the treetop. "O world, I cannot hold thee close enough!" cried the poet Edna St. Vincent Millay in such a moment.

Enthralled, we see as we never saw before. The most important thing in these peak experiences, says Professor Maslow, is the feeling of these people that they had really glimpsed "the essence of things, the secret of life, as if veils had been pulled aside."

We see, too, the unity of all things—a dazzling vision of the kinship we all have with one another and with the universal life around us. Everyone who has ever had such a moment has noted this quality of "melting into." There is a feeling that life is whole; I and my world are part of each other; I and all life are united in a bond of love and understanding. And we feel free to be ourselves. Suddenly we know who we are and what we are meant to be. This is our true self and we have found it.

"To miss the joy is to miss all," wrote Robert Louis Stevenson. For these moments of joy are like flowers in the pastureland of living. Life grows larger, we draw deeper breaths, doors open softly within us. "Where there is joy, there is fulfillment," wrote Paul Tillich in *The Meaning of Joy*, "and where there is fulfillment, there is joy."

The sad thing is that it happens to most of us so rarely. As we grow older, our lives become buried under the pressures of the workaday world. Joy is not likely to come to us when we are going round and round the tormenting circle of our own busyness, our own importance.

What we need is the child's spontaneity and wonder of discovery. "To me every hour of the light and dark is a miracle," wrote Walt Whitman. And English naturalist Richard Jefferies, desperately poor and fighting a deadly disease, could still cry, "Every blade of grass was mine as if I had myself planted it. All the grasses were my pets: I loved them all. Every wild hawk that passed overhead was mine. What more beautiful than the sweep and curve of his going through the azure sky? Oh, happy, happy day! So beautiful to watch; and all mine!"

How can we restore to our lives this eager openness to all the world? Sometimes all that is needed is a chance to see an old experience in a new way. I remember one such occasion. I had been working all night on a manuscript and I felt I could never finish it. But as the clock struck 5, the last sentence fell into place, and I put down my pen, opened the door and stepped out onto the lawn. The stars were thinning out and the sky in the east had that "light is coming" look. A few birds began to sing tentatively. The trees, dark shapes on the horizon, began now to take on form and configuration. More trees appeared, one by one. Then the great maples lighted with brilliance like candelabra in the dark.

The sun was up! Twig by twig the sun set fire to every branch and leaf. The birds now were singing wildly as though they had just been created by the morning itself; and I, too, felt newly created, so full of joy that it seemed I could not hold it.

Most of us need to learn to break out of the prison of self. For joy comes not only from fusion with nature; it comes from love and creativeness; from insight and discovery and great emotion.

Perhaps joy is most likely to come when we forget ourselves in service, or in the pursuit of a great dream. Florence Nightingale, working long, hard hours to become a nurse, could say, "This is life! I wish for no other world than this!"

Most of all, joy may come when we do not run from life—from its sorrows, struggles and hopes. The person who wants above all to avoid risk and suffering sets out no welcome for the moments of joy.

When life's transiency and frailty are omnipresent, what we have grows sweeter. As G.K. Chesterton said, "The way to love anything is to realize that it might be lost."

I remember finding myself seated beside an old gentleman on a train some years ago. He sat quietly looking out of the window. His eyes searched each leaf, each cloud, the lines of passing houses, the upturned faces of children watching the train go by.

"It is beautiful, isn't it?" I ventured at last.

"Yes," he said, and no more for a moment. Then he smiled and waved a hand at a passing hay wagon. "See," he said. "Hay going to the barn." And he made it sound as though there could be no greater event in all the world than a wagonload of hay on its way to the mow.

Overtaken by Joy

He saw the unspoken question in my face. "You think it's strange," he said, "that just a hay wagon means so much. But you see, last week the doctor told me that I have only three months to live. Ever since, everything has looked so beautiful, so important to me. You can't imagine how beautiful! I feel as if I had been asleep and had only just waked up."

Perhaps we are more likely to experience a moment of joy if we can admit that there is more to life than we have yet fathomed; if we can acknowledge a world greater than our own. To be sure the experience of joy is not necessarily religious in any conventional way. Just a distinguishing characteristic of joy is the feeling people have that they have touched the hem of something far beyond themselves.

In my own life there was a moment of this special exaltation. En route by plane to the Midwest, we were flying at a high altitude, and a continent of shining clouds spread beneath us. Often before and since, I have watched these radiant towers and hillocks of cloud go by. But this time the scene was haunted by a strange joy so penetrating that the plane seemed not to be there. I thought of myself as living and walking in a land like that, and I, who am the most gregarious of humans, knew in a flash of deep illumination that there was in the universe a light, a stuff, a tissue, a substance in company with which one would never be lonely. The experience left the compelling certainty that we dwell safely in a universe far more personal, far more human, far more tender than we are.

What if these moments of joy are given us to reveal that this is the way we are meant to live? What if the clarity of joy is the way we should be seeing all the time? To many people, it seems almost wicked to feel this radiance in a world threatened as ours is. But most generations have known uncertainty and challenge and peril. The more grievous the world, the more we need to remember the luminous beauty at the center of life. Our moments of joy are proof that at the heart of darkness an unquenchable light shines.

Originally published in the April 1965 issue of *Reader's Digest* magazine.

Tunnel to Freedom

by Flight Lieutenant Paul Brickhill, Royal Australian Air Forces

This story of astonishing ingenuity and audacity will be remembered after most war tales have been forgotten.

Stalag Luft III, at Sagan, Germany, halfway between Berlin and Breslau, held 10,000 captured airmen in the spring of 1943. Nearly all were from the RAF, although Americans were beginning to arrive.

In April a north compound was added and 700 of us were moved into it. Already, prisoners in the working parties that helped build the compound had studied its layout and paced off its distances—with tunnels in mind. Escape was the one hope that had kept us going.

A few of the officers had dug tunnels at other camps, and around them we built "X," our escape organization. Head of X was Squadron Leader Roger Bushell, a tall South African fighter pilot who had been shot down over Dunkirk. Bushell had already made two remarkable escapes, and once had got almost to Switzerland before he was caught.

North compound was a thousand-foot square enclosed by two tall barbed-wire fences, five feet apart. Ten yards inside this barrier was the warning wire; step across it and the guards shot. Numerous sentry towers were manned 24 hours a day. Twenty-five yards outside the wire on all four sides were dense pine woods that cut off any view of the outside world—but equally would cover an escape. As soon as we moved in, notices were posted asking for volunteers to play cricket and softball. The notices were signed Big X. Everybody knew what that meant, and 500 signed up for the tunnel work. It was decided to start three long tunnels, Tom, Dick and Harry, in the hope that one would be undetected. We never used the word "tunnels"; too many eavesdropping guards understood English.

Tom was to be dug from block 123 to the wire, 150 feet away, and then on to the woods. Dick was to be dug from 122 toward Tom, so that it could either join with Tom's shaft or be dug all the way to the woods. Harry was to begin from block 104, and drive to the woods on the north.

*   *   *

Of course the tunnels would have to start from within our huts. Each hut was 100 feet long, with sleeping quarters, washroom and small kitchen. The Germans had built these huts about a foot off the ground, so that the guards could look underneath to see if we were up to any funny business. There were usually several of these "ferrets" around, easily spotted by their blue overalls. With torches and long steel probes they searched for hidden trap doors and telltale sand from tunnels.

Three teams were organized, each under a veteran tunneler. Every volunteer was interviewed by the X chief of his block. Miners, carpenters, engineers were assigned to tunnel. Tailors were organized to turn out disguises. Artists set up a forgery shop to fake papers. Any man who spoke fluent German was assigned to make friends with a ferret, cultivate him and eventually try to bribe him.

The tunnels were scooped out with coal shovels and iron scrapers made from our cookstoves.

Prisoners without any special skills were assigned either as "penguins," to dispose of sand from the tunnels, or as "stooges," to keep watch on ferrets. For the next year we had 300 stooges working in shifts every day.

Once the security system was working we went ahead on the tunnels. The Germans had overlooked one detail. In each hut, the washroom, kitchen and a small section where there was a stove had concrete floors and stood on brick and concrete foundations that had no openings through which the security guards could probe. These were the places from which we started work.

First, we built secret trap doors. With a little cement left over from building the camp, a Polish team cast a removable block to replace a small slab chipped from the floor of block 123. With sand and dirt rubbed around the edges, nobody could spot it. This was Tom's entrance.

Dick's trap door in block 122 was the most ingenious. In the washroom floor was an iron grating through which wastewater ran into a concrete well three feet deep. The drain pipe that led from this sump was so placed that there was always some water in the well. While stooges kept watch outside, the Poles removed the iron grill, bailed out the well and freed the whole concrete slab that formed one side of the well so that it was removable at will. When the slab was in place, the cracks sealed with soap, the waste water rapidly accumulated to hide it.

Harry's entrance was also tricky. The tall heating stove in room 23 of block 104 stood on tiles embedded in a concrete base about four feet square. The men moved the stove back, chipped the tiles free and reset them in a concrete trap door that looked precisely like the original base. Five of the tiles cracked in the process. They were replaced by tiles stolen from a cookhouse in East compound and smuggled in to us.

Now we were set for the more dangerous business of tunneling. The distances, direction and angles of the three tunnels had been computed by rough trigonometry. We had learned German sound detectors could hear nothing below 25-foot depth, so we decided to sink shafts 30 feet straight down from the three trap doors before heading for the woods.

Early in May 1943, the first of the soft, sandy soil was cut away with little coal shovels and iron scrapers made from our cookstoves.

The penguins had the troublesome job of disposing of the bright yellow sand. Some of it could be stirred into the soil of our tiny gardens, but that didn't begin to solve the problem. So we took dozens of small towels and sewed them into sausage-shaped sacks. A penguin would hang one of these, filled with sand, in each trouser leg and wander casually out to the playing ground. There, stooges would be staging boxing matches, volleyball games or pretended brawls. The penguin, hands in pockets, would pull strings that freed pins at the bottom of the sausage sacks and let the sand trickle to the ground. Scores of scuffling feet would quickly trample it into the surface. When we were going good, we kept 150 penguins busy and we disposed of tons of sand under the very noses of the ferrets.

Tunneling veterans had learned that you could not tunnel far without fresh air and that holes poked up to the surface were not adequate. By luck, a copy of a modern-mechanics type of magazine came into camp and it contained an article that described a homemade air pump. We promptly set to work to make one.

Our "tin bashers" collected Red Cross dried milk tins, cut off the ends and fitted the cylinders together to build pipe. The pipe was laid in a ditch along the tunnel floor and covered with sand. At the far end was a nozzle, which delivered fresh air. The air was forced through the pipe by shifts of pumpers who operated a bellows constructed from kit bags. This first outfit worked perfectly and we promptly built two more. Now we could close the trap doors and work without fear of interruption.

Our electrical specialists rounded up bits of wiring left behind by the builders and then surreptitiously rearranged the camp wiring to gain a few score feet. They wired the three shafts and made hidden connections to the camp circuit. With stolen bulbs, we had light to dig by.

The digging teams evolved a rigid system. Number one digger lay full length on his side and one elbow, hacking away at the tunnel face and pushing the sand back toward his feet. Number two lay facing the other way, his legs overlapping number one's. He collected the sand in boxes that were placed on trolleys and hauled back to the shaft.

These trolleys, strong enough to carry two sand boxes or one man, were first-class installations. They had carved flanged wooden wheels fitted with "tires" cut from tin cans. The hubs even had ball bearings, smuggled in by a tame ferret. The track rails were made from barrack moldings. When the tunnels grew long, the diggers sprawled on the trolleys and pushed their way to the working face.

The diggers learned to take sand falls in their stride. The only warning would be a slight rustle and then the number one digger would be buried under a pile of suffocating sand. Number two man would have to work fast to get him out.

Flight Lieutenant Paul Brickhill.

*   *   *

By the end of May, each of the three tunnels was about 70 feet long. With summer approaching, the X leaders decided to concentrate digging efforts on Tom, which had the least distance to go—about 100 feet more.

Other X groups were busily preparing the equipment we'd need. Some of our guards could be tempted with gifts, and once they had smuggled in one item they couldn't refuse more, because we might give them away to the Kommandant. In this way we got crucial supplies—inks, brushes, paper, radio parts, a camera, hammers, saws and nails.

Our forgery department of 50 men turned out phony passports and identity cards. We called it "Dean & Dawson," after the English travel agency. Forging documents was a finicky business: Whole sheets of simulated typewriting were drawn by hand. Letterheads were "embossed" with toothbrush handles. Stamps were cut from boot heels.

In the tailor shop, 60 men made civilian clothes out of RAF uniforms and turned out close copies of Luftwaffe uniforms. Half a dozen map makers traced maps and ran copies off on a makeshift duplicator.

*   *   *

When it was learned that the Americans were to be moved in six weeks to a separate compound, evening shifts were added to hurry things up. More sand was dug into our vegetable gardens.

One day a probing ferret turned over some bright yellow sand in a garden. This touched off a series of frantic but futile searches. The Germans dug a trench between block 123 and the wire, but it was not deep enough to reveal Tom.

By the end of June we calculated that Tom had reached just under the edge of the wood, and we prepared to dig a shaft straight up to the surface. Just then a horde of Germans suddenly appeared and began to cut away the trees! It was actually mere coincidence; they had decided to build a new compound there. They chopped the trees back for 50 yards, but time for the Americans was short and it was decided to break Tom out anyway, and let the escapers crawl the rest of the way to cover.

We had so much sand coming up that we were desperate. The X leaders decided to take a long chance: Store sand in Red Cross boxes under our beds and hope that the Germans wouldn't find it until it could be properly disposed of.

Tom was now 260 feet long, with a few yards to go to its goal. Bushell decided to lie low for a few days to allay suspicion. Then ferrets found the boxes of sand in our huts! Heavy transport wagons were brought into camp and trundled all around in an effort to collapse any tunnels we might have. They only wrecked our vegetable gardens.

A day or so later, in a last suspicious search of block 123, a ferret accidentally jabbed his probe into the edge of Tom's trap door.

That was the end of Tom.

The ferrets couldn't find how to open the trap, so they broke it in. They dynamited Tom and incidentally blew up the roof of block 123. They were so relieved at discovering Tom that they took no reprisals.

A mass meeting decided that work would go ahead on Dick and Harry. However, it was deemed wise to do no more until winter, when we assumed vigilance would slacken because it is a bad season for escapes.

At the end of August 1943 the Americans were moved to their new compound and we threw a farewell party on home-brewed raisin wine.

While we were waiting for winter, it was decided to try some above-ground escapes. Periodically the Germans escorted small parties of prisoners through the gates for delousing our clothes, and the idea was to stage an unofficial delousing party of our own. Three prisoners, disguised as Luftwaffe Unteroffiziers, took 24 other prisoners in tow, passed the inspection at the gate and made off into the woods. A few minutes later six senior officers, including Battle of Britain fighter ace Bob Stanford Tuck, tried to get through but were detected.

We were all forced to stand on parade for nearly seven hours while the three missing men were identified. Later, all were rounded up. One man, a fluent Spanish speaker, who posed as a foreign worker, got to Czechoslovakia and then by train almost to the Swiss border, where he got out and walked right across a narrow strip of Swiss territory without knowing it and back again into Germany, where a frontier guard nabbed him. The other

A ferret jabbed his probe into Tom's trap door.

two got to a Luftwaffe airdrome, sneaked into an old Junkers trainer and were just warming up the engine when a German pilot coincidentally came along to fly it and caught them.

We were ready to start tunneling again early in 1944. The Germans had started to build a new compound where Dick was to have broken out. That left Harry. But snow lay deep on the ground and sand disposal stumped us. One of the tunnelers suggested we put it under the theater.

We had built the theater ourselves and taken care to leave no openings for the ferrets to peek through. Underneath was a deep excavation that could take tons and tons of sand. Our engineers adjusted one seat so that it swung back on hinges, and under it they cut a trap door. Into this the penguins dumped kit bags full of sand every night.

Three teams, ten veteran diggers in each team, pushed Harry ahead up to 12 feet per day. By the end of January, the first "halfway house" was built 100 feet out. The planners had calculated that 300 feet of tunnel in all would bring us into the shelter of the trees.

It was a long dig, and conditions were getting worse. The ground was cold and damp. Every digger suffered continuously from colds. Most of them were spitting black from breathing the fumes of our fat lamps; we had run out of electric wire. Sand falls kept occurring nearly every day.

But by mid-February another 100 feet had been dug and the second halfway house was put in. Then we got a small break. German workmen hooking up loudspeakers laid down two large coils of electric wire, intending to use them in a few minutes. A prisoner calmly walked off with one coil. A mock fight broke out and in the confusion we got the second coil. The German workmen were afraid to report the loss. (At the end, when the Gestapo found the wire in Harry, three of them were shot.)

That haul gave us 600 feet of wiring, enough for lights clear up to the digging face.

By March 8, 1944, the final 100-foot section was dug and a chamber excavated at the end. In four days four of the best diggers carved straight upward, fitting ladders to the side as they progressed, until they struck pine-tree roots. They estimated that they were about two feet below the surface, just inside the woods. They boarded over the top of the shaft and left the remainder to be dug on the night of the break.

About 500 men had worked on the tunnels but we estimated that only 220 would be able to pass through it during the hours of darkness. Bushell was allowed to draw up a list of 60 workers, 20 more were nominated by secret ballot, and 140 names were drawn out of a hat.

The lucky ones began their preparations. We had enough money to buy train tickets for 40 men; the rest were to walk across country. A Czech pilot described the border mountains of Czechoslovakia, 60 miles away, for which most of the foot travelers intended to head.

On the morning of Friday, March 24, Roger Bushell announced that the escape would take place that night. There was six inches of snow on the ground, which was not good, but there would be no moon.

The "Dean & Dawson" boys filled in their forged documents and stamped them with the correct date, which of course couldn't have been done until then. Some escapers were to go as foreign workers, others as neutrals, others as German officials, soldiers and civilians—and each man's papers had to fit his story.

A digger went out to Harry's end to see how far we had to go to break through. When he jabbed a stick upward three inches he struck daylight. It seemed there wouldn't be any difficulty in getting to the surface.

We laid blankets at the bottom of the shafts to deaden sounds and nailed planks on the trolleys so the escapers could lie on them and be pulled along. When darkness came, the escapers put on their disguises, and improvised iron rations were issued.

By half past eight it was announced that all was ready. Ten minutes later the first escaper went down the ladder, well turned out in a civilian suit and carrying a homemade briefcase. The second, dressed as a workman, followed on his heels. Roger Bushell, carrying an attache case and looking like a smart businessman, went down among the first five.

There was a bad wait when the first man was unable to pry the roof boards loose. It was almost an hour, an agonizing time for the men lying along the tunnel, before the swollen boards came loose and the earth was removed. Down the shaft came the sweet fresh air of freedom.

But when the digger cautiously stuck his head out he got a shock. Instead of being just inside the woods, the hole was ten feet short of the trees, and its gaping opening was a bare 15 yards from a sentry tower.

We were stunned when he broke the news. But the men were in no mood to be stopped. To go out now was risky. To wait a month for the next dark of the moon and dig another 30 feet of tunnel was equally risky. Besides, the forged papers were all dated and would have to be redone. That decided it.

The first man up crawled to a brushwood fence, paying out a rope by which he could signal when it was safe for the next man to emerge. The sentry in the tower paid no attention to the woods but played his searchlight on the barbed wire fence and compound. Two other sentries patrolled back and forth along the wire. When both were out of sight the rope was tugged and the second man slipped across into the woods.

It took more than an hour for the first 20 to make it. They were all going by train, and they headed for the Sagan railway station a quarter of a mile away. From timetables smuggled in by guards we knew exactly when the trains were due.

Back in block 104 the initial delay had been terrible. Obviously something had gone wrong, but what? Escapers sat around, a queer collection of well-dressed civilians, workmen and a German corporal, hoping that ferrets would not appear. Just after half past nine the men at the trap door felt a blast of cold air. It could only mean that we'd broken out. A muffled cheer went around the block.

There were other interruptions. Two bad sand falls held up the show for about an hour and a half in all. Sometimes the trolleys left their rails—more delays. Men going out with suitcases or blankets wrapped around them would find themselves jammed in a narrow tunnel, afraid to pull loose for fear of causing a fall. We were running far behind schedule.

The sentry, startled, shot wild.

At midnight the air-raid sirens sounded and all lights, including our illegal ones in the tunnel, were switched off. It was obvious now that not more than 100 men would get away before daylight. Lamps had to be lighted and passed along the tunnel.

We up above heard the faraway sound of falling bombs, and the huts rattled as RAF blockbusters fell crashing on Berlin, 100 miles away. At any other time we would have cheered, but that night we cursed. It was about two in the morning before the lights came on again. In the meantime, one by one the escapers had been crawling silently from the tunnel mouth and away into the woods.

The worst moment came at about half past four. The sentry in the tower shouted to a guard patrolling below. The guard went up the tower ladder and the sentry descended and walked straight toward the hole. He could hardly miss seeing it. Steam from the heat of the tunnel poured out of it, and from it to the wood led a black trail across the snow where escapers had crawled. The sentry, apparently blinded by looking at his searchlight, came on until he was a bare four feet from the hole, turned around and squatted down. For five minutes he remained there, while the men in the shaft hardly dared breathe. At last the sentry went back to his tower. More escapers slipped through the tunnel and away.

When it was almost five the RAF man in charge decided it was getting too light. "Get the next three men down," he said. "Then we finish. If all of them get away without detection the Huns won't know a thing until morning roll call and the boys will have an extra four hours."

The last three men quickly descended. Just as the third man vanished up the tunnel on the trolley, we heard the crack of a rifle.

Two escaping men had reached the rendezvous tree in the woods, another man, crawling, was halfway to it, and a fourth man had just emerged from the hole when the rope signaler saw a guard approaching. The men outside froze to the ground when they felt two sharp warning tugs on the rope. The German strode on.

Left, right, he continued, probably half asleep, and one foot came down a bare 12 inches from the tunnel mouth. He took one more pace, and then he snapped out of his daze. He didn't even notice the man lying doggo at his feet, but he must have seen the black track across the snow. Then he saw the man lying halfway to the wood and raised his rifle to shoot. At that moment one of the escapers waiting by the tree leaped into sight and waved his arms, shouting, *Nicht schiessen, Posten! Nicht schiessen!* ("Don't shoot, sentry! Don't shoot!")

The sentry, startled, shot wild. The two men at the edge of the wood and the man who had crawled halfway came slowly forward, hands raised. And then, right at his feet, the last escaper, still unseen, rose slowly. The guard jumped back a yard and looked downward. There in front of him was Harry's gaping mouth. He whipped out a torch and flashed it down the hole into the face of the 81st escaper, hanging precariously on the ladder.

The sentry blew his whistle. Guards came running from all directions. Harry's long life had ended.

In block 104 there was a frantic scramble to burn our papers, break up equipment and get rid of civilian clothes. The men in the tunnel were inching back along the trolleys, expecting a shot from behind. When the last man came up, the trap door was sealed down and the stove replaced.

In a few minutes a scratching sound came from below. A ferret had worked back along the tunnel and couldn't get out. We let him stay there.

By six in the morning the compound was swarming with guards, and ferrets combed block 104 calling, *"Aus! Aus! Efferbody aus!"* As each man came out, a ferret grabbed him and forced him to strip in the snow, boots and all, while every article of clothing was inspected.

While the search was going on, an adjutant came running to implore us to open the trap door. The ferret was still down there and they were afraid he would suffocate. The other ferrets couldn't find the trap door. We opened it for them. The ferret down below was not a bad type—he was the only one with nerve enough to go down the tunnel.

* * *

In a matter of hours the whole countryside was roused in the biggest manhunt of the war. The radio warned all civilians to be on the watch. SS and Gestapo men, Luftwaffe men and even naval men from Stettin and Danzig were mobilized by the thousands for the search.

Back in the compound we waited for reprisals. Harry had broken the world's record for the number of escapers who got away and we expected the Germans to take it out on us. The Gestapo arrived to investigate, but its agents, never liked by the regular army, got no help from the ferrets and found nothing. We even managed to filch two of their flashlights. But they did uncover a black market—run by the Kommandant and his staff! The hapless Kommandant was promptly whisked off for a court-martial.

Most of the 76 men who got away were nabbed within a day or so, although some got as far as Danzig and Munich. All were taken to a filthy Gestapo prison in Gorlitz, 40 miles away. From Gorlitz, 15 men were brought back to Stalag Luft III. We could learn nothing more.

Then, a fortnight after the break, our senior officer was called to the Kommandant's office. Stiffly the German read out the official report—of the 76 escaped officers, 41 had been shot!

Our senior officer called a meeting and announced the dreadful news. Under the Geneva Convention, drastic penalties must not be inflicted upon prisoners who attempt escape. We thought most likely the announcement was a bluff to dissuade us from further escape attempts. We held a memorial service in the compound, however, and every man defiantly wore a black diamond of mourning on his sleeve.

When the Germans posted the list of dead it contained not 41 but 47 names, among them the leaders—Roger Bushell; Tim Walenn, who ran the forgery factory; Al Hake, the compass maker; Charlie Hall, the photographer.

For days the compound was shaken with grief and fury. Then three more names were added to the list of dead. The Germans never gave us any reason for the shootings, or why they shot only 50 of 76.

In June, a letter arrived, written in Spanish and signed by a fictitious name. That was the signal that one escaper, a Dutch pilot in the RAF, had reached England. A postcard from Sweden, signed with two false names, revealed that two Norwegians had made it out. With 15 men sent back to Stalag Luft III and 50 shot, that left eight unaccounted for.

Not till long afterward did we learn that they had been sent to the notorious Oranienburg concentration camp. Nobody had ever escaped from a concentration camp, the Gestapo boasted. Within a few months the eight had tunneled out. They were eventually rounded up, but by then Germany was in the chaos of collapse and they were not shot.

If the Germans shot our 50 comrades to frighten us from building more tunnels, they made a psychological blunder. "X" was re-formed and we immediately began work on George, which started under the theater. George was on as grand a scale as Harry and we were almost ready to break out when we were hurriedly evacuated. The Russians were only 30 miles away. We were forced to march for weeks half across Germany. We were at Lubeck on May 2, 1945, when tanks of the British Second Army swept forward and set us free.

Originally published in the December 1945 issue of *Reader's Digest* magazine.

Paul Brickhill published a book about this incident in 1950. Titled The Great Escape, *it became the basis of several films.*

Miracle in the Desert

Two figures in burkas of cerulean blue stand out against a desolate landscape in Afghanistan. Framed against dusty peaks, one woman faces the camera as the other unrolls a blanket on the ground. Photographer Lynsey Addario, on assignment for *National Geographic*, stopped short as she and her translator came upon the scene: In Badakhshan Province, women are rarely seen without a man. But there they were, a mother preparing to deliver the child of her daughter, whose husband had gone to get help when their car broke down on the way to the hospital. Happily, Addario was able to ferry the family to a medical facility a few hours away, where the young woman had a healthy baby girl.
Photograph by Lynsey Addario/Getty Images Reportage

Our America

Word Power
—**C.F. PAYNE**
OCTOBER 2003

The Reader's Digest *Complete Guide to*

Witticisms, Quips, Retorts, Rejoinders and Pithy Replies for Every Occasion

Laughs from Gaffes

Bypass the remark you'd always regret in favor of the version you'll shamelessly repeat.

Instead of saying this ... "It is better to live one day as a lion than 100 years as a sheep." —*Donald Trump (retweeting a Benito Mussolini quote)*
... Say this: "The lion shall lie down with the calf, but the calf won't get much sleep." —*Woody Allen*

Instead of saying this ... "I make Jessica Simpson look like a rock scientist."
—*Tara Reid, actress*
... Say this: "My definition of an intellectual is someone who can listen to the *William Tell Overture* without thinking of the Lone Ranger."
—*Billy Connolly, actor*

Instead of saying this ... "It's really hard to maintain a one-on-one relationship if the other person is not going to allow me to be with other people." —*Axl Rose, musician with Guns N' Roses*
... Say this: "Bigamy is having one husband too many. Monogamy is the same." —*Anonymous*

Fight Ire with Fire
Fend off a cruel or foolish declaration with a zinger
that will have the Hamptons buzzing.

When Mick Jagger insisted that his wrinkles were actually laugh lines, jazz singer George Melly replied, "Surely nothing could be that funny."

A sports columnist recalled the story of a flight attendant who asked Muhammad Ali to fasten his seat belt. Ali replied, "Superman don't need no seat belt." The flight attendant's retort: "Superman don't need no airplane either."

When a fan asked Wolfgang Amadeus Mozart for tips on writing symphonies, the composer is said to have suggested, "Begin with some simple *lieder* and work your way up to a symphony." "But Herr Mozart," replied the fan, "you were writing symphonies when you were eight." "Yes," said Mozart. "But I never asked anybody."

Following an argument, an angry Lady Astor told Winston Churchill, "Winston, if you were my husband, I'd put poison in your coffee." Churchill snapped, "If you were my wife, I'd drink it."

In the 1960s, Joe Pyne, one of the original shock jocks, apparently began an interview with Frank Zappa by saying, "So I guess your long hair makes you a woman." Zappa responded, "So I guess your wooden leg makes you a table."

Katharine Hepburn so hated filming a movie with John Barrymore, she declared, "Mr. Barrymore, I am never going to act with you again." Barrymore replied, "My dear, you still haven't."

Director/writer Kevin Smith told Tim Burton that Burton's *Planet of the Apes* reminded him of a comic book he'd written. Burton responded, "Everyone knows I never read comics." Smith shot back, "That explains *Batman*."

Timed Lines

The right line at the right time is a thing of beauty.
Memorize these tried-and-true replies for any situation.

It's Thanksgiving dinner, and your Luddite uncle Ralph is at it again about how science is bunk:

"I have noticed that even people who claim everything is pre-determined and that we can do nothing to change it look before they cross the road." —*Stephen Hawking, physicist*

"By all means let's be open-minded, but not so open-minded that our brains drop out." —*Richard Dawkins, scientist*

"He was so narrow-minded, he could see through a keyhole with both eyes." —*Molly Ivins, author*

"I've come to learn that the best time to debate family members is when they have food in their mouths." —*Kenneth Cole, fashion designer*

A friend is considering getting married, and you have certain "insights" about the institution you'd like to communicate:

"They say marriages are made in heaven. But so is thunder and lightning." —*Clint Eastwood*

"My advice to you is get married. If you find a good wife you'll be happy; if not, you'll become a philosopher." —*Socrates*

"Life in Lubbock, Texas, taught me that sex is the most awful, filthy thing on earth, and you should save it for someone you love." —*Butch Hancock, country musician*

Someone is pressuring you to do better. Time to lower the bar:

"All the things I like to do are either immoral, illegal or fattening." —*Alexander Woollcott, actor*

"Part of [the $10 million] went for gambling, horses and women. The rest I spent foolishly." —*George Raft, film star*

"I was going to sue for defamation of character, but then I realized I have no character." —*Charles Barkley, TV basketball analyst*

A coworker asks your opinion of an insufferable boss. You're happy to unload:

"He is not only dull himself, he is the cause of dullness in others." —*Samuel Johnson, 18th-century author*

"Her only flair is in her nostrils." —*Pauline Kael, film critic*

"She never lets ideas interrupt the easy flow of her conversation." —*Jean Webster, author*

"He can compress the most words into the smallest idea of any man I know." —*Abraham Lincoln*

"He is a self-made man and worships his creator." —*Henry Clapp, newspaper editor*

"People who think they know everything are a great annoyance to those of us who do." —*Isaac Asimov, science fiction writer*

Point/Counterpoint

How to win the argument, switch sides, then win again.

Dogs vs. Cats

Point: "A dog teaches a boy fidelity, perseverance and to turn around three times before lying down." —*Robert Benchley, humorist*

Counterpoint: "Cats are smarter than dogs. You can't get eight cats to pull a sled through snow." —*Jeff Valdez, producer*

Wine vs. Beer

Point: "Wine; a constant proof that God loves us, and loves to see us happy." —*Benjamin Franklin*

Counterpoint: "Why beer is better than wine: human feet are conspicuously absent from beer making." —*Steve Mirsky, author*

Democrats vs. Republicans

Point: "The Democrats are the party that says government will make you smarter, taller, richer and remove the crabgrass on your lawn." —*P.J. O'Rourke, writer*

Counterpoint: "The Republicans are the party that says government doesn't work, and then get elected and prove it." —*P.J. O'Rourke, still a writer*

Men vs. Women

Point: "I've been married to one Marxist and one Fascist, and neither one would take the garbage out." —*Lee Grant, actress*

Counterpoint: "The trouble with some women is that they get all excited about nothing, and then they marry him." —*Cher*

Fiction vs. Nonfiction

Point: "The difference between fiction and reality? Fiction has to make sense." —*Tom Clancy, author*

Counterpoint: "Be careful about

reading health books. You may die of a misprint." —*Mark Twain*

Optimists vs. Pessimists

Point: "An optimist is someone who falls off the Empire State Building, and after 50 floors says, 'So far so good!'" —*Anonymous*

Counterpoint: "The nice part about being a pessimist is that you are constantly being either proven right or pleasantly surprised." —*George Will, columnist*

Blondes vs. Brunettes

Point: "I'm not offended by dumb blonde jokes because I know I'm not dumb ... and I also know that I'm not blonde." —*Dolly Parton*

Counterpoint: "It was a blonde. A blonde to make a bishop kick a hole in a stained-glass window." —*Raymond Chandler, author*

Critic vs. Artist

Point: "He suffers from delusions of adequacy." —*Walter Kerr, critic*

Counterpoint: "Critics are like eunuchs in a harem; they know how it's done, they've seen it done every day, but they're unable to do it themselves." —*Brendan Behan, Irish author*

Originally published in the October 2016 issue of *Reader's Digest* magazine.

Quotable Quotes, from which this collection was drawn, first appeared in Reader's Digest *in January 1934. One of the most popular and longest-running columns in the magazine, it was proceeded by similar quote departments, including Remarkable Remarks, which ran in the first issue of the magazine in February 1922. Drawn from books, speeches, journals and articles, these columns featured the great minds of the day.*

How to Stop Smoking

by Herbert Brean, from the book *How to Stop Smoking*

The bestselling author provides a guaranteed plan to quit.

If you smoke, and wish you didn't, a wonderful experience lies ahead of you: the experience of freeing yourself of a burden—of rediscovering that you are your own boss. It won't come without effort; but if you make the effort, you will win.

Medically speaking, tobacco is not habit-forming. It does not worm its way into your physique and psyche, as opium or cocaine does. But it is habit-forming in the same way that three meals a day, or eight hours' sleep, or wearing clothes, are habit-forming. If you go without any one of them for a while, you become uncomfortable.

But how comfortable are you with tobacco? Does a cigarette really satisfy you—in the way that a big meal does when you're hungry, or a warm coat when you're cold? You know better. Light a cigarette, smoke it, taste its bitterness, put it out. Even as you do, you know that you'll soon want another. Not that you enjoy it. You simply want it.

Why? When you smoke, nicotine, carbon monoxide, small amounts of hydrocyanic acid, pyridine, and various phenols and aldehydes are absorbed into your lungs and mouth. Your nervous system is momentarily stimulated. Your blood pressure goes up. Your pulse rate increases.

Most important of all, your blood vessels undergo a constriction.

This "slows you down." That is, after the momentary stimulation, smoking depresses, for a far longer period, both the sympathetic and the central nervous systems of the human body.

This means that when you smoke you are artificially slowing down your body's normal activities. Now, suppose you are suddenly confronted with an emotional or psychological emergency: Adrenaline is pumped into your bloodstream, your muscles tense, you breathe faster and get edgy, jittery—"nervous." Tobacco smoke retards these natural processes by slowing the blood circulation and thus "calming you down." You find a smoke is "good for your nerves."

If that were as far as it went, there would be no occasion for worry. In fact, if you smoked only at times of real emotional stress, it might be a good thing for you. But smoking goes much further than that.

If you smoke a pack and a half of cigarettes a day, you smoke an average of one cigarette every 32 minutes of your waking hours. That many crises don't arise every day. Your body has simply come to expect this depressant effect every so often. If it doesn't get it, you begin consciously to want a cigarette. You are unhappy if you don't get it.

There is little pleasure in smoking—until you so inure yourself to it that your body puts up with the harsh taste, the hot dryness, for the sake of a mild narcotic effect. If you were to go without cigarettes for the next 24 hours, and then light one, you would find out how distasteful and noxious tobacco smoke really is. After two deep inhalations of the first cigarette your head would be swimming, your legs and arms shaky. You might even feel faint. If you think this is an exaggeration, try it.

Or think back to the time many years ago when you smoked your first cigarette. Divorced from all the excitement of your first smoke, how did it *taste*? Gaseous, strong, biting, wasn't it?

Yet this is the experience that you give your system 30 to 60 times a day. You are able to do it because the human mechanism is a marvelously adjustable piece of machinery that can get used to living amid coal dust or doing the work of a truck horse—almost anything.

Very well, you say, smoking is a bad habit. What do I do about it?

It ought to encourage you to know that you have already taken one big step toward giving up smoking: You have already read this far—which means that, for this long at least, you have been *thinking* about smoking and about giving it up. And that is an important rule: If you want to stop smoking, *think about giving it up.*

Think of it coolly and calmly, without fear or hopelessness. Think of what it would be like not ever to *have* to smoke. For giving up smoking isn't all asceticism and self-denial; there are compensations. In fact, there are so many that when you give yourself a chance to appreciate them, you will never want to go back to nicotine.

When you give up smoking, your food will taste much better. Your nose and throat and lungs will not be continuously permeated with smoke and smoke's residue, soot. You will begin to *smell* the world around you. When you walk into a garden you will *smell* as well as *see* flowers. When you get up in the morning, you won't find your throat clogged with phlegm, and you won't cough or clear your throat so often.

You will actually feel far less nervous. That's hard to believe—and during the first days of nonsmoking you *will* be nervous. The depressant effect smoking has exerted on your body for years suddenly ends, and the unfamiliar effect is almost overwhelming. You will possibly be more emotional; you may laugh at trivial things and, for a while, be tense, jumpy. But gradually the nervousness diminishes. When you are over it, you'll be surprised at what experiences you can meet and live through without a cigarette.

You'll be calmer, more poised, and you may well find that there now are more hours in the day. For, when you stop slowing down your body and cutting your energy with tobacco, you will find that you have much more energy. There seems to be more time to get things done.

A word of caution here. It is generally believed that a reformed smoker gains weight. If you are of normal weight or underweight, there is nothing to worry about. If you have trouble with your waistline, remember this: When you stop smoking, you will probably gain. Don't worry about it—face it! You will not gain more than a few pounds. For when you stop smoking you will have a great increase in energy; and in using up that energy you will burn away a lot of the weight that you put on.

If you have read this far, you probably think you are about ready to swear off. Don't do it yet. Think about it—during the day and for just a moment as you go to bed. Tentatively, like this: *One of these days, when I feel like it, maybe I'll try going without smoking and see what happens. Just as an experiment, as a little change of pace in my regular routine.*

Watch and wait until sometime when your life is on a fairly even keel. Don't try it when you are leaving on an important trip, or preparing to give a big party, or when you are facing some personal emergency. Don't postpone it too long, either, or you will lose the momentum you are gradually building up.

But some sunny morning you will wake up feeling especially good. You will have had a good night's sleep; you will feel fit for anything. The idea of stopping smoking will pop into your head.

Why foul up a swell morning with the noxious fumes of burning nicotine? Why shoulder for another day the burden you've been carrying for years? Decide, then and there, quietly and firmly, that you're through with smoking! This is the moment, intelligently selected and properly prepared for, when you can get off with the running start of feeling good!

Now let's put to use three pieces of advice from a great psychologist, William James, whose observations on habits and their making and breaking are of extraordinary value here.

One: Start yourself off on the new way of life with as much momentum as you can. Tell your friends that you have given up smoking. Don't be smug or complacent or boastful, but let people know what you are doing. Then, at some point when you are seriously tempted to smoke, the thought of all the derisive laughter you'll get for giving in may well carry you over the crisis.

Most smokers have fixed ideas about the occasions when a smoke tastes best. The first cigarette after breakfast, or the one with a cocktail before dinner. If such associations are likely to tempt you to smoke, try to avoid them for a few days. If that is impossible, brace yourself in advance for such temptations. Tell yourself that such an occasion is coming, and that you will want to smoke badly. If you hold out only for a moment, that sudden strong temptation will die almost as quickly as it arose.

How to Stop Smoking

Two: Don't permit yourself to make a single exception to your new rule until the nonsmoking habit is firmly implanted (and that will be a long time). If a habit is not fed, it dies relatively quickly, but it can subsist for a long time on the slightest food. If you occasionally let yourself have one cigarette or pipe on the ground that "just one won't hurt," you will keep alive the desire to smoke. Just as one drink is too many for an alcoholic, one cigarette is too many for the heavy smoker who is trying to reform.

Win the battle of the moment—forget about an hour from now, or a day from now, or a week from now. Every time you say no to the temptation to smoke, you are making the next "no" easier.

Three: Deliberately expose yourself to small temptations and conquer them. Just as a fighter conditions himself by road work and sparring, you can develop your determination by deliberate "workouts."

Go out of your way at least once every day to demonstrate how you have forsworn tobacco. Carry matches and light cigarettes for your friends. If you are accustomed to riding in the smoking car, continue to do so, and look at all the people around you who are riding there by necessity and not choice, as you are doing! They can't give up smoking. You have!

If you thus deliberately try to make it tough, it will seem far less so, and you will much sooner get over the worst of it, which usually lasts about a week.

Baby yourself in everything else. Most of us are inclined to launch sudden, widely ambitious programs of self-improvement that defeat their own purpose. We try to do more than we can reasonably expect of ourselves. Don't increase the difficulties of stopping smoking by adding others. On the contrary, indulge yourself. Eat what you want and enjoy it. Have an occasional cup of coffee or soft drink when you feel the desire to smoke. Make it a habit to carry mints, gum, salted nuts.

Don't worry about getting the gum or candy habit. As the desire to smoke dies, so will the desire for a substitute. But during the first few weeks keep such substitutes on hand—and pop one into your mouth whenever you feel the urge to smoke.

Let your sleep work for you. On the night of the first day that you give up smoking, think for a moment when you go to bed of how today you did not smoke. Think of the various times during the day when you were tempted to, yet did not. Then tell yourself, "Tomorrow I am not going to smoke." Repeat it to yourself as you get drowsy. This will be the last thing in your conscious mind as you drop off to sleep.

When you wake in the morning, remind yourself that you are going to get through this day, too, without smoking. Don't make a big issue of it. Just—briefly—say: "This day I don't smoke." Even if you don't follow the other rules set down here, this exercise in "controlled sleep" could get you over the hump.

Now, in addition to all the physical pleasures that nonsmoking brings, you will find that a sudden sense of freedom and self-assurance results from simply going a half day, and then a day, and then two days without tobacco. This is a sharp, continuing pleasure, and every minute you live with it will strengthen you against the next minute's temptation.

And above and beyond this pleasant, heartening knowledge is the awareness that you are doing something you will be proud of—as well as healthier and happier for—during the rest of your life. Six months or six years from now, when someone offers you a cigarette, you will refuse it, but not weakly or defensively. You will say, "Thanks—I used to smoke, but I gave it up." And you will be looked at with a glimpse of wistful envy, like a freshman looking at a senior who has been through the mill.

Originally published in the April 1954 issue of *Reader's Digest* magazine.

Beginning with the publication of "Does Tobacco Injure the Human Body?" in November 1924, Reader's Digest was a prominent and persistent voice against smoking, bringing to light both the scientific evidence of its ill effects and the best practical advice on how to quit. This article was condensed from a bestselling book, which was sold with the guarantee that the purchaser's money would be refunded if he was unable to break the habit. Fewer than 50 of the more than 75,000 copies sold were returned.

Humor Hall of Fame

"We all do a lot of stupid things when we're young. So, what'll it take to remove that 'Butterball' tattoo?"

The other day I got carded at the liquor store. While I was taking out my ID, my old Blockbuster card fell out. The clerk shook his head, said "Never mind" and rang me up.

—ANDREA PRICE

For over 40 years my grandfather put in long hours at his job, so I was more than a little curious about the way he filled his days since his retirement.

"How has life changed?" I asked.

A man of few words, he replied, "Well, I get up in the morning with nothing to do, and I go to bed at night with it half-done."

—DENNIS LUNDBERG

A Dog's Life

by Dr. Nick Trout, from the book *Tell Me Where It Hurts*

*This veterinary surgeon can't talk
to his patients—but they speak to him
loud and clear.*

The phone call came at 2:47 a.m., jolting me awake. "Hi. I'm Dr. Sarah Keene, the new surgical resident," I heard a voice say. "I've got a dog here, a ten-year-old spayed female German shepherd. She's bloated and, well … Sorry. My backup's not answering his pager. Can you come in for the surgery?"

Sitting up in bed and reassuring my wife, Kathy, that the call was for me, I said, "No problem, Dr. Keene. Tell me about the patient."

Bloat—or GDV, for gastric dilatation and volvulus—is a true veterinary emergency typically occurring in deep-chested dogs like German shepherds, Great Danes and standard poodles. Often the animal eats a large meal, gets some exercise and develops a serious problem about an hour later. The stomach, distended by fermented gas, twists around and flips over on its long axis. The effect is catastrophic. The animal tries to rid itself of food and gas, but nothing budges. The stomach keeps expanding unchecked, squashing the lungs and the blood flowing back to the heart. A dog can die in a matter of hours.

"Is she stable?" I asked.

"Not really," said Dr. Keene. "Her pressures are off the charts, and

*The author with Sophie,
his Jack Russell terrier, at home.*

we're having a hell of a time finding a decent vein, let alone placing a catheter." The dog needed fluids to prevent shock.

My feet were now swinging out of bed as I fumbled for clean clothes. "Do your best to pass a stomach tube. I'll be there as fast as I can."

At this hour of the morning, my eyes were piggy and I had a jaunty case of bed head, but thankfully my patients didn't judge me on my appearance. I drove quickly to the Angell Animal Medical Center in Boston, one of the largest veterinary hospitals in the country, where I'd worked for the past ten of my 25 years in the field. I saw my patient, Sage, lying across a stainless steel surface in the prep area. Her darting eyes were full of fear; an oxygen mask was on her face. As I approached, her broad and bushy tail offered me a couple of friendly beats.

I liked German shepherds and grew up with one. Yet the wagging tail was utterly surprising and endearing to me given this dog's dire condition. I ran my hand across her soft velvety ear, over the chest and down to the drum-tight abdomen. There was a small shaved square on Sage's flank, where an attempt was made to release the stomach gas with a large-bore needle. The skin was taut; clearly the attempt had failed.

"No luck with a stomach tube?" I asked Dr. Keene after we'd quickly shared hellos and introductions.

"Afraid not. She's in bad shape. Heart rate's 220 with occasional VPCs." She was referring to ventricular premature contractions, or abnormal and ineffective heartbeats.

Sage's tail beat a message of thanks as I relieved her of the oxygen mask and inspected her gums. Instead of healthy, vibrant pink tissue, signifying normal blood flow, I saw an ugly muddy purple. "How much intravenous fluid has she had?"

"This is her fourth liter," said Dr. Keene. Sage's color looked awful. "She's acting like she's near the end," I said urgently. "Start a lidocaine drip, give her some intravenous antibiotics and knock her down. The faster we get her stomach untwisted, the better. I'm changing into scrubs."

"Before I forget," said Dr. Keene, "the owner insisted on meeting with you first."

I hesitated. Clearly the owner did not understand the gravity of the situation. But good client communication was crucial, and I believed in it wholeheartedly. "OK," I said. "If I'm not back in five minutes, get scrubbed in, drape her off and set up."

In a corner of the waiting room, I saw a mature man sitting with his head slightly bowed. He was alone. "Mr. Hartman?" I said as the man looked up. "Hi. I understand that Dr. Keene has explained that your dog is seriously ill and needs emergency surgery. I'm Sage's surgeon."

He got to his feet, and we shook hands. "I'm so sorry for getting you out of bed," he said. "I just don't want to lose her." There was a tremor in his voice as he added, "If she were your dog, would you put her through this surgery given she's ten years old?"

"Absolutely," I said immediately. "Sage seems like a great dog. Any animal prepared to beat me up with her tail, feeling as sick as she does at the moment, is definitely worth saving."

He tried his best to stifle a smile. Then the tears began to fall.

"She's all I've got since my wife died. I can't tell you how much this animal means to me."

I swallowed hard, needing to stay focused. "I know," I said. "My father had a shepherd when I was growing up. They bond tight, like superglue, and never let go."

He gave my shoulders a gentle squeeze. "Just do your best."

"That's the easy part," I said. "Sage has to do hers."

"She will. She's a strong girl. She won't let us down."

The iodine-stained skin yielded easily to my scalpel, revealing the white fatty shellac below. I was in blue scrubs, a sterile gown, a bouffant cap and latex surgical gloves; most of my face was hidden behind a paper mask. Dr. Keene, for her part, was peering through the green window of the sterile drape that covered our anesthetized patient—only to recoil as the bloated stomach burst through my calculated slash.

Dr. Keene and I squeezed our gloved hands into the tight space between Sage's stomach and the abdominal wall, seeing the vat of red that was free and pooled blood.

"Get a good grip of stomach in your right hand, and pull up on it as you push down with your left," I encouraged Dr. Keene, who, somewhere in her 20s, was still learning her trade.

She began to grunt and strain. With every breath Sage took, the abdominal wall was cinching down on Dr. Keene's forearms. A full minute passed.

"Damn it!" she said, retrieving her fingers. "I can't do it."

"Your instinct is to be too cautious, too gentle," I said. She resumed her position, hands grappling the enormous stomach, and this time applied greater force. Finally, with a satisfying whoosh, the big muscular balloon flopped back into its correct position.

> *I saw a dog who managed to say hello with a stomach about to burst.*

"Fantastic," I said.

I reached into the abdominal cavity and placed the stomach tube; a column of liquid food and gas poured into a bucket. My hands fished through the small intestines as I said, "Next we check out Mr. Spleen."

I located the large meaty boomerang of an organ next to the stomach. It was entirely black, no pulse at all. With blood flow cut off by the bloating, the spleen was dead; fortunately Sage could afford to lose it. Within minutes, we had removed it and gone back to the stomach. I pulled a portion of it free of the blood and into the bright light of the surgical lamps.

Dr. Keene sensed my hesitation. "What is it?"

I was noting its color—purple, with a hint of gray. I could almost feel Mr. Hartman's hand on my shoulder. "I don't like what I see," I said. "It may not be viable."

"So why not just staple it off?" she asked.

I wished it were as simple as that. Surgery was replete with nuance, forcing surgeons to make quick, vital decisions based on experience, instinct and faith. Sage had every negative prognostic factor—abnormal heart rhythm, high pulse rate, removal of the spleen and the need to cut out part of the stomach—yet I wanted to give her the benefit of my doubt. In my mind's eye, I could still see a dog who managed to say hello with a stomach about to burst, and a man reduced to tears at the thought of losing his closest friend.

"Here are Sage's three options as I see them," I explained. "One, we take our chances, staple off as much stomach as we dare, and pray nothing breaks down. Two, we seal off the end of the stomach, put a feeding tube into the small intestine, and let the stomach decide whether it lives or dies. In a few days, we see whether we can put Sage back together again."

Dr. Keene asked if I'd ever done that. "No," I told her. "And I hope I never do. But it's possible."

"So what's option three?"

I sighed. "We call it a day. It might be better to let Sage die in her sleep than have her succumb to a slow and painful death if her stomach perforates because I made the wrong decision."

Suddenly I noticed the beating of the heart monitor. It was deafening, filling the silence.

"What do you think Mr. Hartman would want to do?" asked Dr. Keene.

I met the young doctor's stare. I knew the answer. "The right thing. Whatever that may be."

I chose option No. 1.

Dr. Keene separated the good part of the stomach from the bad. She was firing the GIA device—the gastrointestinal anastomosis stapler—as I selected healthy tissue from the dead. "Let's oversew the staple line," I said. "Then you can get on with it." She would do the gastropexy, the surgical fixation of the stomach to the abdominal wall so that it wouldn't perform somersaults in the future.

The resident loaded her needle driver and began passing the suture through the stomach wall. I made her feel for the physical separation between the inner and outer layers of the stomach, and watched as she traced the margin of the flap with the point of her scissors. I approved her design and let her work.

Moments had passed when I heard a curse. Dark brown fluid was spewing from a tiny rip in the stomach where Dr. Keene had been cutting. It was small; the tissue still looked good.

"I'm so sorry," she said, fumbling with sponges, mopping up the contamination that flooded into our sterile surgical field.

"It's OK—it's done," I said. "Don't beat yourself up. Let's fix it, flush half a dozen liters of sterile saline solution through her abdomen, change gloves, change instruments and get out."

"Do you want to finish this? You'll be much faster," she said.

"No way," I said. "I'm useless before my first cup of coffee."

Which was true, but, more important, Dr. Keene would gain nothing if I took over. This sort of experience was critical for the resident's professional development.

Fifteen more minutes and the click of the last staple brought the edges of the skin into perfect alignment. We were done here. I scrubbed out and returned to the waiting room. Mr. Hartman was sitting in the same spot, chewing on his lower lip. I approached and sat beside him.

"Everything went well," I told him. I explained what we had found and how we had deflated the stomach, fixed it in place, and taken out the spleen, how Sage would be fine without it. He hung on my every word. "My biggest concern now is the stomach wall and whether it will live or die. The next 24 hours will be critical."

He sighed deeply, relieved that Sage was still in the fight. When I suggested he go home and rest, he said that rather than drive more than an hour back to Cape Cod, he would stay with his daughter in nearby Wellesley.

"Great. Sage needs you in good shape for visiting hours later."

He smiled, and I promised to call if anything changed. As I watched him go, my mind was in a tumult. Mortality rates for GDV could be as high as 60 percent. Should I have been more cynical in my assessment of the surgery? I'd made a huge decision—either an example of flitting genius or an enduring miscalculation—and like it or not, a stranger and his best friend were along for the ride. For all the years of training, the obsession with a singular performance, I tried my best to be a social

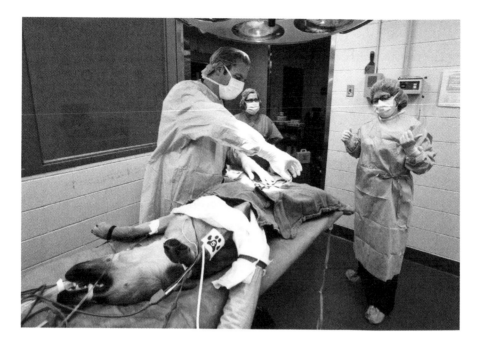

Dr. Trout performs surgery on Hannah, a one-year-old shepherd mix. "It's like playing the piano," he says. "It's a skill that can be learned."

worker, psychologist, grief counselor, mentor, carpenter, plumber, cosmetologist, athletic coach, magician, grim reaper and, occasionally, guardian angel. Sometimes I worried that I'd run out of hats.

For this complicated equation, I thought about the single most important component, the patient herself. When I focused on Sage, the way her eyes locked on mine and the warm greeting from her tail despite the agony, I thought that, if ever a dog deserved a chance, this dog did. We humans would be ripping the arm off every nurse or doctor and screaming for morphine, yet this selfless creature had placed more importance on the simplicity of a connection with us than on the pain she felt.

I prayed I had done the right thing for Sage.

Back at my house several hours later, resigned to hitting the bed and worrying, I was making for the stairs when the phone rang.

Sage was in rapid decline.

I heard every detail over the phone from another veterinarian; Dr. Keene had left by then.

I reached for the keys, headed to my car, and sped back to work and to the decision that must have gone wrong.

*　　*　　*

They were in the waiting room when I got there, Mr. Hartman with an appreciative smile and a woman I took to be his daughter. She was probably in her late 40s, her hair short, dark and damp. Her name was Helen Hancock. I quickly introduced myself, and we shook hands. Mr. Hartman offered a nod and a "thank you for coming out again."

"Can you tell us what's going on with my father's dog?" asked Helen directly.

"I've spoken with the emergency doctor," I said. "Sage has been running a temperature of 104° to 104.2°. High normal would be around 103°, but it could go up with pain and inflammation. The doctor reviewed her pain meds and checked her surgical incision. Everything appeared to be in order."

It was not what I saw that counted, but what I didn't see.

Then I explained about the abdominal tap, which suctioned up a bit of fluid from the belly, allowing us to examine it under a microscope. It showed that there were some free bacteria in Sage's abdominal cavity. "There's most likely a small leak," I said.

"Can anything more be done for her?" said Mr. Hartman.

"There's one more thing we can try." I explained how I planned to take Sage back into surgery to figure out where the leak was coming from. "Believe me," I added, "I will not let this dog suffer. I know when it's time to give up on an animal, and in my opinion, before taking one last look, this is not the time."

I watched father and daughter absorb the news.

"I need to change into scrubs and get started," I said, noticing that Mr. Hartman had begun rummaging for something in his overcoat pocket. He sandwiched my right hand between both of his and jabbed something into my palm that felt hard and plastic.

"Just do your best," he said, as he had earlier.

I managed to secrete the mysterious object into my pants pocket. Soon after, I put it in the breast pocket of my scrubs, assuming that its physical presence in the operating room was what Mr. Hartman had in mind.

I hated going back into an animal's belly. Aside from the glaring proof of failure, it was a slow, untidy process. Sharp, clean lines of white and red were traded for jagged edges of lavender and crimson where tissue had been crushed and bruised by the scalpel, scissors, needle and forceps. Some people, I thought, assumed that surgeons had a God complex, that they relished the power to choose between life and death and to wield it through their hands, their eyes and their scalpel blades. To me, nothing was further from the truth. Surgeons were not God. God didn't have to worry. God didn't feel guilty. God didn't make mistakes. And we most certainly did.

At first all I did was look. And it was not what I saw that counted, but what I didn't see. I didn't see black, gray or green. I didn't see a stomach that had decided to die or an infection out of control. I didn't see disaster or despair. Within seconds of looking, I didn't see a reason to put this dog to sleep.

The area of the stomach that Dr. Keene and I had stapled off was bruised and inflamed, but it glowed with the vibrant pulse of tissue that would survive. I fed the entire small and large intestines, pale and endless, through my fingers, looking for a perforation, a defect, something we might have overlooked. There was nothing. This left only one explanation: the site where the stomach had been inadvertently punctured when Dr. Keene was trying to secure it to the abdominal wall.

I carefully got to the delicate tissue below and then to the tiny defect. When I compressed a pocket of stomach gas into this area, I noticed how a bit of yellow-green liquid bubbled and burst at the cut surface. I repeated the process to convince myself that this truly was the source of the bacteria.

It was not what I expected. I had imagined a raw, gaping wound. What I saw seemed subtle and insignificant. But what else could there be? I revisited the stomach staple line again, ran the intestines one more time. Once more I came up empty.

I had been logical, methodical and conscientious. There was no other explanation. The leak, if it could be labeled that, might have been minor and tenuous, but it had to be the cause.

As I carefully placed additional stitches to reinforce the original repair, I realized I'd been wrong, almost selfish, not to call Dr. Keene back in for this. I had figured she needed her rest. But she would want to know what I'd found. She would need to learn from it. I made a mental note to be sure to relay the news. Then, for the last time, I tested for bubbles, restored the sutures I'd removed, and rewarded Sage's stomach wall with a revitalizing and cleansing bath in ten liters of warm sterile solution.

* * *

Mr. Hartman was sitting in his favorite corner of the waiting room, head slightly bowed as usual. I patted my breast pocket as I walked toward him. "Your friend did the trick," I said, smiling. "Sage is going to be just fine."

I studied his response as I sat next to him, the pain of relief no less than the pain of loss. It took him a moment to contain the tremble in his lips. I patted his shoulder.

"Sage is awake and in the critical care unit," I said. "The leak was tiny and easily fixed. Best of all, the part of the stomach I was worried about pretty much told me it had no intention of quitting anytime soon. It looks good. It should continue to heal fine."

He leaned forward, hand clamped across his mouth. Was he unable to find the words, or afraid to let them out? All he gave me was his eyes; that was enough. They said thank you.

"You'd best have this back," I said, reaching into my pocket to pull out the object. "Sage may need him for another fight."

It was a religious figurine about three inches long, pinged as though it must be hollow. It appeared to be a monk, and therefore I assumed it must be St. Francis of Assisi, the patron saint of animals. The man was dressed in a robe with a pair of twittering gray birds, one in his left hand and one at his feet. His right hand was outstretched with an open palm.

"My wife gave it to me," said Mr. Hartman, his voice small. "It's not St. Francis; it's St. Sergius, saint protector of Russia. It's silly, but it makes me feel better having him around, and I was in such a rush to get here the other night, I forgot to bring him."

I nodded. I understood Mr. Hartman a little bit better. "Your daughter didn't stay?" I asked him.

"She had to leave. She has to work—she's an engineer."

"You should be getting home yourself," I said. "It's late, and I think a certain German shepherd is going to want a visitor come tomorrow morning."

He nodded, got to his feet and pointed to the figure still in my hand. "Keep him," he told me. "You never know—he might be able to help some other sick animal."

I was both surprised and honored. "Are you sure?" I asked.

"Positive," he said. "I know you'll put him to good use."

He adjusted his cap as he eased toward the automatic doors.

He was absolutely right. I have.

Originally published in the July 2008 issue of *Reader's Digest* magazine.

SAVED BY A STRANGER

When I was 16, my parents and I were at a kennel looking
for our next cocker spaniel when I stepped on a 12-inch
rattlesnake. He bit through my thin sock on the instep, and I
immediately felt the poison move through my foot and up my
leg. We raced to the nearest hospital, where it had antivenin
on hand for me. Turns out that years before, a woman had
been bitten but the hospital had had no treatment available.
That dear lady ordered it to always keep antivenin on hand
for emergencies. The ultimate miracle worker!

   P.S. We got the dog free.

—Barb Williams, *Denver, Colorado*

LIFESAVING LUCKY PENNY

I never really believed in the lucky objects that many people
have carried. But one day as I was mowing our five-acre yard,
I was going along a fairly steep side of the road and noticed a
shiny object out in the grass some five yards away. I stopped
the lawn tractor and hopped off to go over and see what had
caught my eye. Just as I bent over to pick up the object, the
lawn tractor exploded behind me, knocking me off my feet.
Later in the emergency room, my family was curious about
the fact that when I was brought in by ambulance they found
a shiny penny clutched in my hand. I now believe in lucky
pennies and stop to pick them up whenever I see them!

—Philip Hayden, *Bloomington, Illinois*

Oak Island's Mysterious "Money Pit"

by David MacDonald, from *The Rotarian*

There is something down there—
but for 200 years no one has been able to
figure out how to get at it.

Just off the rugged southern shore of Nova Scotia lies a tiny island shaped somewhat like a question mark. The shape is appropriate, for little Oak Island is the scene of a baffling whodunit that has defied solution for almost two centuries. Here, ever since 1795—not long after pirates prowled the Atlantic Coast and left glittering legends of buried gold in their wake—people have been trying to find out what lies at the bottom of a mysterious shaft dubbed, hopefully, the Money Pit.

Using picks and shovels, divining rods and drilling rigs, treasure hunters have poured about $1,500,000 into the Money Pit. To date, they have taken precious little out—only three links of gold chain and a scrap of ancient parchment. Despite more than 20 attempts, no one has yet reached bottom: Each time a digging or drilling crew has seemed close to success, torrents of water have suddenly surged into the shaft to drown

131

their hopes. Although it's now known that the Money Pit is protected by an ingenious system of man-made flood tunnels that use the sea as a watchdog, to this day no one knows who dug the pit, or why.

One legend makes it the hiding place for the plunder of Captain Kidd, who was hanged for piracy in 1701. Other theories favor the booty of Blackbeard and Henry Morgan, both notorious buccaneers; Inca treasure stolen by Spaniards; the French crown jewels that Louis XVI and Marie Antoinette were said to be carrying when they attempted to flee during the French Revolution; or Shakespeare's missing manuscripts. Whatever the pit may contain, few other treasures have been sought so avidly.

The long parade of searchers began one day in 1795, when Daniel McInnes, a 16-year-old boy from Chester, Nova Scotia, paddled over to uninhabited Oak Island to hunt for game. On a knoll at one end of the island he noticed an odd depression, 12 feet in diameter. Sixteen feet above it, on a sawed-off tree limb, hung an old ship's tackle block. McInnes's heart raced, for in the nearby port of La Have, once a lair for pirates preying on New England shipping, he had heard many legends of buried treasure.

Next day he came back with two other boys, Tony Vaughan and Jack Smith, and began digging. Ten feet down they hit a platform of aged oak logs; at 20 feet, another; at 30, a third. In the flinty clay walls of the shaft they could still see the marks of pickaxes. As the work grew harder, they sought help. But no one else would go near Oak Island. It was said to be haunted by the ghosts of two fishermen who vanished there in 1720 while investigating strange lights. So the boys gave up, temporarily.

Later, McInnes and Smith settled on the island. In 1804, intrigued by their tale, a wealthy Nova Scotian named Simeon Lynds joined them in forming a treasure company. They again found oak tiers every ten feet down the pit, to a depth of 90 feet. They also uncovered layers of tropical coconut fiber, charcoal and ship's putty, plus a stone cut with curious symbols that one cryptologist took to mean, "Ten feet below, two million pounds are buried." At 93 feet, the diggers drove a crowbar five feet deeper and struck a solid mass. Lynds felt sure that it was a treasure chest.

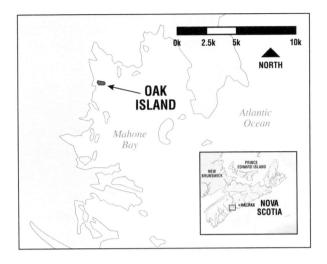

But the next morning he was amazed to find 60 feet of water in the pit. Weeks of bailing proved fruitless; the water level remained constant. Lynds assumed that this was due to an underground freshwater spring. The next year, his hired miners dug 110 feet down, off to one side of the Money Pit, then began burrowing toward it. When they were only two feet from it, tons of water burst through. As they scrambled for their lives, the shaft quickly filled to the same depth as the Money Pit.

Beaten and almost broke, Lynds gave up. McInnes died. But Vaughan and Smith never lost hope. In 1849, they took another stab at the Money Pit, with a syndicate from Truro, Nova Scotia. The results were dramatic.

At 98 feet down, just where the crowbar had hit a solid mass in 1804, a horse-driven pod auger (which picked up a sample of anything it passed through) pierced a spruce platform. After dropping through an empty space, it cut into 4 inches of oak, 22 inches of metal pieces, 8 of oak, 22 of loose metal again, 4 more inches of oak and 6 of spruce, and then into deep clay. To the drillers, this suggested an exciting prospect—a vault containing two chests, one atop the other and laden with treasure, perhaps gold coins or jewels. Moreover, the auger brought up a tantalizing sample of what might be there: three links of a gold chain.

A second 110-foot shaft was dug in 1850. It also flooded. But this time a workman fell in and came up sputtering, "Salt water!" Then someone noticed that the water in the pits rose and fell like the tide. This discovery jogged old Tony Vaughan's memory: Years before, he had seen water gushing down the beach at Smith's Cove—520 feet from the Money Pit—at low tide.

The treasure hunters stripped the sandy beach, searching for a hidden inlet of the sea. Under the sand, to their astonishment, they found tons of coconut fiber and eel grass on a stone floor that stretched, 154 feet wide, the full distance between high- and low-tide marks. More digging uncovered more surprises: Five rock-walled box drains slanted in from the sea and down, converging on a line aimed at the Money Pit.

In effect, the beach acted as a gigantic sponge to soak up tidewater and filter it into a conduit. This conduit dropped 70 feet straight down, later exploration proved, then sloped back to a point deep in the Money Pit—all of it filled with loose rock to prevent erosion. This brilliant baffle was no natural obstacle; it was the work of a genius. As diggers neared the cache at 98 feet, they had unwittingly lessened the pressure of earth that plugged the mouth of the conduit.

Undeterred, the Truro crew built a cofferdam to hold back the sea. The sea promptly wrecked it. Next they dug 118 feet down and burrowed under the Money Pit. But while the diggers were at dinner, the bottom of the pit collapsed into the tunnel, then dropped even farther—into a mysteriously empty space.

Though the Truro syndicate lost $40,000, its discoveries excited wide interest in Oak Island. A series of costly expeditions followed, all dogged by bad luck. One outfit gave up after a huge steam pump exploded, killing a man. In 1893, almost a century after the dig began, still another syndicate was organized, this time by Frederick Blair, a Nova Scotia businessman who was to spend almost 60 years trying to solve the mystery.

His company was the first to locate the flood-tunnel outlet, 111 feet down the side of the Money Pit. To block it at the source, dynamite was set off deep underground near the shore at Smith's Cove. After filling the Money Pit with water, well above sea level, Blair threw in red dye. Not a trace of it seeped back to Smith's Cove—proof that the dynamite had been successful.

But on the opposite shore of the island, 300 feet from the pit, red stains appeared at three places! This meant that there was at least one more flood tunnel to cope with. No one has yet found it.

Blair and his partners also resorted to core-drilling in the Money Pit.

At 153 feet—the deepest yet—their bit chewed into 7 inches of cement, 5 of oak, 32 inches of metal pieces, then more oak and cement. Finally, at 170 feet, it rattled against impenetrable iron.

To Blair, this indicated a treasure chest encased in primitive concrete, larger and buried deeper than the ones drilled through in 1850. This time, along with flecks of gold, the bit brought up a tiny scrap of parchment bearing the letters *vi-* written with a quill pen and India ink, according to analysts in Boston.

"That's more convincing than a few doubloons would be," Blair claimed. "Either a treasure of immense value or priceless historical documents are at the bottom of that pit." But the syndicate never found out. After spending more than $100,000, it folded.

Only Blair carried on. He secured treasure-trove rights to the island for 40 years, then offered to lease them for a share in any bonanza that might be found. The first taker was engineer Harry Bowdoin, of New York. With several prominent backers looking on—including a young lawyer named Franklin D. Roosevelt—Bowdoin dug and drilled in 1909, to no avail. Then he wrote a magazine article, claiming that there had never been any treasure on Oak Island anyway.

Next came syndicates from Wisconsin; Rochester, New York; and Newark, New Jersey. All failed. In 1931, William Chappell of Sydney, Nova Scotia, a wealthy contractor who had run the drill that brought up the piece of parchment, sank $30,000 into the Money Pit. Then the Depression made him quit.

Chappell was followed in 1936 by Gilbert Hedden, a New Jersey millionaire who spent $100,000 more. Hedden ran submarine power lines from the mainland to drive high-speed pumps, and hired a Pennsylvania mining firm to clear the 170-foot shaft. He finally concluded that all the digging and flooding had probably shifted the treasure as much as 100 feet—in *any* direction.

At the time of Blair's death in 1951, Oak Island and its treasure rights were acquired by William Chappell's son, Mel, who had worked with his father's expedition in 1931. Mel Chappell spent $25,000 on one excavation, which quickly became a small lake, then leased portions of his rights to a series of other fortune hunters, the latest being Bob Restall of Hamilton, Ontario. A 59-year-old steelworker, Restall quit his $150-a-week job in 1959 and moved to Oak Island with his wife, Mildred, and their sons, Bobby and Rickey. The Restalls have lived there ever since, in a one-room cabin beside the Money Pit, a caved-in crater filled with sludge and rotting timbers. Restall has managed to clear a 155-foot shaft sunk in the 1930s. He has added eight holes, 25 feet deep, trying to intercept the flood tunnels that have foiled all previous searches. To finance his hunt, Restall has already sold about half of his interest in any treasure to friends and interested strangers who have written from as far away as Texas. In all, including his savings and five years of hard labor, Restall figures that his quest for Oak Island's elusive hoard has cost almost $100,000. Yet all he has to show for it so far are an olive-colored stone chiseled with the date 1704, which he found in one of the holes, and a profound respect for whoever designed the Money Pit. "That man," he says, "was one hell of a lot smarter than anyone who has come here since."

Originally published in the January 1965 issue of *Reader's Digest* magazine.

In August 1965, not long after this article ran in Reader's Digest, *Bob Restall, his son Bobby and two other men were killed by a poisonous gas in a shaft on Oak Island. In 2014, the History Channel premiered the series "The Curse of Oak Island," which follows a team of treasure hunters who have used sonic core drilling, metal detectors and deep ground penetrating radar to try to solve the mystery. The treasure has still not been found.*

Our America

Highway Patrol
—C.F. PAYNE
JULY 2006

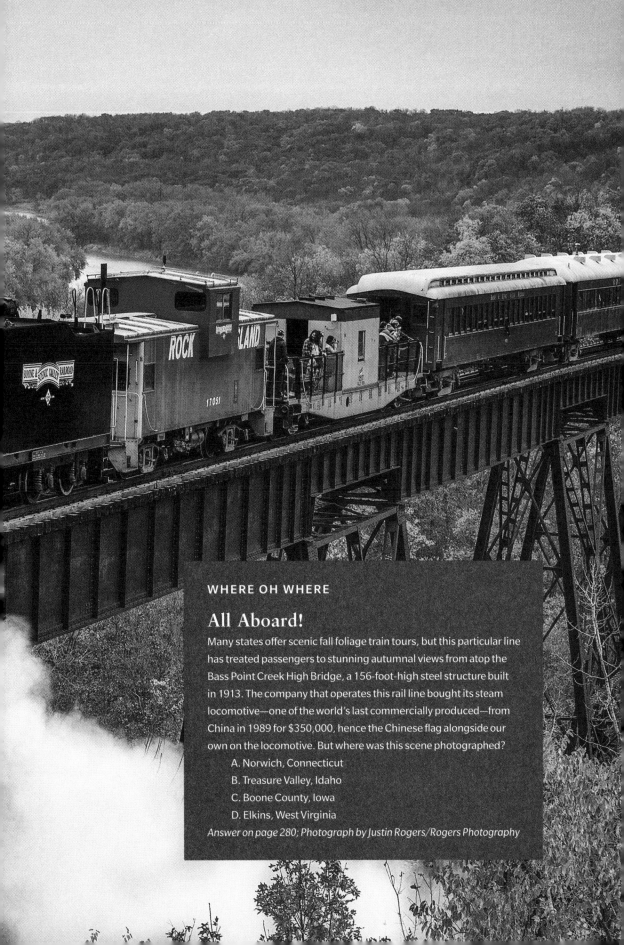

WHERE OH WHERE

All Aboard!

Many states offer scenic fall foliage train tours, but this particular line has treated passengers to stunning autumnal views from atop the Bass Point Creek High Bridge, a 156-foot-high steel structure built in 1913. The company that operates this rail line bought its steam locomotive—one of the world's last commercially produced—from China in 1989 for $350,000, hence the Chinese flag alongside our own on the locomotive. But where was this scene photographed?

    A. Norwich, Connecticut

    B. Treasure Valley, Idaho

    C. Boone County, Iowa

    D. Elkins, West Virginia

Answer on page 280; Photograph by Justin Rogers/Rogers Photography

Letter to Olivia

by Mel Allen, from *Bowdoin Magazine*

*A journalist profiles a young single father
who came to college with
little more than a basketball.*

Dear Olivia,

I am writing this letter to you on November 27, 1999, your father's 31st birthday. I want to tell you about your father, Wil Smith, and about your time together at Bowdoin College. One day you will probably ask him about these years, when he was a single dad with a young daughter, struggling to stay in school, compete in a tough Division III basketball program and provide a home for you. Everyone knows how modest your father is, so I suspect he'll leave out the details.

You are a bouncy, pretty little four-year-old girl with braided pigtails and happy brown eyes. During the games you roam through the stands as the free-spirited, trusting child you are. The students are drawn to you as if by magnet, and it must seem as if the whole world knows your name. Wil says he plays with his head on a swivel, always looking for you during breaks in the action.

You live together in a two-bedroom apartment a few blocks from campus. Both of you eat in the student cafeteria. Most nights you are in bed by nine; Wil turns in soon after so he can get up to study, often as early as 5 a.m.

*After basketball practice,
Wil Smith relaxes with his
young daughter, Olivia.*

You have always come first, but he is also co-captain of the men's basketball team, a four-year starter on a nationally ranked team at 31—an age when other men are playing weekly pickup games at the YMCA. He led Bowdoin in assists and steals, and he made the conference All-Defensive team.

Nearly half the Bowdoin students arrive from private schools. Your father came from the Navy, a decade after graduating from a public high school. His first year at college he had to work twice as hard to keep up with the others.

He is a black student at a college and in a state with few people of color, and he has made it his business to make life better for others who come after him. "I try to educate people about the people I come from," he says.

Wil's story begins in Jacksonville, Florida, with a woman you never knew, your Grandmother Mildred. "My mother was the most incredible person I ever met," Wil says. "I was the last of ten children she raised, pretty much on her own, and she always put us first. She worked every day and still found time to coach boys' and girls' baseball and basketball."

Wil turns in soon after you so he can get up as early as 5 a.m. to study.

Everyone knew the Smith boys because they were athletes. At five-foot-ten, Wil was the smallest of all the boys, but he was fast and tough, and nobody worked harder. He wanted to play on his mother's teams, but she sent her sons to play for coaches who knew the sport better than she did. Wil was an all-star in football, basketball and baseball. Mildred learned to drive at age 49 just so she could get to the games; she never missed one.

* * *

When she died of cancer on November 27, 1983, Wil's 15th birthday, she took much of Wil's passion for sports with her. "My mother was my biggest fan," he says. "When she passed away, I asked myself, 'Why am I still playing?' A lot of my joy in sports came from my mother's look."

Wil struggled to cope. He still played, but he was drifting. "I never reached the heights everyone thought I would," Wil says. When colleges sent recruiting letters, he didn't bother to respond.

Reluctantly Wil attended Florida A&M in Tallahassee for a year and a half. He played a season of baseball, but his heart wasn't in it. Wil left school in 1988 and started spending time with a crowd that was dealing drugs and fighting.

"I was hanging out at a store with my friends," Wil says, "and ESPN came on. It was a baseball highlight. One guy said, 'Wil, man, you don't belong here. You're different. I expected to see you up there, playing ball on TV.' I always remember that. I witnessed heavy stuff, but there's no way to get away from good roots."

Three years after graduating from high school, Wil enlisted in the Navy. He was trained to be an aviation electronics technician. In June 1991 his orders sent him to the Naval Air Station in Brunswick, Maine. In his spare time he volunteered as a football coach for middle-school students.

"I had 60 white kids on my team," Wil says. "Most had never been in contact with a black man. I had no problem with the kids, but the parents said I was too intense. I told them that every day I'd ask the kids, 'Anybody hurt? Anybody not having fun?' The kids always said they were fine. I told the parents, 'As long as your kids are with me, they're mine for three hours a day.'"

By the season's end, some of those same parents told Wil their kids were slipping in their work. As someone they looked up to, would he talk with them? Soon he became a community fixture, coaching basketball and football.

His teams played hard, and they won. In the summer of 1995, while coaching at a basketball camp, Wil's ability and character caught the eye of Tim Gilbride, the men's basketball coach at Bowdoin. Gilbride asked Wil if he'd considered applying to Bowdoin College.

Wil was at a crossroads. He had served seven years in the Navy and was due to re-enlist. But the Navy meant six months overseas every year, and you, Olivia, had been born a couple of months before. He'd met your mother in Portland after returning from overseas duty. Their relationship ended and you lived with your mom, but Wil came for you every Thursday and kept you until Monday.

*   *   *

Wil applied to Bowdoin while on a six-month assignment in Sicily. He decided he would not leave you again for that length of time. His last day of active duty, April 25, 1996, was also the day your mother gave him full custody of you, then 11 months old.

Though Wil had been accepted to Bowdoin, he didn't know the questions to ask—questions that so many parents of college students take for granted. He didn't know how to apply for student aid or room and board. Wil started school in September 1996. You were 16 months old, and he had no choice but to bring you to class. When you were sick, he wouldn't go. The money he'd saved from the Navy went faster than he could have imagined. At times he didn't eat for three days so he'd have enough food to feed you.

"I lost 17 pounds," Wil said. "I couldn't sleep. I got an F in a course that required you to read about 20 books. I didn't have money for books; I didn't know about books being on reserve in the library."

What he told the dean was simply, "Things are hard for me right now." The dean called Betty Trout-Kelly, who oversees Bowdoin's multicultural programs and affirmative action.

"I know you feel you shouldn't need this support," Trout-Kelly told Wil, "but if you don't take our help, you won't make it."

You were 16 months old. He had no choice but to bring you to class.

For the first time, Wil told her about his struggles. Later, after meeting with school officials, Trout-Kelly notified Wil that an anonymous donor would give nearly $25,000 for Olivia's day care and after-school care. Wil would be able to move to campus housing and eat regularly with his daughter. "Thank you," Wil told her. "I'll prove myself worthy."

In four years, Olivia, your father has become as well known off campus as on. A sociology major, he puts what he learns in the classroom to work. He is the community adviser for civil rights teams at Brunswick and Mount Ararat high schools. He travels around the state of Maine giving talks to educators about the problems and challenges of diversity. "I feel like I have an obligation to every young person I come in contact with," Wil says. During the summer he is a counselor at Seeds of Peace International Camp in Otisfield, Maine, where teenagers from regions of conflict around the world live together.

A Navy reservist, Wil served in the Balkans.

None of this has come easily, Olivia. You have asthma, and when you're sick, he has trouble trusting anybody else with your care. Last season you had a fever when the team had a weekend road trip. It took all of Coach Gilbride's skills of persuasion, and his saying his wife had raised three kids and would care for you, before Wil agreed to go.

During spring semester of his junior year, Wil was called to active duty—he's still in the Navy reserves—during the Balkan conflict. Before leaving, he scrambled to get you to your aunt in Florida, finished work for two courses, and took incompletes in the rest. He came back before summer, picked you up, finished some papers and got ready for his final year as a student-athlete.

Wil is torn about what to do in the future. Whatever he decides will be in large part because of you, Olivia, because you are more important to him than anything in the world. "I know people look at it as a disadvantage having Olivia," Wil says. "I see it as an advantage. If it was just me, I'd never have made it. There've been nights I've been so tired, I've been ready to quit on papers. But then I look in on Olivia sleeping, and I go back to my paper."

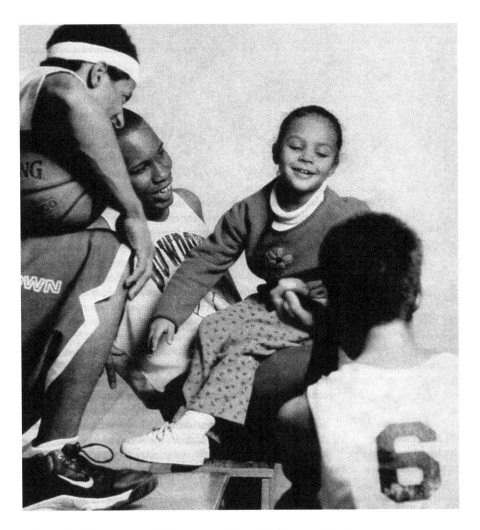

Olivia holds court with the team. Her dad's contribution was so great that Bowdoin renamed a school honor the Wil Smith Community Service Award.

Once when you were two, he was walking you to school, holding your hand. "My mind was in turmoil," he says. "I had midterms, my car had broken down and we had no money. Olivia was talking about leaves and trees. I didn't even realize she had let go of my hand. I had taken ten steps without her, then suddenly turned. 'Dad,' she said, 'talk to me.' She was saying, in her own way, 'None of this other stuff matters.'

"All she cared about is that we were there. She was glad the car had broken down; that meant we could walk to school together. She put life in perspective for me."

Olivia, I hope when you're older you'll read this and understand what an extraordinary man your father is.

Originally published in the May 2001 issue of *Reader's Digest* magazine.

This story, written by Yankee Magazine *editor Mel Allen, attracted national attention when it first appeared in* Bowdoin Magazine *in the winter of 2000. That May, more than 400 students graduated from Bowdoin College. At the ceremony on the campus quadrangle, when Bowdoin President Robert H. Edwards read off the names "Wil and Olivia Smith," the crowd cheered and gave a standing ovation.*

Wil went on to become Bowdoin's coordinator of Multicultural Student Programs and, later, dean of community and multicultural affairs at the Berkshire School in Sheffield, Massachusetts. He died of colon cancer on February 22, 2015, at the age of 46.

Olivia Smith graduated from Howard University in 2018.

"I Get a Lot More Than I Give"

by Bob Hope

The "best friend the serviceman ever had" recalls some of his Christmastime visits to soldiers serving in South Vietnam.

Our huge C-130 droned high over the jungle. The scenery below looked much like Oregon: towering mountains and lush green valleys, the picture of tranquility. We were snapped back to reality when our project officer stood up to make an announcement.

"If there is a mortar attack on the show site, lie down flat to reduce the target," he said. "If your hotel is under attack, lie down on the floor and cover your face and eyes. Do not go to a window. The greatest danger is from flying glass. Your best protection would be to cover yourself with your mattress."

The major's matter-of-fact words brought home to us that we were landing once again in Vietnam. And though we're there as entertainers doing a Christmas show, it isn't all jokes and pretty girls.

People ask if I don't mind leaving my family at Christmas to fly half way around the world to be with the troops. My answer is: I get a lot more than I give! Some say it's an unpopular war we're carrying on in

Bob Hope puts on a show on an aircraft carrier in December 1966.

South Vietnam, but, as far as I'm concerned, we have 500,000 of the most popular Americans I know fighting there. And the satisfaction that comes from bringing a few hours of laughter and home to these men living such hard, dangerous lives is difficult to express.

* * *

You look out over an audience of laughing, applauding GIs, snapping pictures and wolf-whistling at the pretty girls, and you know that a lot of them aren't going to make it home. And there are the wounded who will make it back but never be the same again. Visiting our casualties in hospitals, as I've been doing for three wars now, never gets any easier.

The first time it really hit me hard was on Espiritu Santo in the South Pacific in World War II. I stopped by the bedside of a badly wounded boy who was getting a blood transfusion. "I see where they're giving you a little pick-me-up," I said. "It's only raspberry soda," the boy said, "but it feels pretty good." Then he died. I thought about how in his last moments he'd smiled and tried to say something light, and I couldn't stand it. I had to go outside and pull myself together.

Now it's the wounded from Vietnam, and visiting them and talking with them is just as tough. But you can't let it show through, or it destroys the purpose of your visit—to try to bring them a moment of cheer. They don't want sympathy. They want to exchange laughs, and if they can top you, they love it. I try to breeze into a hospital ward, brash and bouncy, saying something like "All right, get the dice and let's get going" or "What happened to you? Were you driving on the Hollywood Freeway?"

The men's eyes may be glazed with pain or sedation, but they almost always manage a smile when I shake hands. Their courage is inspiring.

* * *

We made our first Christmas trip to Vietnam in 1964. Ten minutes before we arrived at our Saigon hotel, the Vietcong bombed Brink's Hotel, about a block away. Two Americans were killed, and 50 Americans and 15 Vietnamese were wounded in the blast. U.S. Ambassador Maxwell Taylor asked if we'd mind going over to the Naval Hospital to see if we could cheer up the casualties.

The hospital was chaotic, with operating rooms and corridors overflowing. I met a good-looking captain whose head and right arm had just been bandaged. "I'm really embarrassed to meet you here, Mr. Hope," he said with a grin. "I was supposed to be in charge of your security!"

*   *   *

If there's anything that gives our GIs a lift it's the sight of a pretty girl, so I always take plenty along. Exuberant singer Kaye Stevens is particularly good at cheering up casualties. Her approach is to run down the aisles between the beds, saying to each boy, "Hiyah! Wow! How about a kiss for Christmas?" Then she plants a big smack on him. Yet even Kaye sometimes runs into a boy so wounded and disconsolate that he virtually defies cheering up. On one trip, as we walked through the wards of the Third Field Hospital near Saigon, she came to a boy called Frenchy, who'd had an arm and an ear blasted off. "Merry Christmas!" Kaye greeted him, with her usual ebullience. "What's there to be merry about?" the boy asked bitterly, with some reason. "You're alive, aren't you, stupid?" Kaye persisted. "Merry Christmas!"

> *"It's only raspberry soda," the boy said. Then he died.*

Frenchy didn't respond, and Kaye turned away, crushed. That encounter haunted her. "Those sad eyes," she said, "just staring at me."

On the way home, we visited the hospital at Clark Field in the Philippines. Kaye was walking through a ward when one of the boys called out, "Hey, Merry Christmas, stupid!" It was Frenchy, still all swathed in bandages. "How come you're so cheerful now?" Kaye asked brightly.

"I wasn't feeling too good the last time," Frenchy said. "But afterward I got to thinking about it, and you were right. I'm still alive. Can I have my Christmas kiss now?"

*   *   *

They say there's a healing power in laughter, so I always go well supplied with jokes. And I've discovered that our men are pretty quick with the jokes themselves. I found this out in New Guinea in World War II. Our troupe was playing to a group of 5,000 lonely, battle-weary men at Hollandia. Frances Langford came out and began singing, "I'm in the mood for love…" Some sailor yelled, "You've come to the right place, honey," getting the biggest laugh I ever heard in a jungle.

In U.S. hospitals in Vietnam, I've found signs reading "Welcome, Bing" and "We love you, Bing." In one ward, First Lieutenant John J. Fannelli of Brooklyn, a victim of shrapnel wounds in the leg and chest, had a sign on his bed that read "Quiet: Bone Growing." In another ward for orthopedic patients they had a sign: "Welcome, Bob Hope. We'd stand and salute—but at the moment we're all hung up."

Talk about humor. At each show I'm introduced by an enlisted man, and some of them are pretty darn sharp. Last year at Long Binh, I was introduced by Specialist 5 Bruce D. Gaub of Seattle. "Bob's clothes are very unusual," he said. "He has a flak jacket tailored into every suit. His clothes are done by Hart, Schaffner and U.S. Steel."

During that same trip, I talked to Sergeant Bob Stuckey of Richmond, Indiana, one of the "River Rats" who comb the Mekong Delta for the Vietcong. Operating a small boat in choppy water means that Stuckey is wet and uncomfortable most of the time. I asked him how he was chosen for the job. "I knew someone in Washington," he cracked.

The best GI joke I heard last year was told to me by Specialist 5 Steve Ramsey of Denver: A hard-boiled old sergeant was laying into a new recruit. "I know your type," he told the recruit. "You're the kind that's going to wait around for me to die and then spit on my grave."

"No, sir, Sarge," the recruit protested. "When I get out of the Army, I ain't never gonna stand in line again."

Leaving Vietnam is always a wrench, for though we're going back to comfort and safety, the men we have entertained are trudging back to a bloody war. This was especially brought home to me last year at Chu Lai, a sprawling, sandy base where about 15,000 men saw our show.

The audience was a good one, laughing and whistling and cheering

for Ann-Margret and the other pretty girls. When we finished, we drove in a jeep convoy along the dusty red beach roads to the air strip. Believe me, it was the loneliest sight in the world, the thousands of men streaming back to their posts, carrying their rifles. They seemed weary. The brief respite from their drab and dangerous lives was over. Yet they waved goodbye and called out "Merry Christmas!" as we passed.

The most poignant moment of our trips is always Christmas Eve, when our cast joins with the GIs in singing "Silent Night." One reason it is especially touching is that this is when attendants begin carrying the litter patients back to the hospitals. One year at An Khe, Diana Lynn Batts, Miss USA World, cried unabashedly during the song. Afterward she asked Jerry Colonna, a veteran of several of our trips, how it was possible to sing "Silent Night" with the men without breaking down. "Just look over their heads," Jerry said. "If you look into those faces, you've had it." They are great faces and great men. The best we have.

And no matter how bad things are, the men manage to keep their sense of humor. Last year, as I walked off at the end of a show at Chu Lai, a Marine sergeant yelled, "You look tired, Bob. Next year why don't you just send for us?"

Originally published in the January 1970 issue of *Reader's Digest* magazine.

Humor Hall of Fame

My parents had one of those old-time rotary telephones. This drove my brother crazy. Once, he misdialed a long-distance number and had to do it all over again.

"Mom," he asked in frustration, "why don't you replace this thing with a touch-tone phone?"

"If we did," my mother said, "your father would never get any exercise."

—**DEBRA COPELAND**

My husband was going on a diet, but when we pulled into a fast-food restaurant, he ordered a milkshake. I pointed out that a shake isn't exactly the best snack for someone who wants to lose weight. He agreed but didn't change his order.

The long line must have given him time to make the connection between his order and his waist-line. As the woman handed him his shake, she said, "Sorry about the wait."

"That's OK," he replied self-consciously. "I'm going to lose it."

—**KAREN NAZARENUS**

"Then it struck me—nobody originally on the Paleo Diet lived past 35."

The Secret Life of Walter Mitty

by James Thurber, from the book *My World—and Welcome to It*

In this classic short story, a mild-mannered man daydreams of heroic exploits.

W e're going through!" The commander's voice was like thin ice breaking. He wore his full-dress uniform with the heavily braided cap pulled down rakishly over one cold gray eye. "We can't make it, sir. It's spoiling for a hurricane if you ask me." "I'm not asking you, Lieutenant Berg," said the commander. "Throw on the power lights! Rev her up to 8,500! We're going through!" The pounding of the cylinders increased: ta-pocketa-pocketa-*pocketa-pocketa*. The commander stared at the ice forming on the pilot window. He walked over and twisted a row of complicated dials. "Switch on No. 8 auxiliary!" he shouted. "Full strength in No. 3 turret!" The crew, bending to their various tasks in the huge eight-engine Navy hydroplane, looked at each other and grinned. "The Old Man'll get us through," they said to one another. "The Old Man ain't afraid of hell!"

"Not so fast! You're driving too fast!" said Mrs. Mitty. "What are you driving so fast for?"

"Hmmm?" said Walter Mitty. He looked at his wife, in the seat beside him, with shocked astonishment. She seemed grossly unfamiliar, like a strange woman who had yelled at him in a crowd. "You were up to 55," she said. "You know I don't like to go more than 40. You were up to 55."

Walter Mitty drove on toward Waterbury in silence, the roaring of the SN202 through the worst storm in 20 years of Navy flying fading in the remote, intimate airways of his mind. "You're tensed up again," said Mrs. Mitty. "It's one of your days. I wish you'd let Dr. Renshaw look you over."

Walter Mitty stopped the car in front of the building where his wife went to have her hair done. "Remember to get those overshoes while I'm having my hair done," she said. "I don't need overshoes," said Mitty. She put her mirror back into her bag. "We've been through all that," she said, getting out of the car. "You're not a young man any longer." He raced the engine a little. "Why don't you wear your gloves? Have you lost your gloves?" Walter Mitty reached in a pocket and brought out the gloves. He put them on, but after she had gone into the building, he took them off again. He drove around the streets aimlessly for a time, and then drove past the hospital on his way to the parking lot.

... "It's the millionaire banker, Wellington McMillan," said the pretty nurse. "Yes?" said Walter Mitty, removing his gloves slowly. "Who has the case?" "Dr. Renshaw and Dr. Benbow, but there are two specialists here: Dr. Remington from New York and Dr. Pritchard-Mitford from London. He flew over." A door opened and Dr. Renshaw came out, distraught and haggard. "Hello, Mitty," he said. "We're having the devil's own time with McMillan, the millionaire banker and close personal friend of Roosevelt. Obstreosis of the ductal tract. Tertiary. Wish you'd take a look at him." "Glad to," said Mitty.

In the operating room there were whispered introductions: "I've read your book on streptothricosis," said Pritchard-Mitford, shaking hands. "A brilliant performance, sir." "Thank you," said Walter Mitty. "Didn't know you were in the States, Mitty," grumbled Remington. "Coals to Newcastle, bringing Mitford and me here for a tertiary." "You are very kind," said Mitty. A huge, complicated machine, connected to the operating table, began to go pocketa-pocketa-pocketa. "The new anesthetizer is giving way!" shouted an intern. "There's no one in the East who knows how to fix it!"

"Quiet, man," said Mitty, in a low, cool voice. He sprang to the machine, which was now going pocketa-pocketa-queep-pocketa-queep. He began fingering delicately a row of glistening dials. "Give me a fountain pen!" he snapped. Someone handed him a fountain pen. He pulled a faulty piston out of the machine and inserted the pen in its place. "That will hold for ten minutes," he said. "Get on with the operation."

A nurse hurried over and whispered to Renshaw. Mitty saw the man turn pale. "Coreopsis has set in," said Renshaw nervously. "If you would take over, Mitty?" Mitty looked at him, at the grave, uncertain faces of the two great specialists. "If you wish," he said. They slipped a white gown on him; he adjusted a mask and drew on thin gloves; nurses handed him shining ...

"Back it up, Mac! Look out for that Buick!" Walter Mitty jammed on the brakes. "Wrong lane, Mac," said the parking-lot attendant, looking at Mitty closely. "Gee. Yeh," muttered Mitty. He began cautiously to back out of the lane marked "Exit Only." "Leave her sit there," said the attendant. "I'll put her away." The attendant vaulted into the car, backed it up with insolent skill and put it where it belonged.

They're so damned cocky, thought Walter Mitty, walking along Main Street; they think they know everything. Once he had tried to take his chains off, outside New Milford, and he had got them wound around the axles. A man had had to come out in a wrecking car and unwind them, a young, grinning garageman. Since then Mrs. Mitty always made him drive to a garage to have the chains taken off. Next time, he thought, I'll wear my right arm in a sling; they won't grin at me then. They'll see I couldn't possibly take the chains off myself. He kicked at the slush on the sidewalk. "Overshoes," he said to himself, and he began looking for a shoe store.

When he came out into the street again, with the overshoes in a box under his arm, Walter Mitty began to wonder what the other thing was his wife had told him to get. He hated these weekly trips to town—he was always getting something wrong. Kleenex, he thought, razor blades? No. Toothpaste, toothbrush, bicarbonate, carborundum, initiative and referendum? He gave it up. But she would remember. "Where's the what's-its-name?" she would ask. "Don't tell me you forgot the what's-its-name." A newsboy went by shouting something about the Waterbury trial.

... "Perhaps this will refresh your memory." The district attorney thrust a heavy automatic at the quiet figure on the witness stand. "Have you ever seen this before?" Walter Mitty took the gun and examined it expertly. "This is my Webley-Vickers 50.80," he said calmly. An excited buzz ran around the courtroom. The judge rapped for order. "You are a crack shot with any sort of firearm, I believe?" said the district attorney insinuatingly.

"Objection!" shouted Mitty's attorney. "We have shown that the defendant could not have fired the shot. We have shown that he wore his right arm in a sling on the night of the 14th of July." Walter Mitty raised his hand briefly, and the bickering attorneys were stilled. "With any known make of gun," he said evenly, "I could have killed Gregory Fitzhurst at 300 feet *with my left hand*." Pandemonium broke loose in the courtroom. A woman's scream rose above the bedlam, and suddenly a lovely, dark-haired girl was in Walter Mitty's arms. The district attorney struck at her savagely. Without rising, Mitty let the man have it on the point of the chin. "You miserable cur!" ...

"Puppy biscuit," said Walter Mitty. The buildings of Waterbury rose up out of the misty courtroom and surrounded him again. A woman who was passing laughed. "He said 'puppy biscuit,'" she said to her companion. "That man said 'puppy biscuit' to himself." Walter Mitty hurried on. He went into an A&P. "I want some biscuit for small, young dogs," he said to the clerk. "Any special brand, sir?" The greatest pistol shot in the world thought a moment. "It says 'Puppies Bark for It' on the box," said Walter Mitty.

His wife would be through at the hairdresser's soon. She would want him to be waiting for her as usual in the hotel lobby. He found a big leather chair facing a window, and he put the overshoes and the puppy biscuit on the floor beside it. He picked up an old copy of *Liberty* and sank down into the chair. "Can Germany Conquer the World Through the Air?" Walter Mitty looked at the pictures of bombing planes and of ruined streets.

... "The cannonading has got the wind up in young Raleigh, sir," said the sergeant. Captain Mitty looked up at him through tousled hair. "Get him to bed," he said wearily. "With the others. I'll fly alone." "But you can't, sir," said the sergeant anxiously. "It takes two men to handle that bomber, and Von Richtman's circus is between here and Saulier." "Somebody's got to get that ammunition dump," said Mitty. "I'm going over. Spot of brandy?" He poured a drink for the sergeant and one for himself.

War thundered and whined around the dugout and battered at the door. There was a rending explosion, and splinters flew through the room. "A bit of a near thing," said Captain Mitty carelessly. "The box barrage is closing in," said the sergeant. "We only live once, sergeant," said Mitty, with his faint, fleeting smile. "Or do we?" He poured another brandy, tossed it off, then stood up and strapped on his Webley-Vickers automatic. "It's 40 kilometers through hell, sir," said the sergeant. Mitty finished one last brandy. "After all," he said softly, "what isn't?" The pounding of the cannon increased; there was the rattat-tatting of machine guns, and from somewhere came the menacing pocketa-pocketa-pocketa of the new flame-throwers. Walter Mitty walked to the door of the dugout, humming "Auprès de Ma Blonde." He turned and waved to the sergeant. "Cheerio!" he said. ...

Something struck his shoulder. "I've been looking all over this hotel for you," said Mrs. Mitty. "Why do you have to hide in this old chair? How did you expect me to find you?" "Things close in," said Walter Mitty vaguely. "What?" Mrs. Mitty said. "Did you get the what's-its-name? The puppy biscuit? What's in that box?" "Overshoes," said Mitty. "Couldn't you have put them on in the store?" "I was thinking," said Walter Mitty. "Does it ever occur to you that I am sometimes thinking?" She looked at him. "I'm going to take your temperature when I get you home," she said.

They went out through the revolving doors that made a faintly derisive whistling sound when you pushed them. At the corner drugstore she said, "Wait here for me. I forgot something. I won't be a minute." She was more than a minute. Walter Mitty lighted a cigarette. It began to rain, rain with sleet in it. He stood up against the wall of the drugstore, smoking. ...

He put his shoulders back and his heels together. "To hell with the handkerchief," said Walter Mitty scornfully. He took one last drag on his cigarette and snapped it away. Then, with that faint, fleeting smile playing about his lips, he faced the firing squad: erect and motionless, proud and disdainful, Walter Mitty, the Undefeated, inscrutable to the last.

Originally published in the January 1943 issue of *Reader's Digest* magazine.

While Reader's Digest *has mostly published true stories about real people, fiction has appeared in its pages from time to time. This classic short story by journalist and humorist James Thurber was reprinted more than once.*

Our America

Odd Man Out
—C.F. PAYNE
OCTOBER 2007

Explorer of Nothing

"When I was a teenager, my father took me out to dinner and asked me how I would define *nothing*," recounts Amanda Gefter. "He'd been thinking about the concept of nothing and how you can get something from nothing and how the universe could have come from nothing. So we had this conversation, and he recruited me to figure out the nature of reality with him. Now I'm a science writer."
Photograph by Glenn Glasser

FACES OF AMERICA

Fashionable Meteorologist

"I'm a meteorologist," says Ronald Trotta, posing with Schmitty the Weather Dog at the Westminster Kennel Club Dog Show. "We go into schools and teach young kids to be excited about science, mathematics and fashion—all at the same time!".
Photograph by Glenn Glasser

With Wit and Wisdom

by Hedwig Gafga and Burkhard Weitz

A Nobel laureate reflects on life.

Archbishop Desmond Tutu, one of the world's most respected religious figures, sat down for a conversation with *Reader's Digest* in 2008.

Your Grace, you were 19 years old when racial segregation became law in South Africa. What did it mean to you to be seen as a second-class person?
The worst of this evil was that the victim of such injustice gradually began to ask himself if he were not indeed a human being of less value than the others. It was, of course, blasphemous to allow a child of God to doubt that he or she was a child of God.

Despite this discrimination you radiate self-confidence. How do you explain this?
(laughing) I have been influenced by marvelous people. My mother was not well educated, but she was a wonderful person. Some of her spirit, her sympathetic, compassionate manner, I have been able to preserve in myself.

As head of the Truth and Reconciliation Commission (TRC), you heard the stories of both victims and perpetrators of apartheid. How did this affect you?
We were all shocked by the depravity to which human beings can sink. But it amazes me still today that we are left not with desolation but with

elation over the wonderful capacity of human beings for good. Over the magnanimity of their ability to forgive—not just blacks, but whites, too.

Do you not think that some perpetrators of apartheid got off too lightly?
Yes and no. If we had demanded trials like Germany's, we would have endangered the transition, for the security forces still had the weapons. It was my wish that more people would have appeared before the commission. But those who rejected this offer will have to live with themselves.

How has your life changed since the end of apartheid?
When I became archbishop in 1986, it was considered a crime for me to live with my family in the official episcopal residence. It was located in a so-called white area. I said to the government: "I am not asking you for permission. My family and I shall live in this residence now."

There were laws that hindered mixed marriages. If whites had sexual contact with nonwhites, that was said to be "immoral." The police peeked through the windows to spot violations of this law. They broke into rooms and examined the bedclothes to see whether couples had slept with each other. They turned love into something dirty.

Recently I saw a group of young black men and one white girl. She was walking arm in arm with one of the guys. I looked up, and the sky was still there. It had not fallen down. I asked myself: Why were we so dumb for so long?

What can we learn from the principle of Ubuntu?
That you can never be a human being in isolation. We shall never, never win the war against terror as long as people in parts of the world suffer under circumstances that leave them in despair. Ubuntu says: Only together can we be free. Only together can we be secure. Only together can we be prosperous. Only together can we be human.

Originally published in the 2008 *Reader's Digest* International editions.

Archbishop Tutu died of cancer in December 2021 at the age of 90.

An Alcoholic's Letter to His Son

by Anonymous

*The important part, this father writes,
is how it all begins.*

Dear R----:

When I opened your last letter and found the picture of you in a college freshman football uniform, I realized it was time for me to be writing this letter. It's one I've been thinking about for a long time.

Three and a half years have slipped by since—let's be honest—my last drunk. This much you know. What I want to tell you about now is a part of my experience you know nothing about—the beginning of it. My idea is that this may help you to understand some things about yourself, and might even save you from making some of the mistakes I made.

Don't get me wrong. Just because I'm an alcoholic doesn't mean you're going to be one. A special sensitivity to alcohol isn't passed on from a parent to a child. No, I haven't any particular fears for you—only those that trouble any father whose son or daughter reaches the age when it is hard to stay out of the way of a potent chemical called alcohol.

OK, you're probably thinking: "Here it comes—the old man's got religion, and now he's going to start preaching." I promise: no sermons.

I had plenty of them before I found the answer to my problem in Alcoholics Anonymous.

Holidays—what a wreck I used to make of them! Remember Thanksgiving 1959? I'm sure you do, even though your mother shooed you out of the house before the shouting started. Now I can finally let you know that I "got the message" when you slouched through the kitchen to the back door. You knew exactly what was going on, and you stopped for just a second and turned toward me. I was standing by the refrigerator—or, more accurately, propping myself up with it. You didn't say anything. You didn't have to. Your disappointment, resentment, disgust, just plain hatred—it all burned in your eyes.

So what can I possibly tell you that you don't already know about what alcohol can do when it takes control of someone? You lived through too much of it—the nightmarish months before the divorce, then a household without a father, the times when you didn't hear from me and wondered why, the times when you did hear from me and wished you hadn't.

What I want to point out, what is so necessary for you to understand, is that what you saw happen in our home, and what happened to me after I left—the fleabag hotel rooms, the psycho wards—was only the last act of my love affair with the bottle. It all began before you were born; in fact, it began about the time I was your age, which is why you need to be thinking about alcohol and alcoholism right now.

We in Alcoholics Anonymous spend a lot of time sitting over coffee talking about our experiences, and one thing we've learned is that it isn't easy to predict what boy or girl is going to turn up with a drinking problem. As children, some of us went to bed every night in the security of well-knit families. Others were pulling the covers over their heads to shut out the hell of their homes. Some have Phi Beta Kappa keys; others didn't get past the ninth grade. None of us fit any alcoholic "type" as far as background is concerned.

Then how did we get to be drunks? Some people think we became alcoholics from drinking too much. I think we drank too much because we had something else wrong with us in the first place and used alcohol as a crutch. We had the equivalent of a broken leg in our inner selves—a weakness, a fear, a sense of guilt or anxiety, a shadow of uncertain outline that dogged our steps. This is not unusual in itself, especially among young people as they are becoming adults. What was unusual for us was how we reacted when we discovered alcohol and the way it could help us. Its effect was sheer magic. It rid us of that shadow.

The trouble is, our crutch began to play tricks on us. At times it would slip and we'd fall down. By the time we decided that it was bringing us more trouble than help, we made a startling discovery: We couldn't let go of it.

Quite a few of us began drinking regularly because alcohol gave us a deceptive sort of courage to meet situations that scared us. The more we relied on this artificial courage, the less genuine courage we could muster. If we drank to feel more comfortable around people, for instance, the result was that we felt all the more awkward and self-conscious and tongue-tied when we *weren't* drinking. If we drank to fight off boredom or loneliness, the more bored and lonely we became when we had no glass at our side.

I picked up my crutch in the most innocent way, not really knowing that I was slipping it under my arm. There were half a dozen of us kids who knew the secret of acquiring a chilled keg of beer on a Saturday afternoon. There was a little glen on a farm about five miles outside of town that was made to order for our midsummer nonsense. With the right amount of beer under our belts—and not necessarily a dangerous amount—we could laugh ourselves silly at jokes that weren't really funny, and there was a warmth and conviviality that certainly couldn't be condemned.

Human beings have been amusing themselves this way for thousands of years, and I suppose that they always will, whether they gather around a beer keg at a picnic or the cocktail bar in a hotel. This is what is called "social drinking," and it is hard to make a case against it. As far as I know, I am the only one of that group I used to drink beer with who went the route of an alcoholic. It was the only kind of drinking I did for a long time. I had no idea that my fondness for alcohol was out of the ordinary. But in the most subtle and gradual way the occasions which called for my drinking began to multiply.

In the office where I had my first job after getting out of school there was a girl named Judy. She was bright, she had a sense of humor and, as you would put it, she "turned me on." I asked her for a date, and took her to a place I couldn't afford for dinner and dancing. I wanted to impress her.

That evening I discovered that Judy didn't like to drink. She didn't disapprove of drinking—it just didn't appeal to her. But we enjoyed each other, and when I took her home she said good night in a way that made me think she would like to go out with me again.

The significant thing is that I never asked Judy for that second date. I dropped her, flat, and scouted around for another girl. As much as I liked and admired Judy, as much as I wanted to get something going between us, I couldn't face the prospect of spending a lot of time with a girl who didn't like to drink. Some kind of subconscious "radar" told me that I could not have Judy and also drink as much as I wanted to. I made my choice.

I was to make the same kind of choice time and again. I picked companions who liked to spend their spare time—as I did—on a bar stool or nursing a fifth through an evening of cards. I doubt that I would have found their company very stimulating if it hadn't been for the liquid refreshment that was always in the picture. And all this while I was developing two skills that you find in most alcoholics: the ability to conceal from others how much I was drinking, and the ability to conceal from myself how indispensable my alcoholic crutch was becoming.

Your mother didn't recognize this side of my character until after we were married. Our courtship was a whirl of barhopping and parties. Unlike Judy, she enjoyed drinking, or at least I always thought she did. She made a game attempt to keep up with me at first, and then she found herself on that bobsled ride so familiar to wives of alcoholics. From enjoying our life together she shifted to tolerating it and then to rebelling against it. She tried to understand me, to help me, and her only reward was a kick in the teeth. The divorce itself was an anticlimax. Our marriage had ended long before. I was just an overgrown adolescent.

As much as I recoiled at what I saw happening, I couldn't do anything about it. I made promises, sincere ones, time and again, and broke them. Once I left a hospital after a week of treatment for acute intoxication—intravenous feeding, sedatives, vitamins, a sweating-out and shaking-out that brought me back from the brink of delirium tremens—and within 48 hours I was drunk again. It was the same suicidal process, and it took me back to the same hospital in worse shape than before.

From what I've written, you might guess that I'm going to tell you to steer clear completely of demon rum. No, I'll be practical and assume that you have the same curiosity about alcohol that I did when I was your age, and that many occasions may arise when you'll either want to drink or be expected to.

First, test yourself with alcohol in a sensible way. There are wrong times and right times to fool around with beer or liquor. With a bunch of kids in a car is a wrong time; at a party where there are responsible adults is a right time. The best time is in your own home, if you can persuade your mother to cut you in on the action when she's having some friends in.

If you're like the majority of people, you'll find that first drink an interesting experience. You may dislike the taste but like the effect, or vice versa. You may barely be able to "feel" one drink, or one drink may knock you for a loop. Just remember that no matter how mature and responsible you may consider yourself to be when you lift that glass, you're dealing with what is, for all practical purposes, a drug.

Alcohol is a depressant, and the first thing it depresses or slows down is the function of the higher center of your brain, your faculty of self-criticism, judgment and restraint. Remember, too, that in spite of what you see in the movies, in spite of the beer and whiskey ads, it is not necessary to drink to be sociable, to be a success in a business or profession, to sweep a girl off her feet.

Next, if the crowd you are running around with is drinking when you don't want to, or is drinking more than you care to, don't hesitate to say no when the next round is offered, to cut out or to go home. It's stupid enough to get drunk; it's twice as silly to drink too much simply because that's what "everybody else" is doing.

Finally, and perhaps most important, there is always a chance that you have within you the characteristics of an alcoholic, a seed that is hidden now but waiting for circumstances that will let it grow and flower. If you should come to recognize in yourself a fondness for alcohol that seems to be greater than you observe in others—especially in people who impress you as competent, well-adjusted human beings—then the red flag of danger is up.

If you do any amount of drinking in the next few years, there is a simple test I wish you would take from time to time: Try doing without alcohol for a while and see what happens. This way you can get an idea of how much alcohol means to you, how much you value what it does for you. You'll probably find that being "on the wagon" means no more than a moment of awkwardness when one of your buddies suggests having a drink. But if you find that removing alcohol from the picture makes a serious difference in the way you feel, if you are drawn back to it against your own resolve not to drink, this may tell you that alcohol does, indeed, hold a special danger for you, as it did for me. Then there is only one safe course: Avoid the use of alcohol altogether.

You will have problems in life. You will have disappointments, doubts, fears. Try never to make the mistake of seeking an artificial, temporary solution to these problems through alcohol, pills or narcotics. A way of life cannot be built on such flights from reality. My prayer for you is not so much that you will find every happiness you seek, but that you will accept with clear-headed fortitude the times of trial that are sure to come your way, and receive with gratitude the love and good fortune that are always close behind.

Originally published in the November 1966 issue of *Reader's Digest* magazine.

NO SUGAR FOR GRANDMA

We recently had dinner at my son and daughter-in-law's home. She had prepared a beautiful pecan pie for dessert, but I do not eat refined sugar in an attempt to lessen inflammation from my rheumatoid arthritis. My young grandson, sitting to my right, generously set two pecans on my empty plate. "These are for you, Grandma," he said. "Oh, thank you, sweetheart, but I don't eat sugar and these pecans are coated with it," I replied. "No, Grandma," he said, "there is no sugar on these. I licked it all off."

—Sharon Lewandowski, *Hastings, Minnesota*

COWBOY BLUES

Billy was the resident cowboy of my kindergarten class, coming to school each day dressed in chaps, a vest and a cowboy hat. One morning, he excitedly told me that his mother was going to have a baby. "I'm going to teach my little brother all the things every cowboy should know, like how to ride a horse and rope a steer," he exclaimed. "But," I cautioned, "what if your mother gives you a baby sister?" Billy had never considered this, and the possibility stunned him. He gazed out the window for a moment, before saying with resignation, "Then I'm headin' west."

—John Thomas Cimics, *Midland, Texas*

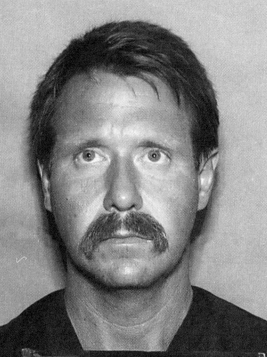

PINELLAS COUNTY
SHERIFF'S DEPARTMENT
SAWYER, TOM F.
2 6 1 4 7 1 11 07 '86

PINELLAS COUNTY
SHERIFF'S DEPARTMENT
MINCHEW, KEITH   020
2 9 7 0 2 0 0 08 29 '87

I Confess

by Derek Burnett

These men each admitted to murdering
Janet Staschak. Which one told the truth?

It's the bleary, wee hours of the morning, and the murder interrogation has yet to yield the confession the detectives are counting on. They have been in this cramped room for 12 hours already. While the suspect keeps inching close to giving them what they need, he repeatedly draws back, as if he can't admit even to himself the enormity of the crime.

The date is November 6, 1986, and the place is Clearwater, Florida. Three days ago, 25-year-old cake decorator Janet Staschak was found dead in the upstairs bedroom of her apartment. Her purse was missing, a window screen had been cut, and her car had been found in the parking garage at the airport. But the detectives, Pete Fire and John Dean, don't believe this was a burglary; they think the killer arranged things to make it look like one because he was someone who knew the victim.

They have no doubt that this someone is the suspect sitting across from them in the interrogation room. His name is Tom F. Sawyer, and on the day Staschak's body was found, the handsome, athletic 33-year-old was caught ducking under the police tape at her apartment complex. When the detectives approached him, they learned he was Staschak's neighbor. He was also a nervous wreck, sweating profusely and mopping his head with a towel. He provided no alibi for Saturday night, probably

175

the time of the murder. And despite his nervousness, he was unusually curious about the case—eager, he said, to help in any way he could.

When it comes to the actual interrogation, however, they find that Sawyer is a tough nut to crack. They initially lured Sawyer down to the station under the guise of asking him to help them solve the case and, over the course of hours, have eased into their questioning by asking him to develop some hypothetical scenarios about how the murder might have taken place. As the hours have worn on, Sawyer's chief scenario has begun to closely match the known facts of the case. So, after a bathroom break, Dean and Fire shift tactics. They read him the Miranda warning, and Dean tells him point-blank, "Tom, I think you did it."

When police approached Sawyer, he was a nervous wreck, sweating so profusely that he actually mopped his brow with a towel.

"No, I didn't."

"Tom," Fire says. "You know too much."

"I didn't kill her," Sawyer protests. "I've never been in her apartment before."

They're losing him. So Fire switches tactics and plays Good Cop. "It was an accident, Tom," Fire suggests. "I know it was. I need you to tell me what happened."

"I was never there. I never did it."

"Tom."

"I'll look you in the eye and say that all night."

"We've got all night."

*   *   *

In the days between the murder and the interrogation, the detectives learned some interesting facts about Tom Sawyer. He had begun drinking heavily in high school, he had been in and out of rehab for years, and he had moved to Florida from Illinois, where his drinking played a role in a difficult romantic breakup. He had not led much of a social life since achieving sobriety 13 months ago. Could the stress of sobriety, coupled with the painful breakup, have made him snap?

He eventually admits that he found Staschak attractive but never worked up the courage to ask her out. A few nights before the murder, she visited him in his apartment. They watched a movie together—*The Shining*—and chatted about life. Had that experience stirred up feelings that could find no other outlet but rape and murder?

Hours into the interrogation, Sawyer agrees to take a polygraph test. When the detectives confront him with the results, his attitude begins to shift. "You

The victim, Janet Staschak.

know what that test says?" Fire asks him. "It says you're a liar. Your heart blew those needles right off the screen."

The detectives also tell Sawyer that they have gathered considerable evidence, including his hairs. It's time to face facts, they tell him. It's not that much different from the first step required in quitting drinking—you have to admit the truth to yourself.

"I don't know," Sawyer finally answers. "I'm thinking I had a blackout. But I never heard of a blackout when you haven't been drinking."

Over time, the detectives get Sawyer to admit that he struck Staschak in the head with an ashtray from her coffee table, dragged her upstairs, stripped and sodomized her, strangled her, placed her on her bed facedown, and pulled the covers over her. By 8:30 a.m., after more than 16 hours of grueling interrogation, they have a narrative that matches the facts of the case: Staschak was indeed found naked facedown in her bed with the covers pulled up; the ashtray is missing from the coffee table in her apartment, as is a single knife from a set in the kitchen, which Sawyer has described using to cut the screen and the ligatures with which Staschak's wrists and ankles were bound. Sawyer says he threw those missing items off the bridge of a causeway. With the details settled, the detectives decide to end the interview. At last, they have their confession.

With their son facing murder charges, Sawyer's parents reach out to a local defense attorney named Joe Donahey. Donahey files a motion to suppress the entire interrogation as evidence, alleging that the detectives had taken too long to read Sawyer his Miranda rights, the confession had been coerced and his pleas to speak with a lawyer were ignored. After hearing six weeks of argument, Judge Gerard O'Brien throws out the confession. The state appeals, but the higher court upholds the decision. After 14 months in county lockup, Sawyer walks free.

Fast-forward 28 years, to January 2014. Fire and Dean have long since retired. Donahey is 80 years old and blind. Tom Sawyer has moved back north and faded into obscurity, quietly working maintenance jobs.

A team of Clearwater Police Department detectives is revisiting cold cases, and it opens the Staschak file. The officers find samples of biological matter that was retrieved from beneath the victim's fingernails—probably produced by Staschak's efforts to scratch at her killer in self-defense. In 1986, DNA evidence was unheard of in Pinellas County, but in 2014, it is an easy matter to run the sample through a federal database. There is a hit. Surprise: The DNA is not that of Tom F. Sawyer. Instead, the alleged match is to the DNA of a 57-year-old man named Stephen Manning Lamont, who, at the time of Staschak's murder, was an escaped prisoner. Police arrest Lamont in Alabama and extradite him to Florida.

But if Tom Sawyer didn't commit the murder, why did he confess to it? And why were Dean and Fire so convinced he was the killer?

Part of Donahey's defense strategy was to have Sawyer psychologically evaluated, and those assessments revealed that Sawyer suffered from an acute social anxiety disorder and a pathological urge to please others. From the outset, Sawyer's unique psychological makeup had thrown the detectives off: He had initially aroused their suspicions by acting nervous and mopping sweat off his brow—but he had been doing that very thing since high school. The mere thought of having people's attention directed on him made him go red in the face and perspire profusely.

When the detectives invited Sawyer to the station, his eagerness to please made him genuinely excited. He was a fan of TV detective shows and relished the thought of helping to crack the case. "I thought this would be a way for me to give something back," he says, referring to the burden he had been to society as an alcoholic. His alcoholism made him even more susceptible to false confession: Decades of drinking shattered his already fragile ego and he had experienced numerous blackouts over the years, so it was nothing new for him to be accused of bad behavior without any memory of the wrongdoing.

Donahey also zeroed in on the "confession" as better proof of his client's innocence than his guilt. The turning point in the interrogation, the point at which Sawyer began to entertain the possibility that he was the murderer, did not come until he was confronted with the polygraph results—which turned out to have been bogus. He had not "blown the needle off the charts," nor had the lab

At one point during the interrogation, Sawyer, hungry and exhausted, told the police, "I keep getting thoughts that say I didn't do it."

returned conclusive hair samples or other evidence linking him to the crime. But Fire and Dean thought it was worth telling him both things were true. "I still didn't believe I'd done it," Sawyer says, "but I believed that the police didn't lie."

*　　*　　*

That was the crux of it: a man already racked by self-doubt, with a lifetime's experience of blackouts, confronted by what to him is inarguable proof of his guilt. He doesn't believe he has committed the crime, and yet he wants to take responsibility for his actions if he did. ("I pray to God that if I did do it, I'm punished for it," he told the detectives.) Donahey has studied the false confessions of American POWs during the Korean War, and he believes that Sawyer's experience closely resembles theirs.

He was badgered, cajoled and lied to until, as he put it at the time, the detectives had driven him "bananas." By the end of the session he was ready to agree to just about anything to make the questioning stop.

But how could the murder scenario suggested by Sawyer have so accurately matched the facts of the case? First, a talkative police officer at the crime scene had told Sawyer several details, including the position of the body on the bed.

Second, the detectives spent all night guiding Sawyer's answers. One example: They needed Sawyer to confess to binding Staschak's wrists and ankles with duct tape, which had left a sticky white residue on her skin. "What was it you used, Tom?" Fire asked.

Nearly out of his mind with exhaustion, Sawyer answered, "A jock?"

"A jock strap? A jock strap won't leave marks like that."

"Scotch tape?" Sawyer asks.

"No, it's white. It's not Scotch tape."

"Well, masking tape, then."

"I feel a little awkward about this, but I think you're owed an apology for what happened to you," said the Clearwater police chief. "I'm sorry."

This game of Twenty Questions goes on until they jointly land on the notion of duct tape. The detectives continued the technique, giving partial descriptions of the crime scene and then asking Sawyer to describe to them the images he was seeing in his mind. To them, and, increasingly, to him, these were flashbacks from the night of the murder rather than images they were producing through their line of questioning. One chilling moment of the interrogation has particular echoes of the brainwashing of the American POWs. Sawyer says, "I just keep getting thoughts that say I didn't do it, you know?"

"But those are thoughts, and that's all they are now," Dean answers. "You've learned to recognize the difference between the reality and the thoughts. What are the pictures you see? Concentrate on the pictures."

As might be expected, the "confession" turned out not to match the evidence after all. The detectives had gotten Sawyer to say that he had sodomized Staschak, but the forensics showed that she had not been sodomized. What about the missing ashtray? Donahey had an investigator track down Staschak's ex-husband and take him to the apartment, where he pulled the ashtray down from the top of the refrigerator. "It was never kept on the coffee table," he said. And the missing knife? "That thing was missing when we moved down to Florida from Pennsylvania."

Without the "confession," the state had no case against Tom Sawyer.

Sawyer has been sober for all these years. He is married and lives a simple life. Despite having spent 14 months in a jail cell, he is remarkably philosophical about his ordeal. "It's part of life," he says, blaming himself for his troubles. "None of this would have happened if I had had a little more sobriety in me. I had no confidence whatsoever. No self-esteem."

Still, a shadow hung over him for 28 years: Because his case never went to trial, there would have been no double jeopardy if the state had decided to prosecute him after all. For the past three decades, he says, every time the doorbell rang, he worried that it would be the police.

The nightmare ended when Sawyer and Donahey flew to Florida to watch Stephen Lamont confess to murdering Janet Staschak and agree to a life sentence with no possibility of parole for 25 years. As the gavel fell, Sawyer clenched his fists and raised them over his head in triumph. He then approached the state's attorney who had prosecuted both him and Lamont. Sawyer stuck out his hand. "Thanks for your hard work," he said. "I just want to let you know there are no hard feelings."

Later, he received a call from the chief of the Clearwater Police Department. "I feel a little awkward about this, since I was in tenth grade when it happened," he told Sawyer. "But I think you're owed an apology for what happened to you. I'm sorry."

The apology was long in coming, but it mattered. When asked what he would do now that it was all over, Sawyer shrugged. "Live my life," he said—the life that was so senselessly interrupted on the night in 1986 when Stephen Lamont almost got away with murder.

Originally published in the November 2015 issue of *Reader's Digest* magazine.

A Rainbow in the Desert

This may be one of the most virtually viewed spots on the planet; Microsoft turned a photo of it into a popular screen saver image in its ubiquitous Windows OS. Viewing it in person is a much rarer feat. These calcified sand dunes—"baroque bands of red, pink, yellow and white Navajo sandstone arcing precipitously up, down and around ancient stone chutes," as one visitor described it—have been around for 190 million years, but to protect it from a stampede of tourists, the Bureau of Land Management lets only 64 lottery winners a day on-site. Where is this?

    A. Little Grand Canyon, Texas

    B. The Wave, Arizona

    C. Painted Desert, New Mexico

    D. Valley of Fire, Nevada

Answer on page 280; Photograph by Sumiko Scott/Getty Images

A Family Discovers Its Rare Gift

by Sarah Gray

When one of her identical twins died shortly after he was born, a brave mother decided to donate his tissue to science. Then she followed it wherever it went.

I was three months pregnant with identical twin boys when my husband, Ross, and I learned that one of them had a fatal birth defect. Our son Thomas had anencephaly, which means that his skull and brain were not formed properly. Babies with this diagnosis typically die in utero or within minutes, hours or days of being born.

This news was devastating, and also confusing. I had never heard of this before, and it didn't run in my family. I wondered, *Was it something I did?* But then, even if it was, why was one of them healthy?

So I was wrestling with a lot of questions that would never have answers. And I had to make peace with that. It was like having an annoying hum in the background.

Six months later, the twins were born, and they were both born alive. Thomas lived for six days. Callum was healthy, and Ross and I moved on the best that we could. We had a beautiful, healthy boy to raise.

We decided early on to tell Callum the truth about his brother. We have a few pictures of Thomas in our home, and it was a few years later that Callum started to comprehend what we were trying to tell him.

Sometimes he said things that were sad, and sometimes he said things that were kind of funny. We visit Thomas's grave a couple of times a year, and one time we told Callum that we were going to bring some flowers to put on Thomas's grave.

Callum picked up one of his little Matchbox cars and said, "I want to put this on the grave too," which I thought was really sweet.

Then, once we were there, Callum said, "Is Thomas scared under there?"

Of course I don't really know the answer to that, you know? But I could pretend, so I said, "No, he's not scared."

Later on, we were on the couch watching cartoons, and Callum said, "Mommy, what is it like in heaven?"

Again, I don't really know, so I did my best. I just said, "You know, some people think it's a place you go when you die. Some people don't believe it's there."

I had also been pondering Thomas's afterlife, but in a totally different way. Ross and I had decided to donate Thomas's organs to science. While his death was inevitable, we hoped it could be productive. He would be too small at birth to qualify for transplant, but he'd be a good candidate to donate for research. We donated his liver, cord blood, retinas and corneas.

We were able to donate his liver, cord blood, retinas and corneas. I was curious about whether these donations made a difference.

A short time later, I was on a business trip in Boston, and I remembered that Thomas's corneas had gone to a division of Harvard Medical School called the Schepens Eye Research Institute. I thought, I would love to visit this lab and learn more about where Thomas's donation went. Because I'd given them a donation, but it wasn't just signing a check or giving a bag of clothes—I had given them the gift of my child.

However, in order to donate, I had to sign away my rights to any

Ross, Callum, one-year-old Jocelyn and the author, in their living room.

future information about the donation. So if they did not welcome me, I would understand. I still felt in my heart that I wanted to visit, that I should be allowed to visit, and that if I asked the right person, I might even be invited for a visit. But I also wondered, *If they reject me, am I emotionally ready for that? What's that going to do to my grief?*

But I called. I explained to the receptionist, "I donated my son's eyes to you a couple of years ago. I'm in town on business for a couple of days. Is there any chance I can stop by for a ten-minute tour?"

Lucky for me, the receptionist was very compassionate. She didn't laugh or say it was weird, when it was a little weird.

She said, "I've never had this request before. I don't know who to

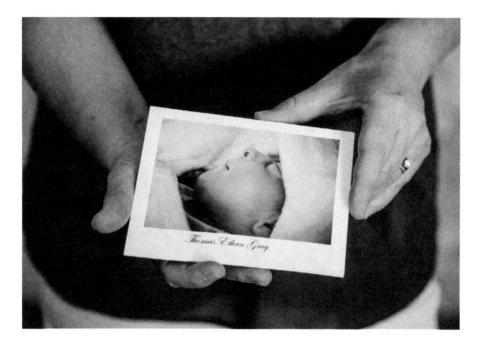

Thomas lived for six days. Years later, doctors still relied on his donated tissue.

transfer you to, but don't hang up. I'm going to find somebody for you."

So she connected me to someone in donor relations. It was not organ donor relations. It was *financial* donor relations, but she knew how to give a tour. So we set an appointment.

I showed up the next day, and she introduced me to one of the people who requested corneas, James Zieske, an associate professor of ophthalmology at Harvard Medical School. I stood in his doorway, and the donor relations woman explained who I was. Dr. Zieske was eating a salad at his desk, and he stood up and thanked me for my donation.

He shook my hand and said, "Do you have any questions for me?"

I was so emotional at meeting him. I said, "How many corneas do you request in a year?"

He said, "My lab requests about ten a year. We would request more, but they are hard to get, and infant eyes are like gold to us."

My heart was just in my throat. I could barely choke out the words. I said, "Could you tell me why?"

He said that infant eyes are unusual because most of us are older when we die, and that's when you donate your eyes. But unlike adult eyes, infant eyes have the potential to regenerate longer in the lab because the cells are younger and divide more easily.

He said, "If you don't mind my asking, how many years ago did your son die?"

I said, "About two years ago."

He said, "We are likely still studying your son's eye cells, and they are probably in this lab right now."

So the tour concluded, and my guide said to me, "I'll never forget you. Please keep in touch with me."

I felt something in me starting to change. I felt that my son had found his place in the world, and that place was Harvard.

So my son got into Harvard, and I'm now an Ivy League mom.

But I also got the bug, and I thought maybe I could visit the three other places too. I made some phone calls, I set up two appointments in Durham, North Carolina, and this time I took my husband and our son.

Our next visit was to Duke University, at the Center for Human Genetics, where the cord blood had gone. We met the director of the center, who had also worked on the Human Genome Project. He explained that being able to study the blood from each twin's umbilical cord was extremely valuable. He was studying a field called epigenetics, which means "on top of genetics." Epi-

"We would request more corneas, but they are hard to get. Infant eyes are like gold to us."

genetic changes can help determine whether genes are turned on or off, and it's one of the reasons that identical twins can still be different. Our twins' cord blood helped the researchers establish a benchmark to learn more about how anencephaly develops.

We then drove down the street to Cytonet, which is the place that got Thomas's liver. We met the president and eight staff members and even the woman who'd held Thomas's liver in her hands. They explained to us that his liver had been used in a six-liver study to determine the best temperature at which to freeze infant liver cells for a lifesaving therapy.

They also said we were the only donor family who had ever visited.

A few years later, I set up the final appointment, in Philadelphia, and Ross, Callum and I went to visit the University of Pennsylvania. That's where we met the researcher who'd received Thomas's retinas. She was studying retinoblastoma, which is a potentially deadly cancer of the retina. She explained that she had been waiting six years for a sample like Thomas's. It was so precious to her that she had saved some of it. She still had some of it in her freezer, did we want to see it?

Yes, we did.

She then gave Callum a Penn T-shirt, and she offered him an internship.

So I had thought when we made these donations—in the abstract, in the generic sense—that it was a nice thing to do. But I was amazed and blown away when I met the researchers and they told me specifically what they were doing with each donation. My feeling of grief started to turn into pride. I felt that Thomas was introducing us to his colleagues and his coworkers. He was introducing me to people I never would have met and taking me to places I never would have been.

The humming that I felt in the back of my mind stopped.

Recently, Ross, Callum and I went to Philadelphia to accept an award from the National Disease Research Interchange for advocacy. We went onstage, and Callum accepted the award. He was so proud. I took the opportunity to ask him a question.

I asked, "Do you know why we are accepting this award?"

And he said, "For helping people."

I know that as he grows older, there will be more questions, tough questions. And I'm going to have to teach him that there are some times in life when there are questions that are important, but you'll still never get the answer. But it's worth the try, and you never know until you ask.

Originally published in the December 2017/January 2018 issue of *Reader's Digest* magazine.

Callum is now in sixth grade and hopes to play soccer professionally. Sarah Gray visits the lab at the University of Pennsylvania once a year.

Are You Missing the Best Thing in Life?

by Norman Vincent Peale,
from the book *The Amazing Results of Positive Thinking*

*The pastor and author offers a simple
solution to a common problem.*

It's been a long time since I've heard anyone whistling a tune on the street. And this isn't just my own observation. Bill Arthur, managing editor of *Look* magazine, mentioned it the other day. Bill remembers his childhood as a time when people seemed to know how to get more fun out of life than they do today.

Why is this? If it is true of you, what can you do to bring the want-to-whistle back into your attitude of living? What can you do to gain the natural, unaffected joy that comes from deep inside?

Your physical condition has a lot to do with your ability to enjoy life. Proper exercise and proper rest are essential ingredients of joyful emotions. When you feel right, your appreciation of everything expands. Dr. Henry C. Link, the psychologist, would never see a patient who was depressed without first prescribing: "Walk rapidly around the block ten times. This will exercise the motor centers of the brain, and the blood will flow away from the emotional-activity centers. When you come back, you will be much more receptive to positive thoughts."

So, the first step in attaining this wonderful sense of the deep fun of life is to treat your body right. The second step is to think right. The positive thinker trains himself in the attitude of joy. He expects it, and he finds it. A good friend of mine says, "I have made it a habit to expect a pleasant surprise each day, and it has seldom failed to come to pass."

Those who look forward, expecting to see great things, are going to be happy. Marcus Aurelius said, "No man is happy who does not think himself so." If the mind is filled with hate or selfishness, the clear light of joy cannot filter through. It is extremely important to clean up sins and errors; then forget them and go forward. "Forgetting those things which are behind, and reaching forth unto those things which are before." (Philippians 3:13) This is to be wise.

Elbert Hubbard said, "Be pleasant until ten o'clock in the morning and the rest of the day will take care of itself." Henry David Thoreau used to give himself good news the first thing in the morning. He would tell himself how lucky he was to have been born. If he hadn't been born he'd never have known the crunch of snow underfoot, or the glint of starlight; he'd never have smelled the fragrance of a wood fire or have seen the love light in human eyes. He started off each day with thanksgiving.

Giving to others is another joy producer. This may mean giving money or time or interest or advice—anything you take out of you and transfer to others, helpfully.

I recall a young businessman who was extremely ambitious. He gave to his job all he had. As a result, he developed tension and anxiety symptoms, in part because he feared he couldn't sustain the fast, competitive pace he had set for himself—a pathetic reaction often experienced by those who "get ahead."

"Why don't I get fun out of life any more?" he asked me.

We checked for the usual causes of unhappiness. We looked into his participation, or lack of it, in activities which would not "get him something."

"You're not giving a thing to anyone except your family," I said.

The church he attended got exactly one dollar a week from him, about a twentieth of what he should have been giving on his income. He gave the Community Chest just as little as he could get away with. Of time and thought to help others, he gave nothing at all.

"No wonder there's no fun in life for you," I said. "You've stopped the creative process. You're run down because everything has been coming in and nothing going out. You're like the Dead Sea, inlets but no outlets, and that means mental and spiritual stagnation."

We gave him this program: First, he was to increase his giving to the Lord's work to 10 percent of his income.

He was to look outside his family and friends for someone who needed help, someone who might never be able to help him in return. The help might be money, or advice, or just friendly interest.

He was to stop rushing long enough to give himself to people—a few leisurely words with those who were part of his daily life: the policeman on the corner, the news vendor, the elevator operator, his own wife and children.

He was to offer to help in some of the church's business problems. More, he was to offer to call on a few people to carry the helpful ministry of the church to them—people in a hospital, for example.

"That sounds time-consuming," he complained.

"That's exactly right," I said. "You must learn to give, not only money and good will, but time for the benefit of others. The payoff will be more than worth it! You'll get back your old sense of fun."

He followed the program; he became active in his community life. The tension and anxiety subsided.

Still another element in the joy-in-living formula is to know that you are able to meet and overcome the hardships, sorrows and trying circumstances of everyday life.

On a plane a man said to me: "I was the world's worst self-defeating person. I blamed everyone for my failures—even the government. But I knew who was my worst enemy: myself."

Then he described a series of defeats and disappointments sufficient to take the heart out of any man. "At first I shied off your philosophy because I didn't go for the religious approach. I noticed that you urged your readers to read and apply the Bible to problems. Frankly, I hadn't opened a Bible in years. But finally I started reading.

"I was reading the 84th Psalm and the 11th verse struck me: 'No good thing will he withhold from them that walk uprightly.' 'Walk uprightly'—what did that mean? I should stand up like a man and quit griping and being sorry for myself. Uprightly! Stand up to things—that was what I should be doing! And I got the idea that if I did that, God wouldn't hold back any good thing. So I started walking as sprightly as I could, not cringing as I had been doing. I also saw that uprightly meant no double-dealing. I decided I'd straighten some things out, with God's help.

"I now see why you tie religion and practical psychology together. Religion makes it work."

Who wants to live with joy? Who wants to feel like whistling on the street again? Pray many times a day. Soak the mind with Bible passages. See how many good thoughts you can think about people. Get outside yourself. Give of yourself to someone else; give of your resources to good causes. It is not easy. It takes self-discipline. But there is no need for you to be unhappy. Simply do a rehabilitation job on your thoughts. Try spiritual living, really try it. You will discover for yourself that there's a lot of fun in life.

Originally published in the February 1960 issue of *Reader's Digest* magazine.

Norman Vincent Peale, the pastor of Marble Collegiate Church in New York, was best known for his book The Power of Positive Thinking, *published in 1952. Criticized by many experts as being unsupported by scientific evidence and potentially even dangerous to mental health, his ideas were nonetheless enormously influential and an example of the variety of writing featured in* Reader's Digest.

Terror in Room 73

by Sheldon Kelly

The 16-year-old pointed the gun at his young hostages. The principal knew the only way to save lives was to risk his own.

Frost sparkled in the early morning sun as Dan Stockwell paused outside the sprawling, one-level school building in Swanzey, New Hampshire. He felt proud and happy. The programs he had started during his two years as principal of Monadnock Regional Junior-Senior High School were reaping benefits. Morale was high; test scores were rising.

As he did every morning, Stockwell went to his office for a quiet period of paperwork. Then, as the school's 1,040 students began pouring in from eight towns in the rural southwestern corner of the state, he walked toward the cafeteria to mingle with them.

"Morning, Mr. Stockwell!" the students greeted him that October 15, 1991. Just as the bell rang, he heard a loud popping sound coming from the cafeteria. Suddenly there was a commotion in the rear of the cavernous room. A girl's piercing scream dissolved into a cacophony of shouts and cries. An instant later, the entire crowd rushed toward the exit, their faces stricken with fear.

A teacher told Stockwell the horrifying news: A teenager had fired a high-powered rifle, wounding at least one student. (Stockwell would later learn that the bullet had been shot into the air, ricocheting off a girder and striking two students. Both were in the lavatory, conscious and stable.) The gunman was last seen heading toward the gym.

The 49-year-old principal moved quickly down the gym hallway. Another teacher approached, his face pale. He had almost bumped into the young man, who had pointed the rifle at him. As the teacher moved out of the way, he saw the gunman going toward the junior-high wing.

A 12-year-old honors student was walking down the hall. She and her girlfriends had been playing basketball in the gym when the bell rang, and she had to stop at her locker before going to class. She hardly noticed the tall young man wearing a long black coat.

Then she heard him yell at two teachers standing near Room 73: "Get back!" At first, she thought it was a joke. Then she saw the rifle.

"Get inside!" he yelled at the 12-year-old and other kids standing nearby. He gestured toward the empty classroom. "I said get in there! Now!" The honors student dropped her books in horror as she saw the rifle barrel come within inches of her. Some of the kids began crying as they entered the room and sat at desks. Others cowered in a corner.

The gunman removed a box of bullets from his coat pocket and placed it on a table. Then he began loading, ejecting and reloading. "Are you going to kill us?" one boy asked.

There was no answer.

Stockwell walked down the corridor, searching for the gunman. He felt he had to act. The students were his responsibility, and, in that sense, almost as important to him as his own three children.

He reached a corridor where several teachers and custodians had gathered. Whispering, they told him how the youth had warned the teachers away and taken a group of seventh graders hostage.

Stockwell breathed deeply to calm himself. Once before, he had faced a life-threatening emergency. While a student at Bates College, he had visited Fox Island off the Maine coast. A huge wave had knocked a student off a cliff and swept him out to sea.

Stockwell had immediately run to the rocky coastline, where some 50 people were being held back by ten-foot waves. He asked someone to tie a rope around his waist and then dived into the icy water. He found the victim floating face down, unconscious, and dragged him to safety. Later, Stockwell was awarded the Carnegie Medal for heroism.

Now, as he edged closer and looked through the door's half-window into Room 73, he felt a sickening chill. A wiry teenager with long dark hair was standing in the front of the room, pointing a rifle at over a dozen students. As he watched, the youth ejected a bullet from the gun.

> *The gunman removed a box of bullets from his coat pocket. He began loading, ejecting and reloading.*

Stockwell crept back to where his staff had gathered. He sent word that one of the secretaries should calmly make a P.A. announcement to evacuate the building. He stationed a staff member at each end of the corridor, sealing off Room 73.

The assistant principal briefed Stockwell on the gunman, a 16-year-old dropout who had been attending a program for troubled kids. Stockwell didn't know him, but after 25 years as an educator he felt he had the experience to handle the situation. *I can talk to this kid*, he thought.

He returned to Room 73 and peered through the window. The boy was half sitting on a table, aiming the cocked rifle at the youngsters.

Stockwell knocked gently on the door. "May I come in?" he asked. He pushed the door open and stepped inside. "Hello, son. I'm Mr. Stockwell, the principal. What's going on?"

Without answering, the gunman turned the barrel of his rifle directly at the principal's head. "Well, I'll just sit here," Stockwell said calmly.

He picked a student's chair from which he could see the inside and outside windows. Stockwell smiled slightly, knowing it was important not to show fear. "What's wrong, son?" he asked.

The gunman stared at him in silence, his finger tight on the trigger. "What do you mean?" the youngster finally said.

Stockwell explained how the students could be emotionally scarred by being held hostage. "You've got to let them go," Stockwell urged. "It's wrong to scare and hurt them. Besides, you don't need them. You've got me. We can work it out."

The gunman turned toward the hostages. One girl sat on the floor, fighting back tears. "Are you kids scared?" he asked.

"Yes," one answered in a barely audible voice; others only sobbed. The young man jerked his head toward the corridor. "They can get out of here," he said.

Instantly Stockwell told the students to use the rear door. They scrambled out.

The principal felt relieved; half of the job was done. Then an episode in Concord, New Hampshire, flashed through his mind. A student armed with a shotgun had entered the high school there and, after pointing the gun at a teacher and a policeman, had been killed. *I've got to save this kid from himself!* He looked at the boy, who sat facing him from a front-row desk, his elbows splayed out for a steadier aim. *Start talking. Don't rush things.*

Stockwell's questions were met with silence and baleful stares. He kept his eyes fixed on the gunman, trying not to look at the barrel, three feet away, pointed at his head.

"I'm not leaving here alive," the youth said finally. "Life isn't worth living."

Life isn't worth living. Stockwell mulled that over. How could he convince this distraught kid how utterly wrong he was?

"We all go through times when things seem hopeless," the principal said, choosing his words carefully. "It's like being in a dark tunnel that seems to go on forever. But there's always light at the end. You've got to believe me. People love and care about you."

Stockwell stared imploringly into the young man's eyes. "I know a lot about kids taking their own lives," the principal added quietly. "In a way, it's a very selfish act. The loss to families is terrible. The young person destroys not only the most precious gift of all, but that of others."

The teenager stared back impassively, his finger still taut against the trigger. So Stockwell changed tack. "You've got to give yourself a chance," he said. "Like you did those kids."

The youngster looked away furtively and muttered, "It's just not worth the hassle."

Stockwell said in an even voice, "It is worth it. I'm here to help you."

Swanzey Police Chief Larss A. Ogren, 40, was alone at headquarters a half mile away when he received the call. He immediately summoned other officers, then radioed police in nearby Keene for backup.

Ogren raced to the school and entered quietly through a door leading to the cafeteria. "Hang in there," he told a teacher attending the wounded. "An ambulance is on the way."

Directed by the assistant principal, Ogren moved cautiously to Room 73. He cracked the door open to listen and peeked through the window in the door. Minutes passed; as other officers began arriving, he sent word of his plan. He needed more time, the right moment. No one was to do anything unless it appeared the principal was about to be killed.

Stockwell told himself to go on talking. *Keep his mind occupied. Try to prove to him you understand.* Ten minutes passed, 20, a half-hour. After nearly 40 minutes, the teenager rose from the desk, keeping his rifle aimed at Stockwell.

The gunman's face grew more anguished as he stood, towering over the seated principal. Stockwell tensed. He could see the machined details along the large-bore barrel; he imagined fire spurting, blackness.

"I have some demands," the teenager blurted. His voice broke, as if he were on the verge of crying. His face was wet with perspiration.

"What are they, son?" Stockwell asked.

The youth wanted a boom-box stereo to play heavy-metal tapes. Stockwell could see one of the tapes sticking out of his pocket.

"I'll try," Stockwell said. For the previous 30 minutes he had caught glimpses of a policeman peering through the door window. Now he hoped to give him a chance to act.

"I'm going to get up," the principal said, louder than usual. "I'm going to open the window." He rose slowly to his feet, watching the youth's eyes and the dark barrel that followed him as he moved away.

> *"I'm going to kill myself," the gunman announced, slipping the barrel of the rifle beneath his chin.*

Feeling uneasy with his back turned to the rifle, Stockwell pushed open the window and called outside with the boy's demands. *Why aren't the police rushing in now that I'm distracting him?* Stockwell wondered.

Returning to his chair, unnerved, he assured the boy that his demands would be met. Still, the youth's shaking had worsened; his reddened eyes seemed afflicted with fluttery tics. He looked into Stockwell's eyes with a deep, probing stare. "I have another demand. I want my friend," he said.

The kid's losing it, Stockwell thought. *There's no time.* He moved back to the window and shouted the demands as loudly as he could: the stereo and the name of the friend.

* * *

Ogren remained crouched outside Room 73, his pistol in the ready position. He had seen Stockwell go to the window, forcing the gunman to turn his back to the door. But the rifle was still pointed at the principal's back; any surprise could cause the young man to pull the trigger.

Suddenly the gunman lowered his rifle while following Stockwell back to the window. *Now!* Ogren opened the door soundlessly and raced across the room, his pistol aimed and steadied in both hands. The youngster turned abruptly when he was six feet away. The police chief crouched into the firing position. "You better leave, Dan," he said to the principal, watching as the teen-ager gripped his loaded weapon.

Stockwell left the classroom; Ogren, six-foot-two and a muscular 200 pounds, stared into the young man's eyes.

"I'm going to kill myself," the gunman announced, slipping the barrel of the rifle beneath his chin.

"No!" Ogren holstered his pistol. Like the principal, he was determined to avoid bloodshed.

Sweating, tremorous, the youngster sat down, the rifle still held below his jaw. Ogren began talking: girls, music, love.

*　*　*

As Ogren talked, Keene Police Sgt. Edward F. Gross, 33, had gone into an adjoining classroom and removed his shoes and equipment. Then, over the course of several minutes, he crept silently into Room 73.

Gross slipped to within inches of the unsuspecting gunman. Then, moving with catlike speed, Gross seized the rifle barrel and pulled it away. He applied a chokehold and lifted the youth, causing his "trigger" hand to become trapped beneath a desk. Following a violent struggle, the young man was disarmed, handcuffed and carried to a waiting cruiser.

Dan Stockwell, after having a gun held to his head for 45 minutes, had walked from Room 73 directly to his office. When he learned the teenager was in custody and the wounded students were recovering, he began telephoning experts for advice on helping his students cope.

Police officers Ogren and Gross were awarded medals and citations for bravery; Dan Stockwell received a second Carnegie Medal for extraordinary heroism while risking his life to save others. Since the award's inception 89 years ago, only three other persons have received the medal twice.

The young gunman was tried before a juvenile court and sent to a detention center. He was released but recommitted after he entered another high school, this time carrying a starter's pistol. Astonishingly, he is free again, having turned 18.

Originally published in the October 1993 issue of *Reader's Digest* magazine.

There have been 140 active shooter incidents in K–12 schools since this shooting, according to the Center for Homeland Defense and Security.

Humor Hall of Fame

When I phoned my employee to find out why she hadn't come to the office, I expected to hear a sob story about how sick she was, blah, blah, blah. Instead, her excuse was pretty plausible. "When I was driving to work, I took a wrong turn," she explained. "And then I just decided to keep going."

—JUDIE SHEWELL

A man saw a job advertised as "problem solver" with a salary of $100,000. He applied, had an interview and was offered the job on the spot. "Do you have any questions?" asked his new employer.

"Just one," replied the man. "How can you afford to pay so much?"

"That," said the employer, "is your first problem."

—COLIN JAMES

"If you want me to give 110 percent, I want a 10 percent raise."

My secretary liked to yammer on the phone with friends. One day I was about to interrupt her chat to tell her to get back to work when she looked up at the clock and put an end to the conversation.

"Sorry, I have to hang up now," she said. "It's time for my break."

—JAMES R. MAXWELL

My brother delivered prescriptions to people too ill to go out. Since the neighborhoods he visited were often unsafe, he decided to get some protection.

"Why do you need a pistol?" asked the clerk at the gun shop.

My brother had to explain, "I deliver drugs at night and carry a lot of money."

—LAURA LOFTIS

Strange Encounter on Coho Creek

by Morris Homer Erwin

*Deep in the Alaskan wilderness,
a prospector comes to the rescue of
an injured mother wolf and her pups,
and a lasting connection is formed.*

One spring morning many years ago, I had been prospecting for gold along Coho Creek on southeastern Alaska's Kupreanof Island, and as I emerged from a forest of spruce and hemlock, I froze in my tracks. No more than 20 paces away in the bog was a huge Alaskan timber wolf—caught in one of Trapper George's traps.

Old George had died the previous week of a heart attack, so the wolf was lucky I had happened along. Confused and frightened at my approach, the wolf backed away, straining at the trap chain. Then I noticed something else: It was a female, and her teats were full of milk. Somewhere there was a den of hungry pups waiting for their mother.

From her appearance, I guessed that she had been trapped only a few days. That meant her pups were probably still alive, surely no more than a few miles away. But I suspected that if I tried to release the wolf, she would turn aggressive and try to tear me to pieces.

A female timber wolf can weigh as much as 100 pounds.

So I decided to search for her pups instead and began to look for incoming tracks that might lead me to her den. Fortunately, there were still a few remaining patches of snow. After several moments, I spotted paw marks on a trail skirting the bog.

The tracks led a half mile through the forest, then up a rock-strewn slope. I finally spotted the den at the base of an enormous spruce. There wasn't a sound inside. Wolf pups are shy and cautious, and I didn't have much hope of luring them outside. But I had to try. So I began imitating the high-pitched squeak of a mother wolf calling her young. No response. A few moments later, after I tried another call, four tiny pups appeared.

They couldn't have been more than a few weeks old. I extended my hands, and they tentatively suckled at my fingers. Perhaps hunger had helped overcome their natural fear. Then, one by one, I placed them in a burlap bag and headed back down the slope.

When the mother wolf spotted me, she stood erect. Possibly picking up the scent of her young, she let out a high-pitched, plaintive whine. I released the pups, and they raced to her. Within seconds, they were slurping at her belly.

What next? I wondered. The mother wolf was clearly suffering. Yet each time I moved in her direction, a menacing growl rumbled in her throat. With her young to protect, she was becoming belligerent. *She needs nourishment*, I thought. *I have to find her something to eat.*

One snap of her huge jaws and she could break my arm ... or my neck.

I hiked toward Coho Creek and spotted the leg of a dead deer sticking out of a snowbank. I cut off a hindquarter, then returned the remains to nature's icebox. Toting the venison haunch back to the wolf, I whispered in a soothing tone, "OK, Mother, your dinner is served. But only if you stop growling at me. C'mon, now. Easy." I tossed chunks of venison in her direction. She sniffed them, then gobbled them up.

Cutting hemlock boughs, I fashioned a rough shelter for myself and was soon asleep nearby. At dawn, I was awakened by four fluffy bundles of fur sniffing at my face and hands. I glanced toward the agitated

With four tiny pups to feed, the mother wolf would need to stay nourished.

mother wolf. *If I could only win her confidence*, I thought. It was her only hope.

Over the next few days, I divided my time between prospecting and trying to win the wolf's trust. I talked gently with her, threw her more venison and played with the pups. Little by little, I kept edging closer—though I was careful to remain beyond the length of her chain. The big animal never took her dark eyes off me. "Come on, Mother," I pleaded. "You want to go back to your friends on the mountain. Relax."

At dusk on the fifth day, I delivered her daily fare of venison. "Here's dinner," I said softly as I approached. "C'mon, girl. Nothing to be afraid of." Suddenly, the pups came bounding to me. At least I had their trust. But I was beginning to lose hope of ever winning over the mother. Then I thought I saw a slight wagging of her tail. I moved within the length of her chain. She remained motionless. My heart in my mouth, I sat down eight feet from her. One snap of her huge jaws and she could break my arm ... or my neck. I wrapped my blanket around myself and slowly settled onto the cold ground. It was a long time before I fell asleep.

I awoke at dawn, stirred by the sound of the pups nursing. Gently, I leaned over and petted them. The mother wolf stiffened. "Good morning, friends," I said tentatively. Then I slowly placed my hand on the wolf's injured leg. She flinched but made no threatening move. *This can't be happening*, I thought. Yet it was.

I could see that the trap's steel jaws had imprisoned only two toes. They were swollen and lacerated, but she wouldn't lose the paw—if I could free her.

"OK," I said. "Just a little longer and we'll have you out of there." I applied pressure, the trap sprang open, and the wolf pulled free. Whimpering, she loped about, favoring the injured paw. My experience in the wild suggested that the wolf would now gather her pups and vanish into the woods. But cautiously, she crept toward me. The pups nipped playfully at their mother as she stopped at my elbow. Slowly, she sniffed my hands and arms. Then the wolf began licking my fingers. I was astonished. This went against everything I'd ever heard about timber wolves. Yet, strangely, it all seemed so natural.

After a while, with her pups scurrying around her, the mother wolf was ready to leave and began to limp off toward the forest. Then she turned back to me.

"You want me to come with you, girl?" I asked. Curious, I packed my gear and set off.

* * *

Following Coho Creek for a few miles, we ascended Kupreanof Mountain until we reached an alpine meadow. There, lurking in the forested perimeter, was a wolf pack—I counted nine adults and, judging by their playful antics, four nearly full-grown pups. After a few minutes of greeting, the pack broke into howling. It was an eerie sound, ranging from low wails to high-pitched yodeling.

At dark, I set up camp. By the light of my fire and a glistening moon, I could see furtive wolf shapes dodging in and out of the shadows, eyes shining. I had no fear. They were merely curious. So was I.

I awoke at first light. It was time to leave the wolf to her pack. She watched as I assembled my gear and started walking across the meadow. Reaching the far side, I looked back. The mother and her pups were sitting where I had left them, watching me. I don't know why, but I waved. At the same time, the mother wolf sent a long, mournful howl into the crisp air.

Four years later, after serving in World War II, I returned to Coho Creek. It was the fall of 1945. After the horrors of the war, it was good to be back among the soaring spruce and breathing the familiar, bracing air of the Alaskan bush. Then I saw, hanging in the red cedar where I had placed it four years before, the now-rusted steel trap that had ensnared the mother wolf. The sight of it gave me a strange feeling, and something made me climb Kupreanof Mountain to the meadow where I had last seen her. There, standing on a lofty ledge, I gave out a long, low wolf call—something I had done many times before.

I had no fear. The wolves were merely curious. So was I.

An echo came back across the distance. Again I called. And again the echo reverberated, this time followed by a wolf call from a ridge about a half mile away.

Then, far off, I saw a dark shape moving slowly in my direction. As it crossed the meadow, I could see it was a timber wolf. A chill spread through my whole body. I knew at once that familiar shape, even after four years. "Hello, old girl," I called gently. The wolf edged closer, ears erect, body tense, and stopped a few yards off, her bushy tail wagging slightly.

Moments later, the wolf was gone. I left Kupreanof Island a short time after that, and I never saw the animal again. But the memory she left with me—vivid, haunting, a little eerie—will always be there, a reminder that there are things in nature that exist outside the laws and understanding of man.

During that brief instant in time, this injured animal and I had somehow penetrated each other's worlds, bridging barriers that were never meant to be bridged. There is no explaining experiences like this. We can only accept them and—because they're tinged with an air of mystery and strangeness—perhaps treasure them all the more.

Originally published in the May 1987 issue of *Reader's Digest* magazine.

Stories about connections between man and animal have been enduring staples of Reader's Digest *for years. When this story was reprinted in the magazine and then shared on rd.com in 2019, it went viral and has now been read by many millions online and in print.*

An Open Letter to America's Students

by Dwight D. Eisenhower

General Dwight D. Eisenhower
writes to young Americans. It will pay
all Americans to listen in.

I receive many letters from young people. Mostly they ask a question that could be put like this:

Shall I keep on with school? Or shall I plunge right off into "life"? I try to answer these letters according to the circumstances of each case. But I sometimes feel that I would like to try to write a general answer to the whole general problem of "school" versus "life" in the minds of my correspondents. I think I would say:

Dear Jack—or Margaret: You say you wonder if it is worthwhile for you to go on with high school. You particularly wonder if it is worthwhile to enter and finish college. The tedium of study, nose buried in books, seems a waste of time compared with a job and the stimulus of productive work.

You say you hate to bother me with this "trifling" problem of yours.

It is not a trifling problem at all. Your decision will affect your whole life; similar decisions by millions of other young Americans will affect the total life of our country. And I know how deeply it must worry you. It worried me and a lot of my schoolmates when I was your age.

In a small Kansas town, 40 years ago, a reasonably strong case could be put up in favor of leaving school early. Outside those few who could afford to pick a profession, most of us knew our lives would be spent on the farm, or in one of the local stores, or at the creamery or elevator.

We could be good farmers, good storekeepers, good mill hands, without much book learning. The quickest road to practical knowledge was to *do*. That was the way we might have argued; and we would have been right if there were no more to successful living than plowing a straight furrow, wrapping a neat package, keeping a machine well oiled.

Fortunately, we came of stock that set the school on the same plane as the home and church. The value of education, above and beyond the immediate return in dollars and cents, had been bred into us. Our families stinted themselves to keep us in school a while longer; and most of us worked, and worked hard, to prolong that while.

Today the business of living is far more complex than it was in my boyhood. No one of us can hope to comprehend all its complexity in a lifetime of study. But each day profitably spent in school will help you understand better your personal relationship to country and world. If your generation fails to understand that the human individual is still the center of the universe and is still the sole reason for the existence of all man-made institutions, then complexity will become chaos.

Consequently, I feel firmly that you should continue your schooling—if you can—right to the end of high school and right to the end of college. You say you are "not too good at books." But from books—under the guidance of your teachers—you can get a grasp on the thing that you most ought to understand before you go to work.

It is expressed in a moving letter I got the other day from a young girl halfway through high school. She said that in her studies she seemed to be a failure all along the line, always trailing everyone else. But then she ended by saying: "I still think I could learn to be a good American."

That's the vital point. School, of course, should train you in the two great basic tools of the mind: the use of words and the use of numbers.

And school can properly give you a start toward the special skills you may need in the trade or business or profession you may plan to enter. But remember:

As soon as you enter it, you will be strongly tempted to fall into the rut and routine of it. You will be strongly tempted to become just a part of an occupation which is just one part of America. In school—from books, from teachers, from fellow students—you can get a view of the whole of America, how it started, how it grew, what it is, what it means. Each day will add breadth to your view and a sharper comprehension of your own role as an American.

I feel sure I am right when I tell you:

To develop fully your own character you must know your country's character.

A plant partakes of the character of the soil in which it grows. You are a plant that is *conscious*, that *thinks*. You must study your soil—which is your country—in order that you may be able to draw its strength up into your own strength.

It will pay you to do so. You will understand your own problems better and solve them more easily if you have studied America's problems and done something toward their solution.

Never forget that *self-interest and patriotism go together*. You have to look out for yourself, and you have to look out for your country. Self-interest and patriotism, rightly considered, are not contradictory ideas. They are partners.

The very earth of our country is gradually getting lost to us. One third of the fertile top layer of our soil has already been washed away into rivers and the sea. This must be stopped, or some day our country will be too barren to yield us a living. That is one national problem crying for solution; it affects you directly and decisively.

In our cities there are millions of people who have little between them and hunger except a daily job, which they may lose. They demand more "security." If they feel too insecure, their discontent might some day undermine *your* security, no matter how personally successful you might be in your own working life. That's another problem—and there are innumerable others—whose solution requires the thought and goodwill of every American.

I cannot put it to you too strongly—or too often—that it is to your *practical advantage* to learn America's character and problems, in the broadest possible way, and to help to bring those problems to their solutions.

It is dangerous to assume that our country's welfare belongs alone to that mysterious mechanism called "the government." Every time we allow or force the government, because of our own individual or local failures, to take over a question that properly belongs to us, by that much we surrender our individual responsibility, and with it a comparable amount of individual freedom. But the very core of what we mean by Americanism is individual liberty founded on individual responsibility, equality before the law, and a system of private enterprise that aims to reward according to merit.

These things are basic—your years in school will help you to apply these truths to the business of living in a free democracy.

Yours is a country of free men and women, where personal liberty is cherished as a fundamental right. But the price of its continued possession is untiring alertness. Liberty is easily lost. Witness the history of the past 20 years. Even the natural enthusiasm of warm youthful hearts for a leader can be a menace to liberty.

It was movements of misguided young people, under the influence of older and more cynical minds, that provided the physical force to make Mussolini the tyrant of Italy and Hitler the tyrant of Germany. Mussolini's street song was *Giovinezza*—"Youth." Hitler based his power most firmly on the *Hitlerjugend*—the Hitler Youth.

Never let yourself be persuaded that any one Great Man, any one leader, is necessary to the salvation of America. When America consists of one *leader* and 143,000,000 *followers*, it will no longer be America. Truly American leadership is not of any one man. It is of multitudes of men—and women.

Our last war was not won by one man or a few men. It was won by hundreds of thousands and millions of men and women of all ranks.

Audacity, initiative, the will to try greatly and stubbornly characterized them. Great numbers of them, if for only a few minutes in some desperate crisis of battle, were leaders.

You will find it so in the fields of peace. America at work is not just a few "Great Men" at the head of government, of corporations or of labor unions. It is millions and millions of men and women, who on farms and in factories and in stores and offices and homes are leading this country—and the world—toward better and better ways of doing and of making things. America exceeds all other lands—by far—in the number of its leaders. Any needless concentration of power is a menace to freedom.

We have the world's best machines, because we ourselves are not machines; because we have embraced the liberty of thinking for ourselves, of imagining for ourselves, and of acting for ourselves out of our own energies and inspirations. Our true strength is not in our machines, splendid as they are, but in the inquisitive, inventive, indomitable souls of our people.

To be that kind of soul is open to every American boy and girl; *and it is the one kind of career that America cannot live without.*

To be a good American—worthy of the heritage that is yours, eager to pass it on enhanced and enriched—is a lifetime career, stimulating, sometimes exhausting, always satisfying to those who do their best.

Start on it now; take part in America's affairs while you are still a student. There are responsibilities about your home, in your neighborhood, that you can assume. There are activities about your school, on your campus, that will be more productive of good by your contribution.

Don't think that you are too young. "Let no man despise thy youth," Paul the Apostle said to Timothy. These words apply to you as an American. Loyalty to principle, readiness to give of one's talents to the common good, acceptance of responsibility—these are the measure of a good American, not his age in years.

Alexander Hamilton—General Washington's aide in war, President Washington's secretary of the treasury in peace—was speaking before applauding crowds of his fellow New Yorkers on the political problems of the American Revolution when he was only 17 years old and still a student in King's College, now Columbia University. The same stuff of which Hamilton was made is in you and all American youth today.

But above all, while you are still at school, try to learn the "why" of your country. We Americans know "how" to produce things faster and better—on the whole—than any other people. But what will it profit us to produce things unless we know what we are producing them for, unless we know what purpose animates America?

To assure each citizen his inalienable right to life, liberty and the pursuit of happiness was the "why" behind the establishment of this Republic and is today the "why" for its continued existence. What that means to you personally, what you must do toward its fulfillment, cannot be answered completely in a letter. But I repeat that the answer can be found in your school, if you seek it deliberately and conscientiously. You need neither genius nor vast learning for its comprehension.

To be a good American is the most important job that will ever confront you. But essentially it is nothing more than being a good member of your community, helping those who need your help, striving for a sympathetic understanding of those who oppose you, doing each new day's job a little better than the previous day's, placing the common good before personal profit. The American Republic was born to assure you the dignity and rights of a human individual. If the dignity and rights of your fellow men guide your daily conduct of life, you will be a good American.

Originally published in the October 1948 issue of *Reader's Digest* magazine.

Our America

Choices
—C.F. PAYNE
JANUARY 2005

Lucky 13

"If we can get all 13 of them to adulthood without any major issues, it would probably be beating the odds," says Kevin Deiter of his brood, "but I think we're on the right track. Plus, it's pretty hard to get away with anything; there are too many people around to catch you!"

Photograph by Glenn Glasser

Pastor of Love

"There are the people who got married here 10, 20, 50 years ago, and they return with their children and grandchildren to renew their vows," says Charlotte Richards. "And then there are the people who get married in California on a Saturday night and come here on a Sunday to do it all over again. Because they just love it; they love what they felt, I guess. And it is a wonderful feeling."

Photograph by Glenn Glasser

HAPPY RETURNS

A long flight of weathered steps led to a hollow wooden door
with rusty numbers beckoning us into Room 1108. Inside
we barely noticed the faded wood paneling, lumpy queen-
sized bed and thin, tacky carpet. We could see the expanse of
seashore from our perch and easily wander down the access
path to feel the sand between our toes. We returned again
and again until the burgeoning resort tore down our orange-
shingled eyesore. Forty years later, my husband periodically
sends me a short email that declares the time: 11:08. "I love
you too," I write back.

—Laurie Olson, *Dayton, Ohio*

ACCIDENTAL PEN PALS

I answered a ringing pay phone. A call that was meant for
another. I was so enamored by the angelic voice of the girl
on the other end of the line, we spoke for what seemed like
hours. She was from Iowa, I from Florida, and I was spending
the summer in the mountains of New Mexico. I immediately
knew that I wanted to know more about her. We exchanged
letters and became pen pals. Six months later I traveled to the
Midwest to meet my mystery girl. It was love at first sight. In
September we will celebrate our 30th wedding anniversary.

—Randy Aronson, *Cooper City, Florida*

Leave 'em Laughing!

by Lizz Winstead, from the book *Lizz Free or Die*

The co-creator of The Daily Show *learned how to be funny from the greatest practical joker ever: her dad.*

When they took Dad to the hospital that last time, he phoned me from his room. "Lizzy, the paramedics asked me if I was on any medications. I told them, 'Everything but Viagra.' Then they put the oxygen mask on me."

It was typical of Dad: dark, inappropriate and funny. And they were the last words I heard him say.

My sister Linda called me the next day: "You need to come home."

In his own way, Dad, who had suffered from emphysema for years, had tried to prepare me for this day. A few months before his death, he had sent me a card and had asked me not to open it "'til after I'm gone."

Of course I opened it immediately. It said, "I love you. You are my favorite. Please don't tell the others."

The sentiment evoked a range of emotions in me. It made me feel elated that I did something right. Then it made me feel bad for my brother and sisters. Finally, I felt horribly guilty for opening it.

I taped it open inside my jewelry box so I'd see it a lot, and as I went to grab my pearls—my last item to pack for the trip to Minneapolis, where he lay dying—I glanced at it and at that moment was selfishly grateful that Dad and I shared this secret.

As my sister Ann and I approached Dad's room, the sound of laughter got louder. When we walked in, Mom was sitting in the chair next to Dad, and my brother and two sisters and sister-in-law were all sitting on the extra bed. Tears streamed down everyone's faces as they laughed.

Dad couldn't speak, but he could hear everything. His stomach was bouncing up and down, as he was laughing too.

"What did we miss?" Ann asked.

"The meat! The gas station meat!" my brother said, choking through what I like to think of as dielarity.

Dielarity (diy-lair'-it-ee) *n*: The dark humor created in the environment of or at the expense of someone dying.

Ahh, the gas station meat. The crown jewel in the pantheon of Dad's many "deal" stories. Dad loved bargains. The merchandise was always stuff that no one wanted, never mind wanted to get a "deal" on. Which brings us to the tale of the bargain steaks he'd brought home once, after a trip across town in search of a cheaper tank of gas.

"I will never forget being halfway through my steak when you told us the story of how you'd bought them," I said, then continued in my best Dad baritone voice: "I was filling up the tank and notice this fella's got a station wagon there with the tailgate open. And the guy says, 'You want to check out my meat?' And at first I thought, 'Who is this weirdo who wants to show me his meat?'"

Dad was so proud of that dumb joke, his belly was in full force. Then the story reached its climax with each of us chiming in.

"That guy had half a cow in an old cardboard box in the back of that station wagon."

"That had come from God only knows where!"

"Or when!"

"And Dad bought all of it!"

"For 40 bucks!"

"We were all sitting around eating black market roadkill."

Mom weighed in. "The ribs were really very good."

Leave 'em Laughing!

We swapped stories for a few more hours until the dielarity had exhausted us all.

Dielarious laughter is different from regular laughter, as it drains you of every emotion. It is an exhausting release of all the pain, fear, love and loss that you had been holding in. If I didn't laugh, I would have spent that energy reminding myself that my life was about to change forever. And Dad's spirit was humor—his and his family's. So ipso facto, if there was still laughter, he would continue to exist.

The next day was a long one. Dad's stomach-bouncing was minimal. A hospice worker suggested we each take some time alone with him to share our private thoughts. Finally, it was my turn.

I climbed into bed with him and grabbed his hand.

"Dad, squeeze my hand so I know you can hear me." He squeezed back. I wanted him to squeeze it off.

"You know I love you, and you are my inspiration to go out and make the world a funnier place."

Squeeze.

"I know you let me win at Jeopardy!"

Squeeze.

"Dad, I opened your card. I couldn't wait. I hope you're not mad. It made me feel so special."

He didn't squeeze my hand, but his belly started to bounce. Right then, that felt better than a squeeze.

I then whispered into his ear, "You couldn't have done a better job of being a dad. I hope you are proud of me. I love you."

Squeeze.

Afterward, everyone filed in. Then a nurse checked on Dad. "It's time," she said. "He'll pass within the hour."

By now, we were about 15 people gathered and sitting on Dad's bed. His breathing became so shallow, so slow, that as a family we tried to breathe for him.

Finally he took his last breath. We didn't know what to do. We just sat there, wept and stared at our dead dad.

"He loved you kids so much," said Mom. She was still holding his

223

hand. "He always hoped he'd told you enough. It's why he sent you kids the cards to open after he died, so you would always have a reminder."

"I keep mine open in my jewelry case," I said. Then I thought, *They all got cards?*

"Oh, you opened it?" Mom asked, knowingly. I guess he had told her he was sending us cards, but did he reveal our secret to her? I couldn't imagine he did.

"And did the rest of you open your cards too?" Mom asked.

Everyone nodded. They were all clearly ashamed, but you could read in each person's face how much Dad's special words gave them peace.

"Dad wanted you to open those cards after he died, and since you all went against his wishes, I would love to hear what he wrote to each of you," Mom said. "Lizz, you start."

"Mom, maybe now is not the time," Linda said, to my relief.

"Let's just focus on Dad and you," Ann added.

Crisis averted. No one wanted to read their cards either. I felt relieved, and now I was not the bad guy who denied Mom.

"Lizz, you start," Mom repeated. She was not letting this go.

The only person who could make this stop was lying there not doing anything. Finally, I started crying.

"The card said, 'I love you. You were my favorite. Please don't …'" And before I'd finished, all my siblings had joined me in unison, "… tell the others."

The room erupted with convulsions of dielarity. Dad had pulled off the greatest gotcha moment of his life. And at his death, no less.

Bravo, Dad. Bravo.

Originally published in the February 2013 issue of *Reader's Digest* magazine.

A Fight for Life at 35,000 Feet

by Per Ola and Emily D'Aulaire

The crew was not equipped to handle the life-threatening premature birth.

TWA Flight 265 from New York to Orlando had just leveled off at cruising altitude the morning of November 23, 1994, when 35-year-old Theresa de Bara in row 28 doubled over in pain.

"What's the matter, honey?" asked her husband, Sandy, 39, as their three-year-old daughter, Amanda, watched in alarm.

"I've never felt this before," she whispered, grabbing Sandy's hand. "It feels like someone's ripping out my insides with a red-hot poker."

Frantically, Sandy beckoned to head flight attendant Meg Somerville. "My wife needs help!"

Nothing about Theresa's slender build suggested that she was pregnant. But Somerville played a hunch. "Are you expecting?" she asked.

Theresa nodded and exhaled through clenched teeth: "Just six months. It's too early, and this doesn't feel like labor pains." But then another searing spasm tore through her body.

I think this woman's going into labor! Somerville thought with a jolt. Quickly she mentally reviewed the rules for emergency childbirth listed in her flight-attendant's manual. "We'll need these seats," Somerville said, ushering Sandy, Amanda and two other travelers from row 28.

Flipping back the armrests, she helped Theresa lie down across the seats. Managing a calm voice, Somerville picked up the public-address microphone: "If there is a doctor on board, please report to row 28."

* * *

From the moment Jeanne Rachlin proposed a trip to Walt Disney World with their three daughters, her husband had resisted the idea. A busy internist practicing on Long Island, New York, Steven Rachlin, 46, protested, "I don't have time for a vacation." But Jeanne had convinced him.

"Tell the captain this is an emergency."

Their plans were almost scuttled twice. A mix-up in reservations meant the Rachlins had to scramble to find last-minute seats on TWA's crowded Flight 265. Then, on departure day, they were late leaving home and nearly missed the plane out of New York's Kennedy Airport.

As Dr. Rachlin was just beginning to relax, he heard the call over the public-address system. Heading to row 28, he told Somerville, "I'm a doctor. What's the problem?" She clutched his arm and whispered, "I think this lady is having labor pains."

* * *

Several rows behind the de Baras were Jim and Jen Midgley of Chelmsford, Massachusetts. Jim, 26, and Jen, 34, were both paramedics familiar with pediatrics. Like the Rachlins, they had changed their travel plans last-minute. Jen nudged a passing flight attendant. "My husband and I are paramedics," she offered. "We'd be glad to help."

"Thanks, but there's a doctor responding," the attendant said. Meanwhile, the couple kept their eyes riveted on row 28.

* * *

When Flight 265 reached its cruising altitude of 35,000 feet, Captain Jerry McFerren throttled back and switched on the autopilot. That

A Fight for Life at 35,000 Feet

McFerren, 58, was piloting the huge Lockheed L-1011 that day was something of a fluke. He had commanded a flight into New York only the day before but had readily agreed to fill in for a colleague. He was among the airline's most senior flight officers and was one of the coolest under pressure—with a touch of the bomber pilot left from his Air Force days.

McFerren was about to start breakfast when a chime sounded in the cockpit. The voice of a flight attendant came over the intercom: "There's a woman back here who's having stomach pain."

"Thank you," McFerren answered. "Make sure she's comfortable, and keep me informed." *Probably indigestion*, he thought.

Residents of Greenfield Park, New York, Theresa and Sandy were looking forward to some time off with Amanda.

The day before departure, she began having stomach cramps and phoned her doctor. He diagnosed Braxton-Hicks contractions—false labor. "You had the same thing with Amanda, and she was fine," the doctor reminded her. "Go enjoy your vacation."

After examining Theresa externally, Rachlin reached the same conclusion that her obstetrician had. "I'm pretty sure this is false labor," he said. "Everything's going to be OK." Suddenly a pool of blood appeared on the seat. *My God!* Rachlin thought. *She's having a miscarriage!* "We have a major problem," the doctor told Somerville. "Tell the captain this is an emergency. He has to land the plane and get this lady to a hospital."

Amanda peered at her mother in terror. "Is Mommy going to die?" she asked, sobbing.

Somerville hugged her close. "Everything's going to be fine," she promised, not sure she believed her own words.

Told of the emergency, McFerren immediately banked the southbound plane in a tight arc near Crisfield, Maryland, and headed northwest toward Dulles International Airport outside Washington, DC. McFerren knew Dulles had paramedic crews on 24-hour call.

Setting course for Dulles, McFerren told co-pilot Strohm Lippert to request clearance to land because of a medical emergency, and to ask that paramedics be standing by.

Normally, the 126-mile flight to Dulles would take almost 30 minutes. McFerren pushed the throttles to the fire wall. The airspeed rose to nearly 600 mph—just within the manufacturer's limits for the jet.

* * *

Back in the cabin, tension mounted. "Get blankets, clean towels and linens," Rachlin directed flight attendant Connie Duquette. "We have to stop this bleeding."

Duquette ran up and down the aisle, commandeering blankets from passengers. Another attendant grabbed a few starched linen tablecloths.

The doctor felt a moment of panic. He'd delivered only one baby in his life, just after his residency 13 years earlier. *Can I remember how to do this?* he asked himself.

"I have to see what's going on," Rachlin told Somerville. "Do you have a pair of latex gloves?"

Somerville handed him the plane's first aid kit. As Rachlin examined Theresa, he suddenly drew back in alarm. "She's having the baby right now!" he exclaimed. "I can see the top of its head!"

"Push!" Rachlin ordered Theresa. "Take deep breaths and push."

In a sudden, smooth motion, the tiny infant slipped from the birth canal. It was a boy. Rachlin saw that the umbilical cord was wrapped tightly around his neck. He didn't stir or cry, nor did his chest move.

Slipping his fingers under the cord, the doctor gently unraveled it from the baby's neck. "Breathe!" Rachlin urged as he turned the infant upside down and gently slapped his back.

* * *

From their seats, paramedics Jen and Jim Midgley continued to follow what was happening. "I don't hear the baby crying," Jen told Jim.

"We're paramedics trained in emergency childbirth and infant resuscitation," Jen told a nearby flight attendant. "Can we help?"

Jen and the attendant stumbled down the sloping aisle of the descending plane. Jim quickly followed. Rachlin, who was still trying to stimulate the baby, was losing hope. "I don't think he's going to make it," the doctor whispered.

The baby was turning an alarming shade of blue from lack of oxygen. Jim mentally assigned him an APGAR Score, a quick test for gauging the health and prognosis of newborns. Rating the baby's pulse, respiration, appearance and activity, the paramedic gave him a score of only one out of ten points. *Still, the little guy has a chance*, Jim thought.

The baby had now been without oxygen for two or three minutes. That was approaching the limit before irreversible brain damage set in.

"Is there an obstetric kit on board?" Jen asked Duquette, hoping for a bulb syringe to suction out mucus blocking the baby's nose.

"We don't carry equipment like that," Duquette replied.

"A straw!" Jen called out. "Somebody, quick—give me a straw."

Flight attendant Denise Booth had brought several small juice cartons on board. Each container came with a small, bendable straw. Booth raced up the aisle for her bag. "Here," she said, returning moments later.

"Perfect!" Jen answered. She slipped a slender straw into one of the baby's nostrils and sucked at the mucus plugging the air passages. Temporarily revived, the baby let out his first whimper. But the premature infant needed more help.

* * *

McFerren flew the plane like the Air Force pilot he used to be, racing toward the airport 110 mph faster than the normal initial approach speed.

As the flight engineer called out altitudes, McFerren descended right on course. The huge jet's main landing gear brushed the pavement with a feathery touch, then the nose wheel settled onto the runway. It was the smoothest landing McFerren had made all year. The plane touched down at Dulles 15½ minutes after turning back.

*   *   *

Jen began administering mouth-to-mouth resuscitation.

"What's the pulse?" she asked.

"Low," Rachlin replied. "Around 40."

Jen knew the pulse should be 140 to 160. Jim continued mouth-to-mouth while Rachlin administered cardiac compressions, pressing lightly and rhythmically on the baby's chest.

Jen realized they needed to tie and cut the umbilical cord. "I need some string," she announced.

Duquette, who knew there was no string on board, had an idea. Dropping to her hands and knees, she crawled quickly down the aisle searching for the cleanest pair of shoelaces she could find. She spotted a pair of shiny new leather shoes and announced to the astonished passenger, "Sir, I need one of your shoelaces. Right now, please."

She rushed the lace to row 28, where Jen tied it tightly around the cord. Then, using a pair of sharp sewing scissors, Rachlin quickly and cleanly sliced through the umbilical cord. Suddenly the baby gurgled, and his skin began turning pale pink. He let out a weak cry.

"He's breathing!" Jen shouted. "He's alive!"

Now filled with hope, Duquette hurried to the public-address system and announced, "It's a boy!" Passengers cheered and applauded. Sandy picked up Amanda and hugged her, his knees weak with relief.

With the baby doing better, Rachlin now turned to Theresa. Her pulse and blood pressure were low. "She needs to be stabilized," he told the Midgleys.

*   *   *

Rolling down the runway, McFerren applied full reverse thrust. He knew that a Dulles turn called Echo Five led off the main runway at midfield. He wanted to make that 45-degree left turn and scoot straight for the terminal, rather than rolling to the end of the runway and heading back. That would then save another five precious minutes.

Normally, McFerren would have taken a turn like Echo Five at

50 mph. But now he made a split-second calculation and dived into the turn at 100 mph. The plane roared to the terminal and stopped.

Moments later, paramedics rushed in. One scooped up the baby, wrapped him in blankets and dashed out to a waiting ambulance. Siren wailing, the vehicle sped toward nearby Reston Hospital Center.

Meanwhile, another paramedic administered oxygen and IV fluids to Theresa. This brought her low blood pressure up toward a safe level.

She spotted a pair of shiny leather shoes and said to the astonished passenger, "Sir, I need one of your shoelaces."

Flight 265 took off from Dulles less than an hour after it had landed, minus the four de Baras. As the plane approached Orlando, a TWA agent at Dulles radioed McFerren to report that both mother and child were doing fine. McFerren relayed the good news over the public-address system, and once more the passengers broke into loud cheers.

* * *

The baby received respiratory care in the hospital for the next ten days. Staff members quickly dubbed their tiny patient Dulles—and the name stuck. Sandy and Theresa christened their son Matthew Dulles.

Six months after his birth, Matthew was an active, alert baby. The de Baras still give thanks for the strange twist of fate that put a physician and two paramedics on the same flight. They will always be grateful to everyone involved that day. "You hear a lot of bad news in the world today," Theresa says. "But Matthew is proof that most people are good, decent folks who pull together in times of need."

Originally published in the October 1995 issue of *Reader's Digest* magazine.

Now 27, Matthew de Bara is a marketing manager for a landscape design firm in Cornwall, New York, and a freelance videographer. He graduated from SUNY New Paltz in 2017.

Humor Hall of Fame

My sister got a call from her son's kindergarten teacher. When he'd gone in to check on little James in the bathroom, he noticed the boy was using a urinal. "That's odd," my sister said. "We never taught him how to use a urinal."

"I could tell," said the teacher. "He was sitting in it."

—ESTHER OLCHEWSKI

When my ex-Marine father-in-law was at my house, our six-year-old neighbor came by to play with my kids.

I asked her if she knew who he was. She looked up at him with her big blue eyes and said, "I don't remember what his name is, but I know he used to be a submarine."

—JANELLE RAGLAND

"I'm considering a run for class president. Do we have any skeletons in our closet I should first know about?"

Miniature Golf to the Rescue

by Elmer Davis, from *Harper's Magazine*

*After the stock market crash,
Americans turned to a novelty game.*

A short time ago America was beating the big bass drum at the head of the world's prosperity parade. Then we fell down and the rest of the world tripped over us. How have the nations responded to the disappointment of their hopes? Revolution sweeps South America; in Germany millions of voters turn to Hitlerite Fascism—the cult of the impossible in politics; even in Canada voters rise up and turn out the government, to install a new ministry which sets itself to build a tariff wall that matches ours. But in the United States, where the disaster might have been expected to have had the worst repercussion because hopes were highest, the citizens find solace by knocking a little ball across a surface of crushed cottonseed hulls and through a tin pipe.

Is this a dire reflection on our national sanity? I think not. Theoretically, we might have done something better with our unwelcome leisure; in fact, we might easily have done something worse.

The great boom in miniature golf began last spring. That was the season in which Americans began to realize, with a sudden dismay, that the stock market crash of October 1929 had been no isolated accident, but a symptom of the temporary breakdown of the business organism of the whole world.

Why did people take up miniature golf? Well, hard times are traditionally good times for the cheaper amusements. Baseball and the movies have had a good year. Men out of work, tired of tramping the streets, want someplace to go; and a good many Americans who consider themselves just now practically destitute are not too destitute to spend a quarter for a movie, or 50 cents for a round of miniature golf. It will be remembered that mah-jongg came to popularity after the slump of 1921, and that the bicycle overspread the land after the great panic of 1893.

There is another reason for the success of miniature golf. Millions of Americans play golf. But there are also, it appears, millions of Americans who would like to play golf but can't afford it. Thanks now to the miniature courses, every man can say that he plays golf; when he drops a casual remark about going around in three under par, it may be that nobody will ask him whether he did it at the Crystal Brook Club or at Joe's place on the vacant lot.

A tricky and inexpensive novelty that we all can play—and feel while playing that we are improving our golf game, or breaking in at last on that sport of the minor aristocracy—its appeal in a year of hard times was hard to resist.

And we needed something like that.

For consider the situation in which we found ourselves at the beginning of last summer. It was that most distressing situation in which, for the average man, there was nothing left to be done.

The American people, in the main, behaved admirably in the face of the great collapse in stocks in the fall of 1929. Some of us were wiped out, most of us had lost money; every one of us had suffered from the destruction of the national faith that nothing like that could happen again. When the impossible happened, the American people took it standing up. It was the fashion to make a joke of disaster, to laugh at our wrecked hopes of unearned riches. Now we must all settle down and acquire our riches by the old and tested method of working for them.

But that riches were still there for the taking if only we worked hard enough, few people doubted, then. We laughed at the stock market crash as no more than a readjustment of security values. So stock prices rose, the hopes of the nation rose with them—and then the clouds returned after the rain.

It was the collapse of May, not the collapse of October, that really broke the great heart of the world and unloosed a hysterical defeatism that was almost as unreasonable as the hysterical optimism of the year before. October had seen a stock panic. But May registered the realization that Humpty-Dumpty had actually tumbled off the wall—and that we did not know how to put him together again.

American prosperity had traditionally been attributed by respectable opinion to three agencies—God, hard work and Republican policies. We still had the Republican policies; presumably we still enjoyed the divine favor; so we proposed to settle down to work hard once more. But something went wrong. Men who wanted to go back to work found, all too often, that there was no work to go back to; men who had work, who were producing something, found no place to sell it. People began to realize that work, in and by itself, could not be counted on to produce anything but fatigue. The basic cause of the slump of 1930 lay in the fact that we and the whole world can make more than we can use. Work may still be an indispensable ingredient in the recipe for prosperity, but you must mix something else with it if you want a prosperity that will stick. Something, perhaps, not yet discovered.

Hence the gloom that enveloped business last summer. People began to remember that, as James Truslow Adams lately observed, "over and over again in the past the problems of government have become so complicated that no one was able to solve them." The Roman Empire, for example, broke down because it grew so large and complex that the Romans did not know how to make it work. Men have wondered, lately, if our own economic and political machine has not similarly outstripped the grasp of the human mind.

That is defeatism, and probably unwarranted defeatism. But it is true that the situation has outstripped the mental powers of most of us.

We can only wait while men with superior brains, the world over, try to think their way out; while they try to devise some method not only of reviving business—it is certain to revive, eventually—but of making sure that when it has been revived, it will not run headlong into the same old business cycle. And it seems to me a mark of great good sense that the average man in the United States seems to have decided that the best thing to do was to have as good a time as possible, as cheaply as possible, till things took a better turn.

Other nations have done that. Herodotus, for example, says of the Lydians, "In the reign of Atys there was a terrible famine throughout their country. Then it was that they invented dice, and knuckle bones, and hall games. And having invented these diversions—every other day they would play games all day long, so as not to have to hunt for something to eat; and on the intervening days they played no games but ate instead. Thus they got along for 18 years."

The Lydians, you note, were a resourceful and philosophic people. Why didn't they work? No doubt they did, until they saw that, under those weather conditions, the hardest work brought nothing. Then they showed rare good judgment in finding harmless occupations that would enable them to forget their troubles till business picked up again.

So with us. If we cannot find bread, we are satisfied with the circus. Revolutions and political upheavals are not our style. And perhaps miniature golf has done its part, and a large part, in carrying us past a crisis.

Originally published in the January 1931 issue of *Reader's Digest* magazine.

Our America

The Cookout
—C.F. PAYNE
SEPTEMBER 2005

Unfinished Business

On April 18, 1955, just hours after Albert Einstein's death, a *Life* magazine photographer captured the Nobel laureate's office in Princeton, New Jersey. "This is the photo that changed my life," says Michio Kaku, theoretical physicist and author of *Einstein's Cosmos*. "As a child of eight, I was fascinated that on his desk were the unfinished notes of his 'theory of everything.' I decided then and there that I would try to finish it. This, to me, was greater than any adventure story."

Photograph by Ralph Morse/ Time & Life Pictures/ Getty Images

"I Think We've Lost Them"

by Michael Cabbage and William Harwood,
from the book *Comm Check...*

The space shuttle Columbia *was on track for a triumphant homecoming when Mission Control lost contact with the crew.*

Plunging back to earth after a 16-day mission, the space shuttle *Columbia* streaked through the darkness at almost five miles per second, eight times faster than a bullet from an M-16 assault rifle.

No one was better qualified to bring *Columbia* home than Commander Rick Husband, a 45-year-old Air Force colonel. Data tapes charting his every move at the controls of NASA's shuttle training aircraft were frequently used to show other pilots how to make a textbook approach and landing. Even still, Husband avoided the macho image in which many astronauts reveled, and he went out of his way to make personal contact with engineers and technicians who were the shuttle's keepers.

As he prepared *Columbia* for entry, Husband chatted easily with his crewmates. Husband's rookie copilot, William McCool, was a boyish-looking Navy commander with an engaging grin. An Eagle Scout from San Diego, the 41-year-old pilot was, in the words of his wife, Lani, "an incredibly passionate person. Whether it was running through trails in forestlands, flying at low level or reading a bedtime story to one of our boys, he never took anything in life for granted."

Seated behind Husband and McCool was 41-year-old flight engineer Kalpana Chawla. Chawla enjoyed acrobatics in open-cockpit biplanes and frequently took friends aloft for dizzying spins above Texas. Her interest in flying dated back to her childhood in Karnal, India, a small town with an active airport and flying club. Now on her second shuttle mission, Chawla was a role model for women in her home country.

The fourth person on the flight deck was mission specialist Laurel Clark. The 41-year-old physician made time with her family a priority. Her eight-year-old son, Iain, had not wanted his mother to fly on the shuttle. Just two months before, he, his parents and the family dog had survived a harrowing crash in his father's single-engine plane. The experience haunted him. During a family video conference in late January, while *Columbia* was in space, Iain asked his mother, "Why did you go?"

"He had a premonition he was going to die, to burn up in space."

Strapped into a seat on the split-level crew cabin's lower deck was payload commander Michael Anderson, 43, a lieutenant colonel in the Air Force and one of only a handful of African American astronauts at NASA. It was his job to oversee the scores of scientific experiments scheduled to be conducted during the shuttle's mission. Like all astronauts, Anderson was aware of the risk of a shuttle flight, and had told a former pastor not to be concerned if he didn't make it back. "Don't worry about me. I'm just going on higher."

Seated near Anderson was 48-year-old Israeli colonel Ilan Ramon. As a fighter pilot in the Israeli air force, he helped lead a daring 1981 bombing raid that reduced an unfinished Iraqi nuclear reactor to rubble. At the viewing site at the Kennedy Space Center, a group of Israeli journalists were waiting, along with Rona Ramon and the couple's four children.

Even in the world of superachieving astronauts, mission specialist Dave Brown stood out: a former circus acrobat and varsity gymnast, a Navy flight surgeon and aviator who graduated first in his class in

Columbia's crew, their different colored shirts indicating their shifts on the mission, pose for a weightless group shot. Counterclockwise from left: Chawla, Husband, Clark, Ramon, Anderson, McCool and Brown.

pilot training. Brown, 46, was the only single member of the crew; his constant companion was his aging Labrador retriever, Duggins. While Brown was as outwardly enthusiastic as the rest of the crew, he had told a few people that he wasn't sure he would make it back to Earth. "He had a premonition he was going to die, to burn up in space," astronaut training manager Darla Racz said.

Now, mere minutes from home, Brown had little reason for concern. In the 111 previous space shuttle reentries, there had never been a catastrophic "in-flight anomaly," as NASA refers to out-of-the-ordinary events. The only disaster in the history of the program, the *Challenger* explosion, had occurred during launch.

* * *

At Florida's Kennedy Space Center, a joyful mood had settled in. A crowd of VIPs, NASA managers and reporters occupied bleachers in the midfield viewing site, and the astronauts' families gathered at a set of bleachers cordoned off from the other guests. Astronauts were assigned to each family to answer questions and provide any needed assistance.

After hours of tense meetings, the team determined that the foam strike posed no risk to the shuttle's safe return.

It was 8:44 a.m. Eastern time on February 1, 2003, and just west of Hawaii, *Columbia* was descending through 400,000 feet.

In Mission Control at the Johnson Space Center in Houston, a huge screen showed *Columbia*'s location on a map. The shuttle was right on course. But as *Columbia* streaked toward the California-Nevada border, mechanical systems officer Jeff Kling noticed something unusual in the flow of data appearing on his computer screen. Downward-pointing arrows appeared beside readings from sensors measuring hydraulic fluid temperatures in the shuttle's left wing.

Concerned, Kling notified flight director LeRoy Cain. Cain's thoughts flashed back to *Columbia*'s launch 16 days ago. A briefcase-sized piece of foam insulation had broken away from the shuttle's 15-story external fuel tank almost 82 seconds after liftoff and slammed into the left wing. An unsettling thought crossed Cain's mind. Was the loss of the left-wing temperature sensors related to the insulation hit?

Linda Ham, chairwoman of the Mission Management Team, was also worried about the foam strike. When shuttle managers had viewed tapes of the liftoff, they saw the debris smash into the ship's left wing, producing a spectacular shower of particles. But they couldn't be sure what the particles consisted of: Were they foam, ice or bits of the special material designed to protect *Columbia* from the fierce heat of reentry?

The sight had felt horribly familiar to the NASA staffers. Seconds after the shuttle *Atlantis* had lifted off in October 2002, foam had broken free from the external fuel tank at a similar location and hit one of the shuttle's twin rocket boosters. Examination of the recovered booster showed that the foam had struck close to a critical electronics box. Had the box been disabled, the result could have been catastrophic.

Damage to a shuttle from flying debris was something that had concerned NASA for years. The official agency guidelines laid out the requirements clearly: "The Space Shuttle System shall be designed to preclude the shedding of ice and/or other debris from the Shuttle elements." But shuttle managers, after trying various unsuccessful measures to prevent the foam shedding, had deemed the situation "an accepted risk."

During the time that *Columbia* had been in orbit, engineers had conducted intense analyses of the possible damage, using a computer program originally designed to predict the threat to spacecraft from tiny rock fragments in space. The formula had later been modified to assess damage from foam, ice and other debris, but no tests had been done with larger pieces of foam like the chunk that hit *Columbia*. When estimates of the size, trajectory and impact site of the latest foam strike were loaded into the computer program, the model calculated that the strike would have penetrated completely through *Columbia*'s heat tiles. That meant that the wing's vulnerable aluminum airframe could be exposed to temperatures well above its melting point during reentry.

However, after hours of tense meetings, the Mission Management Team went with the opinion of some analysts that the computer program "was designed to be conservative due to large number of unknowns" and "reports damage for test conditions that show no damage." The bottom line: The foam strike posed no risk to *Columbia*'s safe return.

In just three minutes, the shuttle would be moving out of the zone of maximum heat buildup. There was reason to hope that all was well.

Suddenly Rick Husband called down, his first query since *Columbia* had entered Earth's atmosphere 15 minutes earlier. "And, uh, Hou …" he began. His transmission was cut off. Such dropouts were not unusual during reentry as the shuttle banked left and right, its big vertical fin occasionally blocking signals from reaching a communications satellite stationed over the western Pacific.

A few seconds later, Jeff Kling saw more down arrows appear on his computer screen, this time signaling a loss of data from the shuttle's left main landing-gear tires. His heart sunk. "We just lost tire pressure on the left outboard and left inboard, both tires," he told Cain.

Astronaut Charles Hobaugh, the ground flight controller responsible for talking directly to the shuttle crew, heard Kling's report to Cain and promptly radioed Husband: "*Columbia* ... we see your tire pressure message and we did not copy your last." Seconds later, Husband made another attempt to contact Mission Control, replying to Hobaugh with "Roger, uh, buh ..." Again the transmission was cut off and, along with it, the flow of data from the shuttle.

Much of the crowd in Florida was oblivious to the drama unfolding in Mission Control. But a few reporters huddled around a television set inside the runway's public affairs building had noticed something odd. On the big map broadcast by NASA Television, the red triangle representing the ship had inexplicably stopped moving over central Texas.

Back at Johnson, Hobaugh radioed Husband: "*Columbia*, Houston, comm check." There was no reply.

The shuttle had now been out of communication for nearly five minutes. At the runway, cell phones started ringing. Sean O'Keefe, NASA's administrator, was standing next to William Readdy, a former shuttle commander and the top manager for manned missions. He heard Readdy say, "This is not right, something is not right." Readdy was trembling, his face ashen.

At the north end of the runway, astronaut Jerry Ross got word that *Columbia* had not been picked up on radar approaching Florida. He knew what that meant. He started calling the family escorts at the midfield viewing site. "We think we've lost the vehicle," Ross said. "We need to get the families rounded up and send them back to crew quarters as soon as you can. Don't say anything."

Evelyn Husband and her children, Laura, 12, and Matthew, 7, were

There was comfort in these salvaged images of reentry, shot by Laurel Clark. They show Chawla and Husband (top, from left); Clark (center); and McCool and Husband (bottom) busy and upbeat in their final moments. The tape ended before any hint of trouble.

awaiting the sonic booms that would herald *Columbia*'s arrival. The two distinct booms, caused by the shape of the shuttle's wings, usually arrived about two minutes before touchdown. Later Evelyn told the Amarillo *Globe-News*, "I asked what direction the boom would come from and our [astronaut] assistant had the most horrible look on his face." Evelyn called her father on her cell phone. "He was crying," she told the Amarillo newspaper. "I asked him if it looked bad. He said yes."

* * *

Hundreds of miles away, in Hemphill, Texas, 59-year-old Roger Coday heard a crackling, ground-shaking roar. Coday, an industrial engineer and Vietnam-era veteran, instinctively dropped to the ground beside his mobile home as his wife, Jeannie, screamed, "What was that?"

His face was ashen. "This is not right. Something is not right."

The roaring lasted more than a minute. "It was just a continuous sonic boom," said Coday. "I ran on around the corner of the house and then I saw the vapor trails."

Meanwhile, Jeannie Coday had turned on a television and learned that NASA had lost contact with the shuttle. The couple soon realized the noise might have had something to do with *Columbia*.

After NASA was contacted, search teams located remains of all seven shuttle fliers within a few miles of Coday's home. On February 5, the remains were flown to Dover Air Force Base in Delaware. An honor guard stood by as the flag-draped caskets were carried off an Air Force transport. It was a painful moment for NASA.

In the week of memorials, Robert Crippen, one of the pilots on *Columbia*'s maiden voyage, offered a moving tribute to the lost spacecraft, a machine many at Kennedy had spent decades maintaining.

"*Columbia* was hardly a thing of beauty, except to those of us who loved and cared for her," Crippen remarked. "She was often bad-mouthed for being a little heavy in the rear end. But many of us can relate to that. Many said she was old and past her prime. Still, she had a great many missions ahead of her. There is heavy grief in our hearts, which will diminish with time, but it will never go away and we won't ever forget."

Amateur photographer Dr. Scott Lieberman captured this image of the catastrophe taking place over Tyler, Texas.

"Hail, Rick, Willie, KC, Michael, Laurel, Dave and Ilan. Hail *Columbia*."

While the families and the public mourned, the newly formed *Columbia* Accident Investigation Board (CAIB) and a huge team of NASA and contractor engineers and others kicked off an around-the-clock effort to find out what had gone wrong. It was a daunting task. The spacecraft broke apart around 39 miles up, traveling 18 times the speed of sound, and the wreckage was spread across a vast area. It would not be an easy search, and it would not be quick. But there was a sense of urgency. One of the shuttle program's primary missions had been to serve the orbiting space station. The three-man crew then aboard the space station were nearing the end of their normal tour of duty. NASA had planned to launch a replacement crew aboard the shuttle *Atlantis* a month after *Columbia*'s landing to bring Ken Bowersox, Don Pettit and Nikolai Budarin back to Earth after three and a half months in space. (Bowersox and company wound up waiting until May 2003, when a Russian craft ferried them home.)

One week after the disaster, searchers Carl Vita and Marty Pontecorvo were called to an address near Palestine, Texas. The residents

Taken from below as Columbia streaked toward Texas, this photo shows a deformity in the shuttle's left wing and an unusual plume trailing behind it.

weren't home, but they had placed a small American flag by the foot-long piece of aluminum shuttle wreckage in their yard. As Vita, a technician with United Space Alliance at Kennedy, and Pontecorvo, a senior NASA engineer, walked back to their truck, they spotted what looked like a discarded tape cassette in the dirt by the road. It was wider than a normal audiocassette, and the plastic case had only one visible reel. "It'll probably turn out to be Waylon Jennings or Merle Haggard, and the lab guys will get a kick out of it," said Vita.

Their jaws dropped when they learned that the tape contained 13 minutes of footage of the reentry shot by astronaut Clark. It was a final glimpse of the four crew members on *Columbia*'s flight deck—Husband, McCool, Chawla and Clark—all in good spirits and looking forward to landing. The video ended more than a minute before the first signs of trouble. Many saw that as a blessing for the families. "They were still living large and having a great time," said astronaut Jerry Ross.

On March 19, Art Baker, a firefighter from Florida, was walking a search line over hilly terrain near Hemphill. He saw a square metal box, painted black, about the size of two or three pizza boxes stacked on top of one another. It was lying flat on the ground and appeared to be in pristine condition. It was *Columbia*'s modular auxiliary data system (MADS) recorder, an item near the top of a list of high-priority objects. In one of those breaks that defy explanation, the device had survived *Columbia*'s disintegration, fallen 39 miles and landed intact.

Columbia's MADS recorder was the most elaborate in the shuttle fleet; had the disaster befallen any of the other orbiters, the cause might never have been known. But the 28-track tape from the doomed spacecraft gave investigators the data they needed to determine that a breach had occurred in the leading edge of the left wing, where some people believed the foam had struck. Still, doubts remained about whether a small piece of lightweight material could have done such damage.

To resolve the issue, NASA conducted tests, using a powerful nitrogen-gas-powered cannon used to fire rubber projectiles at various aircraft components to test resistance to bird strikes and similar unexpected collisions. On July 7, a block of foam weighing 1.67 pounds—the approximate size of the chunk that had struck *Columbia*—was fired at a panel from the wing of shuttle *Atlantis* at 530 mph, the speed at which engineers had calculated it had likely hit. To the crowd of reporters and NASA officials looking on from a safe distance, the foam's path was too swift to see. But the results were instantly obvious. A ragged 16-inch-wide hole appeared on the lower side of the panel. The crowd gasped.

Few had any remaining doubts about the cause of the tragedy. As flight director Paul Hill put it, "The most complicated machine we have ever built got knocked out of the sky by a pound and a half of foam."

On August 26, the CAIB unveiled its report. After pinpointing the foam strike as the physical cause of the accident, the panel took aim at the larger culture that had allowed such a known safety problem to go unchecked. "The accident was probably not an anomalous, random event," it said, "but rather likely rooted to some degree in NASA's history and the human space flight program's culture." The report cited "reliance on past success as a substitute for sound engineering practices (such as testing to understand why systems were not performing in accordance with requirements); organizational barriers that prevented effective communication of critical safety information; and stifled professional differences of opinion." In short, NASA had a "broken safety culture."

The CAIB had decided early on to dodge the question of accountability and punishment, leaving that to the space agency. No heads rolled; by the time the report came out, NASA had already reassigned some of the senior managers on the *Columbia* mission to other jobs. Diane Vaughan, a consultant to the CAIB, expressed the opinion that it might not be a bad thing for these people to remain in the organization. "It keeps the institutional memory alive of what happened," she said.

NASA then began the hard work of fixing the problems the report had spotlighted. In the meantime, shuttle missions were put on hold.

One painful question that lingered throughout the investigation was what, if anything, could have been done to save the astronauts if the damage done by the foam strike had been understood early on. The CAIB called for a study of repair and rescue scenarios. Repair was deemed to be "very difficult with a low probability of success." Rescue by the shuttle *Atlantis* was considered to be theoretically possible, but very, very risky.

Frank Buzzard, director of the task force that operated as a liaison between the CAIB and NASA, summed up the feelings of many when he said, "I am not sure we would have committed that next shuttle [to a rescue effort]. Two of the last three had had foam come off [at launch]. But the fact that we didn't try made us feel like we let them down."

Shuttle commander Eileen Collins had been scheduled to fly the first post-*Columbia* mission aboard *Atlantis* at the beginning of March. Collins, an Air Force colonel and former test pilot, was NASA's first female shuttle pilot and the first woman to serve as commander, carrying a $1.5 billion X-ray telescope into orbit aboard *Columbia* in July 1999.

Just six weeks before *Columbia* blasted off on its final voyage, Collins decided it was time to have a talk with her daughter.

"She had just turned seven," Collins recalled. "I said, 'Bridget, have you ever heard about the space shuttle *Challenger* accident?' And she said, 'No, Mom.' So I said, 'OK, I am going to tell you about it. I want you to know this from me before you hear it from someone at school.'

"I got out a picture of the accident," Collins said. "I told her this will never happen again, because it has been fixed."

Originally published in the March 2004 issue of *Reader's Digest* magazine.

On January 6, 2004, NASA administrator Sean O'Keefe announced that the rover Spirit's *Mars landing site would be named* Columbia *Memorial Station, in honor of the seven lost astronauts.*

My Dog Reviews the Furniture

by Andy Simmons

Hudson Simmons gives Andy's House three-and-a-half stars.

I had just spent a busy afternoon barking at motorcycles, lunging at joggers and digging holes in the backyard, so I was famished when I sat down for dinner. Luckily, the proprietor of Andy's House does not skimp on portions, offering entire banisters, whole couches and the complete American Girl doll collection.

Unable to control myself, I first attacked the cold antipasti plate: an exciting assortment of remote controls, lamp cords and children's art projects. The remotes were crisp and enthralling, with a touch of maple syrup from when the owner's daughter clutched them at breakfast. Inside was the real treat: two AA batteries (Eveready, not store brand!), which I swallowed whole, a delightful departure from the chewy lamp cords. That dish's saving grace? It was served still plugged in to the outlet, the electricity adding a much-needed dash of spice. The kids' art projects were light and simple, though the diorama of a Native American village did lodge in my throat. After a few minutes of retching, the tepee came up, and I promptly gobbled it up again. It was just as good the second time around. It was now time to dig in to the next course.

Great-Grandma's Heirloom Wing Chair was aged to perfection. Shards of wood tore easily from its back, exposing Egyptian cotton filling and tufting threads, both of which maintained their aura of faded splendor all the way down. This was Chef Andy's mic drop.

I moved on to the comfortingly thick and tasty Leg of Table. I like my table legs pine, bathed in a rich, dark stain. Thus was the case with the Amish Mission Table from Macy's au Jus. This dish is served in a reduced mahogany varnish, its flavor both deep and long, with extraordinary balance, no gamy edge, and only a few splinters left in my gums. Fortuitously, Andy's House offers an extensive drinks menu with which to wash down the shards. After passing on the overwatered fern, I stopped at the fish tank. This was self-serve, so with a gentle nudge on the stand, the water poured out, along with the gravel, air-filtration system, fake scuba diver, real fish and the 50-gallon tank itself, a heady brew enlivened by algae extract.

For dessert, I had the rug. The rayon fibers were al dente, just how I like them. One downside—it was bland, as Sam's Club rugs tend to be. Fortunately, my dining partner, Chester the beagle, had rolled in something dead only minutes earlier and thoughtfully seasoned the meal.

If there is a drawback to Andy's House, it's the service. I can't say I enjoyed having my nose swatted after each course. Nor was I pleased to

be torn away from the sumptuous, palate-cleansing first edition *Adventures of Huckleberry Finn* and dumped in the yard. But that won't keep me from returning for the restaurant's inaugural theme meal: Hawaiian Shirt Night—all you can eat.

Originally published in the October 2016 issue of *Reader's Digest* magazine.

Our America

Street Fare
—C.F. PAYNE
AUGUST 2004

FACES OF AMERICA

Putting On a Brave Face

Civil War reenactor Wolfgang Landers of Dublin, Virginia, explains, "What I respect most about the soldiers who fought the American Civil War is their bravery. Think about it: You were told to march across an open field and open fire, and if you ran, you were shot. You had to be pretty brave to do that."

Photograph by Glenn Glasser

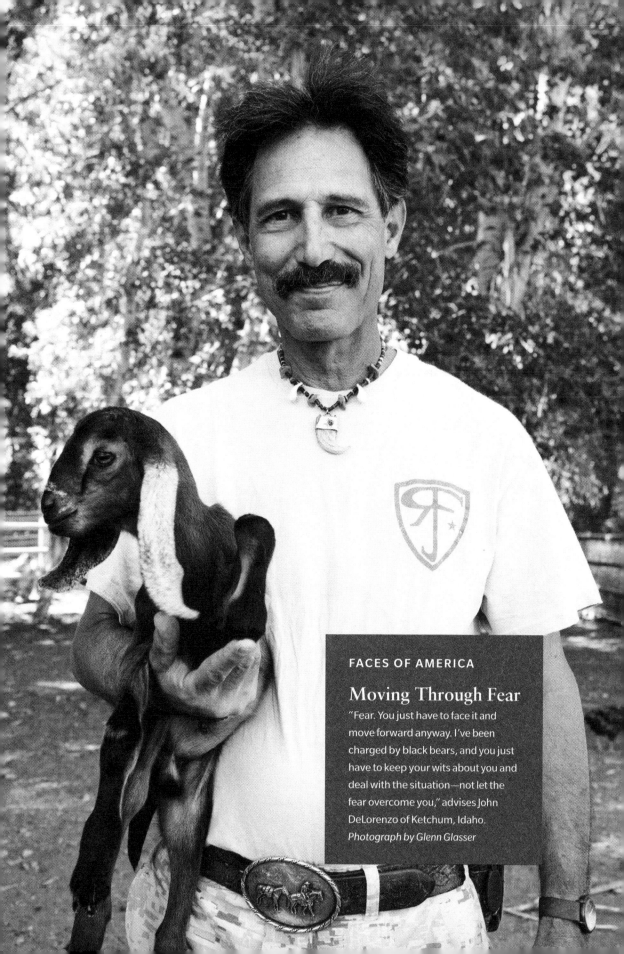

Moving Through Fear

"Fear. You just have to face it and move forward anyway. I've been charged by black bears, and you just have to keep your wits about you and deal with the situation—not let the fear overcome you," advises John DeLorenzo of Ketchum, Idaho.

Photograph by Glenn Glasser

Why I Remain a Negro

by Walter White, from *The Saturday Review of Literature*

An activist's autobiography opens with a statement of unusual power—and faith— in this provocative declaration of identity.

Not long ago I stood on a subway platform in Harlem. As the train came in I stepped back. My heel came down on the toes of the man behind me and I turned to apologize. He was a Negro; his face was hard and full of the piled-up bitterness of a thousand lynchings and a million nights in tenements and "nigger towns." "Why don't you look where you're going?" he said sullenly. "You white folks are always trampling on colored people."

Just then one of my friends came up and spoke to me. The man on whose toes I had stepped listened, then asked: "Are you Walter White of the Association for the Advancement of Colored People? I'm sorry I spoke to you that way. I thought you were white."

I realize that the only characteristic which matters to either race—the appearance of whiteness—is mine. My skin is white, my eyes are blue, my hair is blond. The traits of my race are nowhere visible upon me. Yet nothing within my heart tempts me to think that I am white.

Walter White, an early activist in the NAACP, stands by the rails of a ship.

Every year approximately 12,000 white-skinned Negroes disappear—people whose absence cannot be explained by death or emigration. Nearly every one of the 14 million discernible Negroes in the United States knows at least one member of his race who is "passing"—the magic word which means that a Negro can get by as white, and escape the humiliation which the American color line imposes on him. Many marry white people; sometimes they tell their husbands or wives of their Negro blood, sometimes not. Who are they? Mostly people of little importance, but many have achieved success in business, the professions, the arts and sciences—including a few members of Congress and several organizers of movements to "keep the Negroes and other minorities in their places." Some of the most vehement public haters of Negroes are themselves secretly Negroes.

Why, then, do I insist that I am a Negro, when nothing compels me to do so but myself? An experience in my childhood may help explain.

I stood with my father, a mail carrier, and watched Negroes, male and female, killed by mobs in the streets of Atlanta. The next night the mob, perhaps 5,000 strong, entered the Negro section near our modest home. The whites resented our prosperity; so at times did the Negroes. The Negroes resented our white skin and the ethical standards which my parents maintained and required of their children.

My father was deeply religious, opposed to physical violence. Never before had there been guns in our house, but now, at the insistence of friends, we were armed. As we watched the mob go by, their distorted faces weird in the light of the torches—faces made grotesque and ugly by hate—my father said, "Don't shoot until the first man puts his foot on the lawn. Then don't miss."

A voice cried out, the voice of the son of our neighborhood grocer: "Let's burn the house of the nigger mail carrier! It's too nice for a nigger to live in!"

In the flickering light the mob swayed, paused and began to flow toward us. In that instant there opened up within me a great awareness; I knew then who I was. I was colored, a human being with an invisible pigmentation which marked me a person to be hunted, abused, discriminated against, kept in poverty and ignorance, in order that those whose skin was white would have readily at hand a proof of their superiority. It made no difference how intelligent or talented I might be or how virtuously I lived. A curse like that of Judas was upon me.

The mob moved toward the lawn. I tried to aim my gun, wondering what it would feel like to kill a man. Suddenly there was a volley of shots. The mob hesitated, stopped. Some friends of my father's had barricaded themselves in a building just below our house. It was they who had fired. Some of the mobsmen shouted, "Let's go get the nigger." Our friends fired another volley. The mob retreated up the street.

In the quiet that followed, a tension different from anything I had ever known possessed me. I was sick with loathing for the hatred which had flared before me and come so close to making me a killer; but I was glad I was not one of those made murderous by pride. I was glad I was not one of those whose history is a record of bloodshed, rapine and pillage. I was glad to be of a race that had not fully awakened, and which therefore still had the opportunity to write a record of virtue.

Years later, when my father lay dying in a dingy, cockroach-infested Jim Crow ward in an Atlanta hospital, he put it into words for me and my brother.

"Human kindness, decency, love—whatever you wish to call it," he said, "is the only real thing in the world. It's up to you and others like you to use your education and talents to make love as positive an emotion in the world as are prejudice and hate. That's the only way the world can save itself. No matter what happens, you must love, not hate." Then he died. He had been struck by a car driven by a reckless driver—one of the hospital doctors.

I have remembered that when, sitting in the gallery of the House or the Senate, I have heard members of our Congress spill vilification on the Negroes. I remembered it when, in the Pacific, where I went as a war correspondent, a white officer from the South told me that the 93rd Division, a Negro unit, had been given an easy beachhead to take at Bougainville, and had broken and run under fire. I presented the facts to him. Bougainville was invaded in November 1943. The 93rd was ordered there in April 1944.

I remembered my father's words when I talked with my nephew for the last time, as he lay in a bitterly cold, rain-drenched tent on the edge of an airfield near Naples. He, like me, could have passed for a white man. By sacrifice and labor his parents provided him with a college education. He won a master's degree in economics, and the next day enlisted in the Army Air Corps, as a Negro. He went to the segregated field at Tuskegee, Alabama.

He hated war. But he believed that Hitler and Mussolini represented the kind of hate he had seen exhibited in Georgia by the Ku Klux Klan and degenerate political demagogues. He believed that the war would bring all of that hate to an end.

He was a fighter pilot. He fought well. Over Anzio he was shot down, bailing out and escaping with his right leg broken in two places. He was offered an opportunity to return home but refused. Later, returning from a bomber escort mission, his plane was hit by antiaircraft fire, and struck a tree and burst into flames. That was the end of one of the men described as "utter and dismal failures in combat in Europe."

Suppose the skin of every Negro in America were suddenly to turn white. What would happen to all the notions about Negroes on which race prejudice is built? What would become of the Negroes' presumed shiftlessness, alleged cowardice, dishonesty, stupidity and body odor? Would they not then be subject to individual judgment as are whites? How else could they be judged?

Once on a Harlem subway I fell into conversation with a white man who as usual thought I was white too. "This used to be a pleasant line to ride on," he said. "But now there are too many Negroes. They smell."

"Suppose you and I had to do the same work Negroes are forced to do because they are Negroes—on the docks or over a hot kitchen stove," I replied, "would we be odorless, particularly if forced to live in crowded tenements because we were Negroes? Would we reek like lilies of the valley? Do you imagine the manufacture of deodorants is exclusively for a Negro market? I notice that the advertisements invariably feature a young and beautiful girl—a white girl."

The man looked at me with amazement. "You're the first white man I've ever heard talk like that."

During the early part of the war, a plant manufacturing a secret war machine refused to hire Negroes but did hire persons of German descent. Most of these were loyal, but a few were arrested by the FBI for stealing the secret and convicted. But it was too late. Germany got the information and then passed it on to Japan. Nevertheless, one of the company officials told a friend: "I'd close down the plant rather than hire niggers."

I recall with uneasiness the grimness on a Negro soldier's face when he told me, one day in the Pacific, "Our fight for freedom will start the day we arrive in San Francisco."

There are times when I have felt with a sweep of fear that the patience of the colored man is close to its end. I remember how I felt when I stood beside my father and knew that the whites would not let me live, that I must kill them first and then be killed. Yet I know there is no reason for this killing, this hatred, this demarcation. There is no difference between them. Black is white and white is black. When one shoots the other he kills his reflection. Only hate, the negative force, can separate them; only love, the positive force, can bind them together.

I am one of the two in the color of my skin; I am the other in my spirit and my heart. I love one for the fight it has made to conquer the sins it has committed—and conquer them, in great degree, it has. I love the other for its patience and sorrows, for the soft sound of its singing, and for the great dawn which is coming upon it, in which its vigor and faith will serve the common aims of civilization.

Originally published in the January 1948 issue of *Reader's Digest* magazine.

Walter White started working as an undercover investigator for the National Association for the Advancement of Colored People (NAACP) in 1918, passing as white to join Ku Klux Klan groups and expose those involved in lynchings. From 1929 to 1955, he led the organization as executive secretary. This story is the introductory chapter to his auto-biography, A Man Called White.

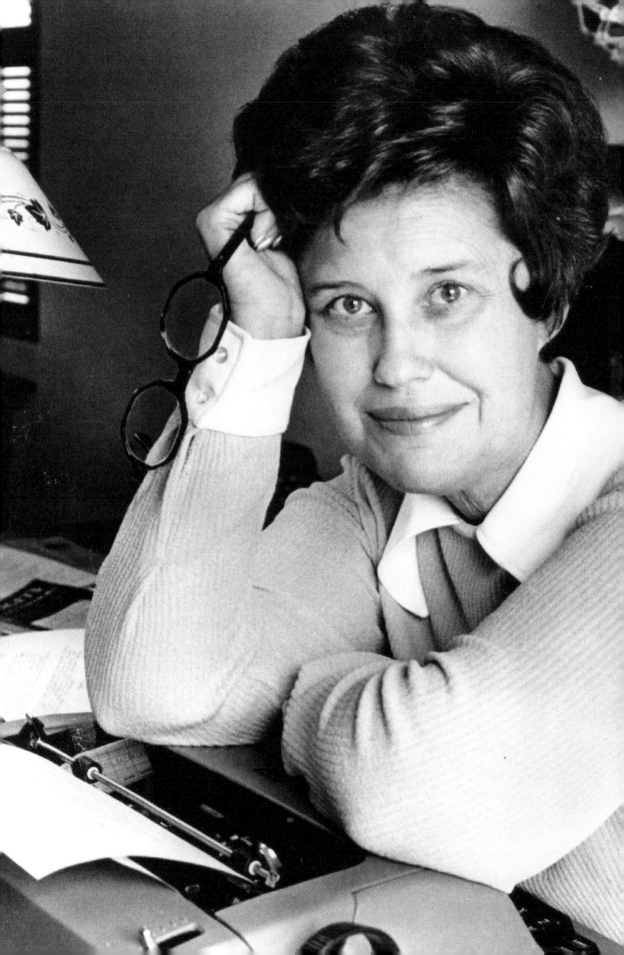

If Life Is a Bowl of Cherries— What Am I Doing in the Pits?

by Erma Bombeck

Here is the latest battle report from
suburbia's favorite housewife.

I've always worried a lot, and frankly I'm good at it. I worry about a snake coming up through the kitchen drain. I worry about getting into the *Guinness Book of World Records* under "Pregnancy: Oldest Recorded Birth." I worry about what the dog will think when he sees me getting out of the shower. But these days I worry most about the family—about its survival in a world that changes daily.

Foremost of the villains that rip the American family to shreds is Education. Before the New Math, for example, I had a mysterious aura about me. I never said anything, but my children were convinced that I had invented fire. Then we began to have "input" with one another, and one day my daughter said to me, "Mamma, what's a variable?"

"It's a weirdo who hangs around the playground. Where did you read that word? On a restroom wall?"

"It's in my New Math book," she said. "I was hoping you could help me." She went to her room and locked her door, and I never saw her again until after she graduated.

The metric system is no better. Once a child knows that a square millimeter is 0.002 square inch, will he ever respect a mother who once measured the bathroom for carpeting and had enough left over to slip-cover New Jersey?

And what modern-day mother isn't intimidated when she has to communicate with a child's teacher? Nothing makes my morning like a kid looking up from his cereal and saying casually, "I gotta have a note saying I was sick or my teacher won't let me back into school."

"I suppose it has to be written on paper," I asked, slumping miserably over the bologna.

"The one you wrote on waxed paper she couldn't read. But if you can't find paper, I could stay home for another day."

I tore a piece of wallpaper off the wall and said, "Get a pencil." After a 15-minute search, we finally found a stub in the lint trap of the dryer.

"Dear Mrs. Weems," I wrote. "Please excuse Brucie from school yesterday. He complained of stomach cramps and ..."

"Cross out stomach cramps," he ordered. "The last time you wrote that she put me next to the door and kept her eyes on me all day long."

"OK, then, get me the dictionary and turn to the D's."

He looked over my shoulder. "What does d-i-a-r-r-h-e-a mean?"

"It means you sit by the door again," I said, licking the envelope.

To me, modern education is a contradiction. It is like your daughter going to college and taking all your linens, furniture, TV set and car, and then saying, "I've got to get away from your shallow materialism."

My kids always talk a great game of ecology. Yet they harbor the No. 1 pollutant in this country: gym clothes. A pair of shorts, a shirt and a pair of gym shoes walked into the utility room under their own steam last Wednesday and leaned helplessly against the wall. As I stood there watching, a pot of ivy shriveled and died before my eyes.

If Life Is a Bowl of Cherries— What Am I Doing in the Pits?

Blinking back the tears, I yelled to my son, "How long has it been since these clothes have been washed?"

"Since the beginning of the school year," he shouted back.

"What school year?"

"'74–'75."

There are other aspects of children for which I profess complete ignorance. For example: Who is "I. Dunno"?

Ever since I can remember, our home has harbored a fourth child—I. Dunno. Everyone sees him but me. All I know is he's rotten.

Who left the front door open?

I. Dunno.

Who let the soap melt down the drain?

I. Dunno.

Frankly, I. Dunno is driving me nuts. He's lost four pairs of boots and a bicycle. Once, he left a thermos of milk in the car for three weeks.

I firmly believe kids don't want your understanding. They want your trust, your blinding love and your car keys. And not in that order. But try to understand them and you're in big trouble.

I have never understood, for example, how a child can climb up on the roof and rescue the cat, yet cannot walk down the hall without grabbing both walls with his grubby hands for balance. Or how a child can kiss the dog yet refuse to drink from a glass his brother has just used.

Child raising can be summed up in one word: frustration. Take the car incident. My oldest used my car last week while hers was in the garage being fixed. The day her car came back, she returned my keys and said, "Hey, Mom, you owe me three dollars for the gas I put in your car."

I could not believe it. These words were uttered by a child down whom I had poured $887 worth of vitamins. For whom I footed the bill for 186 skin preparations to kill a single pimple.

Then I remembered a letter that a teenager had written me after reading one of my books. Maybe that would get through to my daughter.

"Listen to this," I said, reading from the letter. "Parents go through life saying to their children, 'I've worked my fingers to the bone for you and what do I get in return?'"

"'You want an answer, Mrs. Bombeck? You get messy rooms and raided refrigerators. You get something else, too. You get someone who loves you but never takes the time to tell you in words. Someone who'll defend you at every turn even though you do wear orthopedic socks.

"'And when we leave home, there will be a little tug at our hearts because we know we will miss home and all it meant. But most of all, we will miss the constant assurances of how very much you love us.'"

My daughter looked up. Her eyes were misty. "Does that mean I don't get the three bucks?" she asked.

When you're an orthodox worrier, some days are worse than others. But not even a professional pessimist would believe what I went through last week.

It began on Monday morning. The kids filed into the kitchen completely dressed. I asked, "Who wants something pressed before school?" No one spoke! Then my car with the new battery actually started. I found a parking place in front of the supermarket and got a cart with four wheels that all went in the same direction at the same time.

All of this made me feel edgy, but I figured things soon would get back to normal. They didn't.

On Thursday I ran for a bus and made it. The Avon lady refused me service, saying I already looked terrific. The checkbook balanced.

On Friday, I was inconsolable. "Things were never meant to go this well," I said to my husband, sobbing into a dish towel. "I'm worried."

"Now, now," he said, patting my shoulder. "Things can't go rotten all the time."

"But this isn't like us," I whined. "The bad times I can handle. It's the good times that drive me crazy. When is the other shoe going to drop?"

Just then we heard a car turn into the garage, followed by the sickening scrape of a fender meeting a wall. We looked at each other and smiled.

Things were looking up.

Originally published in the July 1978 issue of *Reader's Digest* magazine.

Humor Hall of Fame

It's a problem that the machine I use to do my work also has a function where you can shop for a new duvet cover for three hours.

—@CAITIEDELANEY

I was visiting a friend who could not find her cordless phone.

After several minutes of searching, her young daughter said, "You know what they should invent? A phone that stays connected to its base so it never gets lost."

—MIRIAM SCOW

Footprints in the Snow

by Ty Gagne, from the *New Hampshire Union Leader*

She knew that the tracks ahead meant someone was in trouble. But she had no idea they would lead to a rescue mission that has become legendary.

Pam Bales left the firm pavement of Base Road and stepped onto snow-covered Jewell Trail. She planned a six-hour loop hike through New Hampshire's Mount Washington State Park. She had packed for almost every contingency and intended to walk alone.

A piece of paper on the dashboard of her Nissan Xterra detailed her itinerary: start up Jewell Trail, traverse the ridge south along Gulfside Trail, summit Mount Washington, follow Crawford Path down to Lakes of the Clouds Hut, descend Ammonoosuc Ravine Trail, and return to her car before some forecasted bad weather was scheduled to arrive. Bales always left her hiking plans in her car, as well as with two fellow volunteers on the Pemigewasset Valley Search and Rescue Team.

It was just before 8 a.m. on October 17, 2010. She'd checked the higher summits forecast posted by the Mount Washington Observatory before she left:

In the clouds w/a slight chance of showers. Highs: upper 20s; wind-chills 0–10. Winds: NW 50–70 mph increasing to 60–80 w/higher gusts.

Based on her experience, Bales knew that her hike was realistic. Besides, she had two contingency plans and extra layers of clothing to better regulate her core temperature as conditions changed; the observatory had described conditions on the higher summits as "full-on winter."

The hike up the lower portion of Jewell was pleasant. Bales felt excited as she walked up into snowy paths. At 8:30 a.m., still below the tree line, she stopped and took the first in a series of on-the-trail selfies; she was wearing a fleece tank top and hiking pants, and no gloves or hat because the air was mild and the sun was shining.

Less than an hour later, she took another photo, after she'd climbed into colder air and deeper snows. She now donned a quarter-zip fleece top and gloves. An opaque backdrop had replaced the sunshine, and snow shrouded the hemlock and birch.

She was still smiling. Above her, thick clouds overloaded with precipitation were dropping below Mount Washington's summit, where the temperature measured 24 degrees and the winds gusted about 50 mph.

At 10:30 a.m., the weather was showing its teeth. Bales added even more layers, including goggles and mountaineering mittens, to shield herself from the cold winds and dense fog. She made her way across the snow-covered ridge toward Mount Washington and began to think about calling it a day. Then she noticed something: a single set of footprints in the snow ahead of her. She had been following faint tracks all day and hadn't given them much thought, because so many people climb Jewell Trail. But these, she realized, had been made by a pair of sneakers. She silently scolded the absent hiker for violating normal safety rules and walked on.

By 11 a.m., Bales was getting cold, even though she was moving fast and generating some body heat. She put on an extra top under her shell jacket and locked down her face mask and goggles system. Good thing I packed heavy, she thought. She decided to abandon her plan. Summiting Washington was just an option. Returning to her SUV was a requirement.

Pam Bales took selfies at 8:30 a.m. (left) and 9:15 a.m. to document her climb up Jewell Trail on Mount Washington, which is known for its extreme weather swings.

Howling gusts of wind attacked her back and left side. The cloud cover had transitioned from canopy to the equivalent of quicksand, and the only thing keeping Bales on Gulfside Trail was the sneaker tracks in the snow. As she fought the wind and heavy sleet, her eyes searching for some type of shelter, the tracks made a hard left-hand turn off the trail.

Now she felt genuinely alarmed. She was sure the hiker could not navigate in the low visibility and was heading toward the challenging trails of the Great Gulf Wilderness. The temperature and clouds were in a race to find their lowest point. Darkness was hours away. If Bales followed the tracks, she'd add risk and time to the itinerary she'd already modified to manage both. But she could not let this go. She turned to the left and called out "Hello!" into the frozen fog. There was no response.

She called out again: "Is anybody out there? Do you need help?"

The strong westerly winds carried her voice away. She blew into her rescue whistle. For a fleeting moment she thought she heard someone reply, but it was just the wind playing games with her mind. She stood listening, then turned and walked cautiously in the direction of the single set of tracks. Her bailout route would have to wait.

* * *

Bales followed the tracks gingerly for 20 to 30 yards, struggling to remain upright. She rounded a slight corner and saw a man sitting motionless, cradled by large boulders. He stared in the direction of Great Gulf, the majesty of which could only be imagined in the horrendous visibility. She approached him and uttered, "Oh, hello."

He did not react. He wore tennis sneakers, shorts, a light jacket and fingerless gloves. His head was bare. He looked soaking wet. Thick frost covered his jacket. His eyes tracked her slowly, and he barely swiveled his head.

A switch flipped, and Bales's informal search was now a full-on rescue mission. She leaned into her wilderness medical training and tried to assess his level of consciousness. "What is your name?" she asked.

He did not respond.

"Do you know where you are?"

Nothing. His skin was pale and waxy, and he had a glazed look on his face. It was obvious that nothing was connecting for him. He was hypothermic and in really big trouble. Winds were blowing steadily at 50 mph, the temperature was 27 degrees, and the ice pellets continued their relentless assault on Bales and the man who was now her patient.

The prospect of having to abandon him in the interest of her own survival was horrifying, but she'd been trained in search and rescue; she knew not to put herself at such risk that she would become a patient too. She also knew she didn't have much time. As he sat propped up against the rocks, she stripped him down to his T-shirt and underwear. Because he wouldn't talk and she was in such close contact with him, she gave him a name: John. She placed adhesive toe-warmer packs directly onto his bare feet. She checked him for any sign of injury or trauma. There was none. From her pack, Bales retrieved a pair of soft-shell pants, socks, a winter hat and a jacket. She pulled the warm, dry layers onto his body. He could not help because he was so badly impaired by hypothermia.

Bales next removed a bivouac sack from her pack, holding it firmly so the winds would not snatch it. She slid it under and around his motionless body. She activated more heat packs and placed them in his armpits, on his torso and on each side of his neck. Bales always brought a thermos of hot cocoa and chewable electrolyte cubes. She dropped a few cubes into the cocoa, then cradled the back of the man's head with one hand and poured the warm, sugary drink into his mouth.

*　*　*

Over the next hour, John began to move and speak. Slurring his words, he said that when he had left Maine that morning it had been 60 degrees. He had planned to follow the same loop as Bales. He had walked that route several times before. He said he had lost his way in the poor visibility and just sat down here. Even as he warmed up, he remained lethargic.

Bales recognized that he would die soon if they didn't get out of there. She looked her patient squarely in the eyes and said, "John, we have to go now!" She left no room for argument. She was going to descend, and he was going with her. The wind roared over and around the boulders that had protected them during the 60-minute triage. She braced him as he stood up, shivering, and with a balance of firmness and genuine concern, she ordered, "You are going to stay right on my ass, John." This wasn't the way she usually spoke to people, but she had to be forceful. He seemed moments away from being drawn irrevocably to the path of least resistance—stopping and falling asleep. Not on her watch.

She figured that the only viable route was back the way they'd come. As the pair retraced their steps on the ridge, visibility was so bad that they inched along. Bales followed the small holes that her trekking poles had made earlier. Leaning into the headwinds, she began to sing a medley of Elvis songs in an effort to keep John connected to reality—and herself firmly focused.

He seemed moments away from stopping and falling asleep.

She was trying hard to stay on the trail, and trying even harder not to let John sense her concern, when he dropped down into the snow. She turned and saw that he seemed to be giving up. He curled in a sort of sitting fetal position, hunched down, shoulders dropped forward. He told her he was exhausted and had had enough. She should

By 11 a.m., the weather had turned and Bales was about to turn back. Fortunately for one distraught hiker, she wouldn't quit.

just continue on without him. Bales would have none of it. "That's not an option, John. We still have the toughest part to go, so get up, suck it up and keep going!" Slowly he stood, and she felt an overwhelming sense of relief.

Bales and her reluctant companion had traveled just under half a mile when they arrived back at the junction of Gulfside Trail and the somewhat safer Jewell Trail. It had been around 2 p.m. when they'd started down. The sun would set in three hours. Although the trees would protect them from the wind, it was darker under the canopy. Bales switched on her headlamp, but with only one light between them, she had to move slowly down a steeper section, then turn to illuminate the trail so John could follow. She offered continuous encouragement—"Keep going, John; you're doing great"—and sang a dose of songs from the 1960s.

Their descent was arduous, and Bales dreaded that he would drop in the snow again and actively resist her efforts to save him. Just before 6 p.m., they arrived at the trailhead, exhausted and battered. Her climb to the spot where she located John had taken about four hours. Six hours had passed since then.

Bales started her car engine and placed the frozen clothing she had taken off John inside so that the heater could thaw them. She realized he had no extra clothing with him.

"Why don't you have extra clothes or food in your car?" she asked.

"I just borrowed it," he told her. Several minutes later, he put his now-dry clothes back on and returned the ones Bales had dressed him in up on the ridge.

"Why didn't you check the weather forecast dressed like that?" she asked. He didn't answer. He just thanked her, got into his car and drove across the empty lot toward the exit. Right around that time, at 6:07 p.m., the Mount Washington Observatory clocked its highest wind gust of the day, at 88 mph.

Standing there astonished and alone in the darkness, Bales said to no one, "What just happened?"

∗   ∗   ∗

Bales wouldn't get an answer until a week later, when the president of her rescue group received a letter in the mail, a donation tucked between its folds. It read:

"I hope this reaches the right group of rescuers. This is hard to do but must try, part of my therapy. I want to remain anonymous, but I was called John. On Sunday, October 17, I went up my favorite trail, Jewell, to end my life. Weather was to be bad. Thought no one else would be there. I was dressed to go quickly. Next thing I knew this lady was talking to me, changing my clothes, giving me food, making me warmer. She just kept talking and calling me John and I let her. Finally learned her name was Pam.

"Conditions were horrible and I said to leave me and get going, but she wouldn't. Got me up and had me stay right behind her, still talking. I followed, but I did think about running off—she couldn't see me. But I wanted to only take my life, not anybody else's, and I think she would've tried to find me.

"The entire time she treated me with compassion, confidence and the impression that I mattered. With all that has been going wrong in my life, I didn't matter to me, but I did to Pam. She probably thought I was the stupidest hiker dressed like I was, but I was never put down in any way—chewed out, yes, in a kind way. Maybe I wasn't meant to die yet. I somehow still mattered in life.

"I became very embarrassed later on and never really thanked her properly. If she is an example of your organization, you must be the best group around. Please accept this small offer of appreciation for her effort

277

to save me way beyond the limits of safety. NO did not seem to be in her mind.

"I am getting help with my mental needs. They will also help me find a job and I have temporary housing. I have a new direction thanks to wonderful people like yourselves. I got your name from her pack patch and bumper sticker.

"My deepest thanks, John."

* * *

In the nine years since she saved John, Bales has become something of a hiking legend. It's a title she never sought or wanted, but one she certainly has earned. All that matters to her is that she was moved deeply by the man's gesture and his reference to the fact that she made him feel that he mattered.

"Maybe I wasn't meant to die," he wrote. "I somehow still mattered."

Some people have asked me whether I, in finally recounting this story for the public, tried to find John. The thought of searching for him felt wrong. As I've reflected more on this story and its relation to mental health, my response to that question has evolved. I have in fact found John, and he is very close by me. John is my neighbor; he is my good friend, a close colleague, a family member. John could be me.

At some point in our lives, all of us have found ourselves walking with a sense of helplessness through a personal storm. Alone, devoid of a sense of emotional warmth and safety, and smothered by the darkness of our emotions, we've sought that place just off trail where we hoped to find some way to break free of our struggles. Sadly, some do follow through. Many are able to quietly self-rescue. Others, like John, are rescued by people like Pam Bales.

Originally published in the October 2019 issue of *Reader's Digest* magazine.

CREDITS AND ACKNOWLEDGMENTS

"Where Does Education Stop?" by James A. Michener condensed from an address delivered at Macalester College; *Reader's Digest*, December 1962

"The Undelivered Letter" by Fulton Oursler; *Reader's Digest*, December 1950
Photograph by Isha_Ray/Shutterstock

"Code of the Navajos" by Bruce Watson, *Smithsonian* (August 1993) © 1993 Smithsonian Institution. Reprinted with permission from Smithsonian Enterprises. All rights reserved. Reproduction in any medium is strictly prohibited without permission from *Smithsonian* magazine; *Reader's Digest*, December 1993
Photograph on page 12 by U.S. Marine Corps Collection/National Archives/Charles H. Phillips

"The Husband Who Vanished" by Joseph P. Blank; *Reader's Digest*, January 1987

"Sit, Stay, Whoa!" by P.J. O'Rourke, *Garden & Gun* (February/March 2010) © 2011 P.J. O'Rourke; *Reader's Digest*, March 2011
Illustration on page 28 by John Cuneo

"A Soldier's Last Bedtime Story" by Kenneth Miller; *Reader's Digest*, March 2017
Photograph on page 32 by Burcu Avsar; page 35 courtesy of United Through Reading

"'Don't Go Away! I'm Alive!'" by Joe Austell Small; *Reader's Digest*, February 1982

"Surviving Whole Foods" by Kelly MacLean, Huffingtonpost.com (September 16, 2013) © 2013 Kelly MacLean; *Reader's Digest*, April 2014
Illustration by Steve Wacksman

"The Lady and the Gangster" by Lester Velie; *Reader's Digest*, January 1957

"Back to the Wild" by Matthew Shaer, *Smithsonian* (February 2015) © 2015 Smithsonian Institution; *Reader's Digest* International Editions, 2017
Photograph on page 62 by Mark Carwardine; page 65 courtesy WCS Russia; page 66 Patrick Evans; page 70 courtesy Bastak Nature Reserve

"I Can't Find My Apron Strings" by Louise Dickinson Rich, *Woman's Day* (August 1957) © 1957 Woman's Day, Inc.; *Reader's Digest*, October 1957

"'They'll Never Find Us'" by Margot McWilliams; *Reader's Digest*, October 1993
Photograph by Tom Stewart

"Overtaken by Joy" by Ardis Whitman; *Reader's Digest*, April 1965

"Tunnel to Freedom" by Paul Brickhill; *Reader's Digest*, December 1945
Photograph on page 88 by Yulia Moiseeva/Shutterstock; page 93 by ANL/Shutterstock

"The *Reader's Digest* Complete Guide to Witticisms, Quips, Retorts, Rejoinders and Pithy Replies for Every Occasion"; *Reader's Digest*, October 2016
Illustrations by John Cuneo

"How to Stop Smoking" by Herbert Brean. Reprinted by permission of Don Congdon Associates, Inc. © 1957 by Herbert Brean, renewed 1986 by Dorothy Brean; *Reader's Digest*, April 1954

"A Dog's Life" from *Tell Me Where It Hurts: A Day of Humor, Healing, and Hope in My Life as an Animal Surgeon* by Nick Trout, © 2008 by Nick Trout. Used by permission of Broadway Books, an imprint of Random House, a division of PenguinRandom House LLC. All rights reserved; *Reader's Digest,* July 2008
Photographs by Jason Grow

"Oak Island's Mysterious 'Money Pit'" by David MacDonald, *The Rotarian* (January 1965) © 1964 Rotary International; *Reader's Digest*, January 1965
Map based on illustrations by Rainer Lesniewski/Getty Images and Vektori Cetiri/Getty Images

"Letter to Olivia" by Mel Allen, *Bowdoin Magazine* (Winter 2000); *Reader's Digest*, May 2001
Photographs by Mark Alcarez

"'I Get a Lot More Than I Give'" by Bob Hope; *Reader's Digest*, January 1970
Photograph on page 48 by Bettmann/Getty Images; page 53 by Moviepix/Getty Images

"The Secret Life of Walter Mitty" by James Thurber, *My World—and Welcome to It*, © 1942 by Rosemary A. Thurber. Reprinted with arrangement with Rosemary Thurber and The Barbara Hogenson Agency. To read more about James Thurber, go to www.ThurberHouse.org and www.JamesThurber.org; *Reader's Digest,* January 1943

"With Wit and Wisdom" by Hedwig Gafga and Burkhard Weitz from www.chismon.de; *Reader's Digest* International editions, 2008
Photograph by David Turnley/Getty Images

"An Alcoholic's Letter to His Son" by Anonymous, *Denver Post* (October 15, 1966), © 1966 The Denver Post, Inc.; *Reader's Digest,* November 1966

"I Confess" by Derek Burnett; *Reader's Digest,* November 2015
Photographs on page 174 courtesy Pinellas County Sheriff Office; page 177 courtesy Clearwater Police

"A Family Discovers Its Rare Gift" by Sarah Gray; *Reader's Digest,* December 2017/January 2018
Photographs by Ariel Zambelich

"Are You Missing the Best Thing in Life?" from *The Amazing Results of Positive Thinking* by Dr. Norman Vincent Peale. © 1959 by Prentice-Hall, Inc. Copyright renewed 1987 by Dr. Norman Vincent Peale. Reprinted with the permission of Fireside, a division of Simon & Schuster, Inc. All rights reserved; *Reader's Digest,* February 1960

"Terror in Room 73" by Sheldon Kelly; *Reader's Digest,* October 1993

"Strange Encounter on Coho Creek" by Morris Homer Erwin; *Reader's Digest,* May 1987
Photograph on page 204 Yuliya Razukevichus/Shutterstock; page 207 by Volodymyr Burdiak/Shutterstock

"An Open Letter to America's Students" by Dwight D. Eisenhower; *Reader's Digest,* October 1948
Photograph on page 210 by FPG/Archive Photos/Getty Images

"Leave 'em Laughing!" by Lizz Winstead, *Lizz Free or Die,* © Lizz Winstead, Shoot the Messenger Productions, Inc., published by Riverhead Books, a member of Penguin Group (USA) Inc.; *Reader's Digest,* February 2013

"A Fight for Life at 35,000 Feet" by Per Ola and Emily D'Aulaire; *Reader's Digest,* October 1995

"Miniature Golf to the Rescue" by Elmer Davis, *Harper's Magazine* (December 1930), © 1930 Harper & Bros.; *Reader's Digest,* January 1931

"'I Think We've Lost Them'" from *Comm Check: The Final Flight of Shuttle Columbia* by Michael Cabbage and William Harwood. © 2004 by Michael Cabbage and William Harwood. Reprinted with the permission of The Free Press, a division of Simon & Schuster,

Inc. All rights reserved; *Reader's Digest,* March 2004
Photograph on page 240 by HUM Images/Getty Images; pages 243, 247, 250 courtesy of NASA; page 249 by Dr. Scott Lieberman/AP Wideworld Photos

"My Dog Reviews the Furniture" by Andy Simmons; *Reader's Digest,* October 2016
Illustration on page 253 by Nishant Choksi

"Why I Remain a Negro" by Walter White, *The Saturday Review of Literature* (October 11, 1947), © 1947 Saturday Review Association, Inc.; *Reader's Digest,* January 1948
Photograph by Bettmann via Getty Images

"If Life Is a Bowl of Cherries—What Am I Doing in the Pits?" by Erma Bombeck condensed from *If Life Is a Bowl of Cherries—What Am I Doing in the Pits?,* © 1971 though 1978 by Erma Bombeck, published by McGraw-Hill Book Co.; *Reader's Digest,* July 1978
Photograph by Denver Post via Getty Images

"Footprints in the Snow" by Ty Gagne, *New Hampshire Union Leader* (January 5, 2019), © 2019 Ty Gagne, Unionleader.com; *Reader's Digest,* October 2019
Photograph on page 270 by David Boutin/ Shutterstock (mountain) Alexander Chaikin/Shutterstock (footprints)/Roberto Caucino/Shutterstock (person); pages 273, 276 courtesy Pam Bales

Where Oh Where Answers 30: C. Rainbow Falls in Watkins Glen, New York. (Not to be confused with the Rainbow Falls 200 miles north in Keene, New York, or the dozens of other Rainbow Falls in the U.S.) **138: C.** Boone County, Iowa **182: B.** The Wave, Arizona